# Handbook of Basic Writing Skills

# Handbook of Basic Writing Skills

## CORA L. ROBEY

## ALICE M. HEDRICK

## ETHELYN H. MORGAN

*Tidewater Community College*
*Frederick Campus*

**HARCOURT BRACE JOVANOVICH, INC.**

*New York   San Diego   Chicago   San Francisco   Atlanta*

ISBN: 0-15-529170-X

Library of Congress Catalog Card Number: 77-83605

Printed in the United States of America

# To the Instructor

The *Handbook of Basic Writing Skills* was written in response to a need that has existed for many years — a need for a reference and writing aid that could be readily understood by all students, regardless of their background in English. In writing this handbook, we have attempted to use clear and simple language in both explanations and examples, and to provide an abundance of exercises.

This handbook offers assistance in all the areas covered by the traditional handbooks and gives special emphasis to the problems that trouble beginning writers — particularly verb endings, subject–verb agreement, noun plurals, possessive endings, fragments, and sentence logic. It helps the student in each step from constructing a sentence through researching and organizing a full-length paper.

There are twenty-eight sections. You should be able to refer students to the appropriate section of the handbook for virtually any error found in a student paper. The first eight sections, Sentence Basics, cover such basic writing concerns as agreement, verbs, and fragments. These introductory sections do not include a review of grammar but consider immediately such fundamental concerns as locating the subject and verb, making statements negative, and forming plurals. The verb section (Section 7) is the largest in the book and contains much useful drill. Sections 9 through 11 cover other important elements of sentence structure. Sections 12 through 19, Spelling and Punctuation, focus on questions inexperienced writers are most likely to ask about these matters. Sections 20 through 23 represent a simple approach to the use of words. The dictionary section (Section 20) should be helpful to students who need to build reading skills. Sections 24 through 28 move from sentence improvement and variety through the paragraph (Section 25), the full-length short paper (26), and finally the research paper and the question of manuscript form (27, 28)—illustrated with a sample complete student paper. These sections offer practical suggestions on subjects like the selection and limitation of topics and the organization of material. You might also want to use these sections for beginning the teaching of rhetoric.

The explanations are given with few references to traditional grammar; therefore, the student who does not know what a misplaced modifier or an adverbial clause is will not be at an immediate disadvantage. Students who do feel comfortable with traditional grammatical terms will find most of those terms in the index. Our simple explanations also leave ample room for instructors to use traditional grammatical terms in their own class discussions if they choose to do so.

The exercises are aimed particularly at areas where students need practice. Not all exercises will be helpful for all students, of course, so you will probably want to use some as general class exercises and assign certain others—especially those in Sections 1 through 8—to students with particular writing problems on an individual basis. The examples used in the explanations and in the exercises are mainly student sentences; they are frequently interesting in themselves and are close to the style students use in their own writing.

Throughout the book, we have used such labels as RIGHT and WRONG, FINISHED and UNFINISHED, or WEAK and BETTER to identify example sentences. These labels are designed to help students recognize correctly written Standard American English. We are not commenting in any way, however, on the acceptability of the language that students use in their own informal speech.

Many people have offered welcome help and advice with the preparation of this handbook. We offer thanks to Roberta Matthews, La Guardia Community College; Charlotte Glickfield, Cumberland County College; and Joanne

McCarthy, Tacoma Community College, who read and helped improve the manuscript, and to our editors and friends at Harcourt Brace Jovanovich, particularly Eben Ludlow, Jim Medley, Irene Pavitt, and Eleanor Lahn. We warmly thank our colleagues at Tidewater Community College, Frederick Campus, who offered advice and sympathy all along the way, especially Sarah Kreps, Helen Maloney, and Ramona Mapp. We also thank our students and the administrative officers of Tidewater Community College for allowing us to use paragraphs from the T.C.C. *Anthology of Student Writing* in our rhetoric sections. Finally, we thank our families, who assisted and cheered us all along the way.

*Cora L. Robey*
*Alice M. Hedrick*
*Ethelyn H. Morgan*

# To the Student

This handbook is designed to help you express your ideas correctly and clearly in writing. When you talk with your friends, you may use informal language or even leave out words and still be understood; but when you write for college classes or in your work, you need to be careful in your selection and use of words.

Since the words you use and the way you use them must be understood by both you and the person who reads what you have written, certain forms have been accepted as usual, or standard, ways to write what you want to write. In this book you will see examples with labels such as UNFINISHED SENTENCE and FINISHED SENTENCE or WORDS THAT DO GO TOGETHER and WORDS THAT DO NOT GO TOGETHER to help you recognize and use those standard forms.

Unlike most handbooks, this handbook does not use many of the formal terms for the elements of grammar. However, if you know those terms and wish to use them, you can find them in the index to help you locate the sections you need.

Each section of the book covers a different area of writing skills. Your instructor will usually let you know, by section number, what sections you need to refer to in order to correct errors in your papers. You do not have to start at the beginning of the book unless directed to do so. By doing the exercises in each section, you will have a chance to practice what you have learned.

If you are confused about which form of a word to use or how to say clearly what you mean to say, you may want to look at a particular section for help while you are writing a paper. Sections 1 through 23 help you construct sentences and choose correct words. Sections 24 and 25 tell how to arrange sentences into paragraphs, and Sections 26 through 28 help you plan a complete paper, do research, and prepare the final version.

Learn to use this handbook both to correct your finished work and as a reference book while you are writing. Let it help you prevent errors as you fulfill your writing assignments.

# Contents

## *Sentence Basics*

## *More About Sentences*

## *Words*

## *Moving Toward the Complete Paper*

## *The Complete Paper*

# PART ONE

# Sentence Basics

# 1

# *Sentence Make-Up*

## Learn some basic facts about sentences.

**1a**  What is a sentence?

You probably think about a sentence in one of three ways. Let us look at these ways one by one.

**1a(1)**  A sentence is a group of words beginning with a capital letter and ending with a period, a question mark, or an exclamation point.

The first way of viewing a sentence is the easiest to see. The most common type of sentence makes a statement. It begins with a capital letter and ends with a period.

> Some mothers never learn from experience.
> The Beatles changed the course of modern music.

Sometimes a sentence asks a question. It begins with a capital letter and ends with a question mark.

> Do mothers ever learn from experience?
> Did the Beatles change the course of modern music?

A sentence showing strong feeling or surprise begins with a capital letter and ends with an exclamation point.

> It's a miracle!
> Show me a 1964 Oldsmobile, and I'll show you a great car!

A command begins with a capital letter and ends with either a period or an exclamation point.

> Show me a 1964 Oldsmobile, please.
> Hold your horses!

**1a(2)**   A sentence contains a subject and a verb.

Throughout this book, we will be using these two words. The *subject* of the sentence is the person or thing you are writing about.

A simple subject is one word.

> Hubcaps are not essential parts of automobiles.

A subject may be two or more words, joined by *and, but, or,* or *nor*.

> Fathers and sons frequently don't get along.

A subject with some descriptive words in front of it or after it can be called a complete subject.

> My uncle Fred has eaten too much lunch.
> Part of my lunch is gone.

The *verb* tells what the subject is doing or what is happening to the subject.

A subject may have a one-word verb.

> Few domestic geese fly.

A subject may have a verb of more than one word.

> She should have waited at least an hour.

A subject may have more than one verb.

> Alice just sits and looks out of the window.

There are usually many words other than a subject and a verb in a sentence, but the subject and verb are the only two words necessary to make a sentence.

> Frank cried.
> After many days of waiting and wondering, she finally left.

**1a(3)**   **A sentence finishes by saying something about what the subject is doing or what is happening to the subject.**

Not every group of words with a subject and a verb is a sentence.

> After <u>I</u> had <u><u>looked</u></u> for my pet
> skunk for over an hour          (I finally found him)
>
> Since <u>you</u> will not <u><u>tell</u></u> me any
> more about your plans          (I will not wait for you)

Both of the examples on the left have a subject and a verb, but they are not sentences. Words like *after* and *since* suggest that the writer has not finished saying what the subject is doing or what is happening to the subject. In each case, the words on the right suggest a way the sentence could have been finished. (If you need help in telling whether a sentence is finished, see Section **2.**)

**EXERCISE 1**

Add a period, a question mark, or an exclamation point to mark the end of each sentence in the following paragraph.

> My friend Keith is a short, active fellow whose number one interest is dancing you can bet your bottom dollar that if there's a dance in town, Keith will be there as soon as he enters the D. J. will ask, "Is that you, Hollywood" Keith will grin from ear to ear do you know that he thinks if he isn't there, the dance can't go on the D. J. will then spin one of Keith's favorite records Keith will dance until his clothes are soaking wet, but nothing will keep him from dancing with every woman in the place he really knows how to have a ball show me someone like Keith, and I'll show you someone who can do it all

**1b**   **Recognize the subject and verb.**

Before you can really understand and correct most writing problems, you have to be able to pick out the subject and verb of a sentence. In a very short sentence, this is no problem.

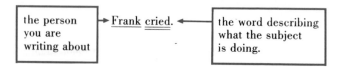

**1b(1)**    A sentence often begins with the subject and verb.

> Judgment is a necessity in surfing.
> I wanted a job working in a bank.
> We have enjoyed painting in our spare time.
> Stews are cooked slowly.

**1b(2)**    Words may come between the subject and its verb.

Although the subject and verb often appear first in the sentence, this is not the only possible word order, especially when a word like *one, all, each, everyone, any, some, many, none,* or *nobody* is the simple subject.

> One of my father's ties fell from the rack.
> All of the patients in the hospital want you to show a personal interest in them.
> None of the women have a different idea on the subject.
> After such a narrow escape, he never went there again.

When trying to locate the simple subject of a sentence, ask yourself *who* is doing something or *what* is happening. That *who* or *what* is the subject. Then look for the word that tells you what the subject is doing. That word is the verb.

> One of my father's ties fell from the rack.

The thing being written about in this sentence is *one* of the ties — not all of them. The verb *fell* goes with the subject *one*.

Do not let expressions beginning with *of* mislead you when they come between the simple subject and its verb.

> The <u>children</u> of today <u><u>will</u></u> be our salvation.
>
> > [*Children*, not *today*, is the subject; *children* will be our salvation.]
>
> <u>Some</u> of the players <u><u>are</u></u> doing different things. [*Some*, not *players*, is the subject. *Some*, not *all*, of the players are doing different things.]

### EXERCISE 2

Underline the simple subject once and the verb twice in each of the following sentences. Before you tackle each sentence, ask yourself: "What is the person or thing written about?" (subject); "What is that person or thing doing?" (verb).

**Example**    The <u>girl</u> of my dreams <u><u>is</u></u> Mimi.

1. The cause of all my troubles is lack of money.
2. Almost every customer in this restaurant asks the chef to cook bluefish.
3. The rules of that school seem very strict to me.
4. The eyes of everyone were on that one man.
5. A machine used in cutting all types of wood and metal is called a lathe.
6. All of the people involved in that project should feel a sense of accomplishment.
7. Many of the men on that ship surely miss home at this very minute.
8. Some of the most enthusiastic former supporters of that candidate voted for his opponent.

**1 b(3)**    The verb sometimes comes *before* the subject.

You usually expect the subject to come before its verb in a sentence, but that is not always the case. In a *there is (are)*, *here is (are)*, *where is (are)* sentence, the verb comes before the subject.

> There <u>are</u> <u>mosquitoes</u> all over the place.
>
> Here <u>is</u> the best <u>reason</u> for buying a new car.
>
> Where <u>are</u> my old <u>friends</u>?

*There, here,* and *where* are not subjects. The simple subjects of the sentences above are *mosquitoes, reason,* and *friends. There, here,* and *where* only introduce the subject.

Be sure that when you use *there* to introduce the subject you do not confuse it with *they* or *it. They* and *it* refer to definite persons or things, and, unlike *there, they* or *it* can be the subject of a sentence.

> <u>They</u> are late for dinner.   [They (certain persons) are late for dinner.]
>
> <u>It</u> is too early to visit your sister.   [It (the time) is too early to visit your sister.]

Do not use *they* or *it* in place of *there* to introduce the subject of a sentence.

> WRONG   Is they a place in Germany more dangerous than Berlin?
>
> RIGHT   Is *there* a place in Germany more dangerous than Berlin?

> WRONG   It is a very nice girl living on our block.
>
> RIGHT   *There* is a very nice girl living on our block.


## EXERCISE 3

Copy the following sentences, changing *it* or *they* to *there* in any sentence where *it* or *they* is incorrectly used to introduce the subject.

> **Example**   They was a good reason for my mother's decision.
>
> *There* was a good reason for my mother's decision.

1. It was something special about this particular room.
2. They were left by the side of the road.

3. In New York, they were more jobs, but they were also more people applying for the jobs.
4. They are many differences between a truck and a car.
5. On that block they is a pool hall with a smoky ceiling.

The verb comes before its subject in sentences other than those beginning with *there is (are), here is (are),* and *where is (are).*

Next to his desk <u>are</u> four filing <u>cabinets</u>. [The subject is *cabinets;* the cabinets are near the desk.]

On the wall <u>hang</u> the <u>racks</u> that hold the cue sticks. [The subject is *racks;* the racks hang on the wall.]

**1 b(4)** **In a command, the subject is not written out in the sentence.**

Since you are talking to someone when you command or request him or her to do something, the subject is *you* (understood).

| *Subject* | *Verb* |
|---|---|
| (You) | <u>Leave</u> my house immediately! |
| (You) | Please <u>wear</u> hiking boots if you are going into those woods. |

**EXERCISE 4**

Underline simple subjects once and verbs twice. If the subject is understood, write *you* next to the sentence.

1. All up and down the stairs are my brother's toys.
2. In the room there are three chairs, a sofa, a loveseat, and a cedar chest.
3. Please walk the dog on the other side of the street.
4. On top of the lockers sit all of our books.
5. Listen carefully to the news this evening.

**1b(5)**    **A sentence may have more than one subject and more than one verb.**

When a sentence is not limited to one subject and one verb, be sure you can pick out the main verbs and their subjects. Only the main verb finishes saying something about its subject.

### Sentence 1

I forgot to call my boss, but luckily he was not angry.

Sentence 1 is really two finished sentences. Each part has a subject and a main verb; each part would, therefore, be a finished sentence if it stood by itself.

FINISHED    I forgot to call my boss.
FINISHED    He was not angry.

### Sentence 2

While Elvira lived in New York, she was looking for a good job.

Sentence 2 has two parts containing a subject and a verb, but only one verb is a main verb. Only one part would be a finished sentence if it stood by itself.

UNFINISHED    While Elvira lived in New York
FINISHED    She was looking for a good job.

### Sentence 3

The check that I have been expecting finally arrived.

Sentence 3 also has two parts containing a subject and a verb, and, like sentence 2, it has only one main verb. Only one part would be a finished sentence if it stood by itself.

FINISHED    The check finally arrived.
UNFINISHED    That I have been expecting

In locating the subject and verb, remember that

1. words may separate a subject from its verb — particularly a simple subject like *one, all, each, some,* and so on.
2. in a *there is (are), here is (are),* and *where is (are)* sentence, the verb comes before its subject.
3. in other sentences, the verb sometimes comes before its subject.
4. in a command, the subject (you) is understood.
5. a sentence may have more than one subject and verb, but it must have at least one subject and main verb.

## EXERCISE 5

Copy these sentences, underlining the simple subjects of the finished sentences once and the main verbs that go with them twice. Do not underline the subject and verb of any unfinished part. When the subject is understood, write *you* next to the sentence.

**Examples**    When I finally met my roommate, I really got a shock.
Go home immediately.   (You)

1. Since Gail had her baby, she stays home all the time.
2. In 1865, he sold dressed pork to get enough money to buy leather to make shoes for his children.
3. I saw that diamond ring, and I wanted it.
4. Of all the things that I like, my favorite pastime is fishing.
5. He stepped on the accelerator again and finally started his car.
6. Stop the car immediately!
7. According to the newspaper reports, none of the relatives or friends of Howard Hughes ever really knew him.
8. All the way across the hardening cement are the unmistakable pawprints of my curious cat, Tagi.
9. In order to be ready for any emergency, have plenty of fuses in the house.
10. One of our aircraft has disappeared.
11. Mr. Vernon, who considered work in his garden more a labor of love than a weekly duty, grew some of the most marvelous vegetables that I have ever seen.

12. In order to learn the essentials of automotive maintenance, people often sign up for some courses at a nearby community college.
13. The boy who was chosen most likely to succeed actually served a jail sentence.
14. Here in the newspaper, after the news, the comics, and all of the classified ads, is the notice of that great sale.
15. After all the kind words of encouragement and the frequently given, but not unwelcome, words of advice, I never dreamed of such an outcome.

## 1c    Write correct negative sentences.

### 1c(1)    The most common negative sentence uses one negative word, such as *no, not, never, nothing,* or *nowhere.*

In addition to telling the reader what is happening to the subject, a sentence can also tell what is not happening.

> There are *no* drill bits in that drawer.
> English is *not* my favorite subject.
> You can *never* cheat an honest person.
> I have *nothing* to do today.

Sometimes a contraction is used instead of the word *not.*

| | | |
|---|---|---|
| There are not any drill bits in that drawer. | OR | There *aren't* any drill bits in that drawer. |
| English is not my favorite subject. | OR | English *isn't* my favorite subject. |
| You cannot ever cheat an honest person. | OR | You *can't* ever cheat an honest person. |
| I do not have anything to do today. | OR | I *don't* have anything to do today. |

Remember to use an apostrophe before the *t* in a contraction, since the *o* of *not* is omitted.

**Note:** *Ain't* is not a correct contraction for *am not, is not, are not, has not,* or *have not.*

> WRONG    That ain't any way to run a railroad.
> RIGHT    That *isn't* any way to run a railroad.

**1c(2)** Use only one negative word, like *no, not, never, nothing,* or *nowhere,* to say that something is not true.

English is unlike most other languages in its negative sentences. In Spanish, for example, the more negative words you use, the more you deny that something is true.

> No vi a *nadie* ni *oí* *nada* en *ninguna* parte.
> I didn't see no one nor hear nothing nowhere.

An English teacher would shriek in horror at that sentence. Remember not to use two negative words such as *no, no one, not, never, nothing, nowhere,* or *hardly* when you want to say that something is not so.

WRONG  I had never seen nobody as pretty as she.
RIGHT  I had *never* seen *anybody* as pretty as she.

WRONG  I did things for them no other person would never have done.
RIGHT  I did things for them *no* other person would *ever* have done.

WRONG  He is not hardly old enough to stay by himself.
RIGHT  He is *hardly* old enough to stay by himself.

To avoid using two negative words, you can usually do one of the following:

1. Eliminate one of the negative words.

WRONG  There are not hardly any peaches left.
RIGHT  There are *hardly* any peaches left.

2. Substitute *ever* for *never.*

WRONG  They're not never here.
RIGHT  They're not *ever* here.

3. Substitute *any* for *no* or *none.*

WRONG  I can't find him nowhere.
RIGHT  I can't find him *any*where.

WRONG  I don't see none on the shelf.
RIGHT  I don't see *any* on the shelf.

*Note:* The only time you do use two negative words to say

that something is not true is when you use the pair *neither . . . nor.*

*Neither* my English teacher *nor* I can understand why I continue to make verb errors.

### EXERCISE 6

Correct the following sentences by changing any incorrect negative words.

**Example**   I don't have no more money.
I don't have *any* more money.

1. I wouldn't trade my dog in for no one else's.
2. They knew we wouldn't like the idea of working in nobody's field.
3. It's not hardly early enough to call Sally.
4. I don't have no more coffee left.
5. Bowser ain't eaten nothing since the start of dog days.
6. I hate to tell you this, but you don't have no gas in that car.
7. Joey feels so bad he can't hardly hold his head up.
8. I don't never expect to do nothing with my education.
9. No wonder they didn't know how to act at her house; they've never been nowhere outside of New Jersey.
10. Didn't nobody figure out the ending to that story?
11. J. J. sits in front of the store and won't let nobody enter.

## 1d   Use singular and plural words correctly.

Sentences make statements about persons and things. The words you use should show whether you are naming one person or thing or more than one.

### 1d(1)   Words like *a, one, each,* and *every* describe single persons or things.

Do not add an *s* or another plural ending to the name of the person or thing when it is used with a singular describing word.

WRONG   each members of the group
RIGHT   each *member* of the group

WRONG  a new records
RIGHT  a new *record*

**1 d(2)**  Words like *six, ninety, many, all, some, several,* and expressions like *a number, a few,* or *a group of* describe more than one person or thing.

When these words are used, add an *s* to or use another plural form for the name of the person or thing being described.

WRONG  five acre of wheat
RIGHT  five *acres* of wheat

WRONG  many young ballplayer
RIGHT  many young *ballplayers*

WRONG  all of the specified adjustment
RIGHT  all of the specified *adjustments*

WRONG  at least three time
RIGHT  at least three *times*

WRONG  a number of test
RIGHT  a number of *tests*

WRONG  I am sometime late.
RIGHT  I am *sometimes* late.

WRONG  these kind of things
RIGHT  these *kinds* of things

Even when the number of persons or things is not mentioned in the sentence, do not carelessly forget the *s* or other ending when you mean to name more than one person or thing.

WRONG  He invites guest to perform.
RIGHT  He invites *guests* to perform.

**1 d(3)**  Some names of persons and things have special plural forms.

Learn them, and use them when needed instead of a singular or another incorrect word. Some common plurals are *women, feet, teeth, people,* and *children.*

WRONG  He is five foot tall.
RIGHT  He is five *feet* tall.

Do not use a plural form when you mean to use a singular one for the name of a person or thing.

WRONG  a women
RIGHT  a *woman*

## 1d(4)  Some words have no plural forms.

Do not add an ending to these words. Some examples are abstract words like *happiness*, *violence*, *sincerity*, *laziness*, and the common words *fish*, *deer*, and *sheep*.

WRONG  Think of the violences in the world!
RIGHT  Think of the *violence* in the world!

### EXERCISE 7

Correct any incorrect singular or plural words naming persons or things.

1. Anesthesia is used in many hospital.
2. He uses hydrochloric acid as a cutting substances for glass.
3. His workshop has many tools and electric motor.
4. He eats at least six time a day.
5. He planted only seven acre of wheat last year.
6. She has finished only a few piece of furniture.
7. At one time a phone call cost five cent.
8. Bob's Pool Hall has eight table and two soda machine.
9. Lazy persons are peoples who never learned the value of work.
10. Sometime the problem can be detected by inspection.
11. Before I let my daughter leave the house in the morning, I inspect everythings she has done to get ready for school.
12. It is a time when all my relatives get together to spread the latest gossips and enjoy themselves.

# 2

# *Unfinished Sentences*

## Be sure that your sentences are finished.

A complete, or finished, sentence has a subject (the person or thing you are writing about) and a main verb (the word that describes what the subject is doing or what is happening to the subject). Remember that when you write a finished sentence, you are saying something about the subject and you finish saying it. When you write an unfinished sentence, you do not complete your statement about the subject.

UNFINISHED SENTENCE
As a traveling salesman.   [What are you saying about a traveling salesman?]
FINISHED SENTENCE
He works as a traveling salesman.

UNFINISHED SENTENCE
And gets no fixed salary.   [Who gets no fixed salary?]
FINISHED SENTENCE
He works as a traveling salesman and gets no fixed salary.

UNFINISHED SENTENCE
Since he gets no fixed salary.   [What happens since he gets no fixed salary?]
FINISHED SENTENCE
Since he gets no fixed salary, it is hard for him to plan his expenses.

Usually a sentence can be finished in two ways:

    1. You can rewrite the unfinished part completely.

        UNFINISHED
        Fear that I would be unable to do the work.
        FINISHED BY REWRITING
        I was afraid that I would be unable to do the work.

    2. You can join the unfinished part to a finished sentence next to it.

        UNFINISHED
        Fear that I would be unable to do the work.
        FINISHED BY JOINING
        One of my biggest problems was fear of returning to school, fear that I would be unable to do the work.

It is often better to join an unfinished sentence to either the sentence before it or the sentence after it. This is because an unfinished sentence is just a group of words that was left out of the sentence next to it. When you find an unfinished sentence in one of your papers, look to see if you really meant to join it to a sentence next to it.

## 2a Finish an unfinished sentence that has no subject or verb.

Remember that a group of words that does not have a subject and a verb is not a sentence. Whenever possible, join these words to a sentence right next to them.

| UNFINISHED | JOIN | FINISHED |
|---|---|---|
| Without thinking about the danger. | People going downhill sometimes coast and ride their brakes. ⟵ Without thinking about the danger. | People going downhill sometimes coast and ride their brakes without thinking about the danger. |

**2a(1)**   When a subject and verb are missing, join a group of words with a beginning like *as, in, into, from, to, with,* and *without* to the sentence next to it.

| UNFINISHED | JOIN | FINISHED |
|---|---|---|
| As a bouncer. [What is being said about a bouncer?] | Bill worked in a disco club in New York. ◄—— As a bouncer. | Bill worked in a disco club in New York as a bouncer. |
| Without any money. [What are you saying about the lack of money?] | You can't do very much in New York. ◄—— Without any money. | You can't do very much in New York without any money. |

**2a(2)**   When a subject and verb are missing, join a group of words introduced by an *-ing* word to the sentence next to it.

| UNFINISHED | JOIN | FINISHED |
|---|---|---|
| Having no income of his own. [What happens because he has no income?] | Having no income of his own. ◄—— George is always borrowing from his brother. | Having no income of his own, George is always borrowing from his brother. |
| Checking myself, proofreading, and correcting errors. | I have to write my paper very slowly. ◄—— Checking myself, proofreading, and correcting errors. | I have to write my paper very slowly, checking myself, proofreading, and correcting errors. |

### EXERCISE 1

Copy the first sentence of each of the following pairs of sentences. Then complete the unfinished sentence below it by joining a finished sentence to it.

**Example** *I can imagine myself shopping at the fanciest shops in the world* with every sales person at my beck and call.

*I found myself all alone in the house* with nothing to do.

1. *I was born in 1955* in a small town called Rocky Mount.
_____ in a small apartment on the next block.

2. *They tried to keep the homesteaders away* by burning their houses.
_____ by locking the front door.

3. On the first day of spring, *Ernie started working in the garden.*
On my eighteenth birthday, _____.

4. *After you have finished playing your guitar, put it back in its case,* making sure its strings are slightly loosened so they won't expand and break.
_____, trying to forget everything that has happened to you.

5. In roles requiring wit and cunning, *Darren McGavin plays the part with a style most actors lack.*
In situations requiring much patience, _____.

6. By cutting small lawns for five dollars and large ones for ten dollars, *Betsy earned enough money to buy a motorcycle.*
By conserving energy all last winter, _____.

7. *She jumped up on her mother's lap,* kissing her, hugging her, and wishing her a happy Mother's Day.
_____, hoping she was not too late.

## EXERCISE 2

Finish all of the following sentences by joining the unfinished sentences to the finished ones. Do not join any sentences that are already complete. Do not change or add any words to the sentences.

**Example** For the entire week. I sat waiting for the telephone to ring.
For the entire week**,** I sat waiting for the telephone to ring.

1. Don't waste time moving the person to a better place.

Loosening the clothing or draining water from the lungs. Begin emergency treatment.
2. It's always a good day. For buying a house.
3. My mother never could get us all to supper. My brother was always practicing. In the gym.
4. Harry doesn't want to stay in that house. The windows are all boarded up. Making the rooms seem like jail cells.
5. You can't go far in this town. Without friends. Anyone who has ever lived here can tell you that.
6. Let me give you an example. My friend Al is always riding his brakes. Causing himself to coast downhill.
7. My friend Lenore lives in Passaic. In a great place. With beautiful oaks and pine trees.

**2b**  Finish an unfinished sentence containing a subject and verb.

A group of words with a subject and verb is not always a sentence.

**2b(1)**  Words like *because, as, although, when, after, before,* and *since* at the beginning of a group of words help you recognize that something needs to be explained before the sentence is finished.

UNFINISHED SENTENCE
Because gossip can get people into serious trouble.   [What is true because gossip can get people into trouble?]
FINISHED SENTENCE
Telling tales is bad because gossip can get people into serious trouble.

UNFINISHED SENTENCE
As I was hanging out my wash.   [What happened as I was hanging out my wash?]
FINISHED SENTENCE
As I was hanging out my wash, I saw a beautiful puppy on my neighbor's steps.

**2b(2)**   Finish an unfinished sentence that describes a person or thing and begins with the words *who, which,* or *that.*

Although such a sentence has a verb, it is not a main verb, and it does not finish saying something about the subject.

UNFINISHED SENTENCE
That often gets him into trouble.   [What gets him into trouble?]
FINISHED SENTENCE
It is his good taste in clothing that often gets him into trouble.

UNFINISHED SENTENCE
Which eats nasty house flies.   [What eats nasty house flies?]
FINISHED SENTENCE
This is a Venus' flytrap, which eats nasty house flies.

## EXERCISE 3

Copy the first sentence of each of the following pairs of sentences. Then complete the unfinished sentence below it by joining a finished sentence to it.

**Example**   Even though Lynn sets her alarm clock, *she still has trouble getting up and ready by seven.*
Even though I am late, *I am not going to rush*.

1. If I see him, *I'll let you know.*
   If I ever think of that answer, _____.
2. After the dance was over, *we all went out for a pizza.*
   After the trial was over, _____.
3. Although Steve is much older than I am, *we are best friends.*
   Although Jerry is never really angry, _____.
4. Remember, if this is your first try, *pick something that is simple to make.*
   Remember, if you take a vacation this summer, _____
   _____.
5. *This is the chair* that I wrote you about.
   _____ that I have been worrying about.
6. *Where are the letters* which the postman delivered yesterday?
   _____which I described to you last month?
7. *Marilyn has many friends* who seem a bit strange.
   _____ who wear the latest fashions.

## EXERCISE 4

Finish all unfinished sentences. Write *F* next to each sentence that is finished.

1. Although there are many jacks-of-all-trades who can produce quantity and not quality. We have a need for craftsmanship.
2. There are many steps. That lead up to the house.
3. If you didn't know better, you'd think she was a model.
4. There is always one person. Who must prove he is the best lover this side of the Mississippi.
5. As Helen walked through the swinging glass doors, she saw the display area.
6. When I picked up the telephone and the medical secretary gave me the decision of the board.
7. If you have to drive on rocks and mud. You need a heavy-duty tire.
8. Fishing is a sport. Which I really enjoy!
9. This is the best dinner that I have ever eaten.
10. The chair matches the wall. Which is dull pink.

**2c**    Finish an unfinished sentence that contains a verb but no subject.

The best way to finish such a sentence is to join the unfinished sentence to the finished sentence that comes before it.

| UNFINISHED | JOIN | FINISHED |
|---|---|---|
| And in a lot of cases share the bills. [Who shares the bills?] | Roommates share their food and time ◄——— And in a lot of cases share the bills. | Roommates share their food and time and in a lot of cases share the bills. |
| And avoid going whenever possible. [Who avoids going?] | Most people hate to go to a dentist. ◄——— And avoid going whenever possible. | Most people hate to go to a dentist and avoid going whenever possible. |

## EXERCISE 5

Copy the first sentence of each of the following pairs of sentences. Then complete the unfinished sentence below it by joining a finished sentence to it.

**Example** *I considered myself as stubborn as anybody* and as able to take as much punishment.

*I considered myself as strong as my sister* and just as smart.

1. *We saw a diamondback rattlesnake* and decided to take it home.
   _____ and stopped to visit her.
2. *Bob and Marion drank all the beer they could hold* but were afraid to leave without paying for it.
   _____ but forgot to let anyone know.
3. *I entered the house quietly* and hoped no one would hear me.
   _____ and listened as she told her story.
4. *Helen counted sheep for an hour* but still couldn't get to sleep.
   _____ but hadn't gotten in line early enough.

## EXERCISE 6

Finish each of the following sentences by adding words to the beginning that will give the sentence a subject.

**Example** And is one of the top actors in my book.
*Bela Lugosi plays in vampire movies* and is one of the top actors in my book.

1. But are unable to appreciate such movies.
2. And has a very surprising ending.
3. But makes Sid worry at times.
4. Or didn't sell at all.

**2d** Finish an unfinished sentence that contains a subject but no verb.

Often you accidentally write a new sentence when you are saying more than one thing about the subject. By mistake, you separate the extra subject or the words describing the subject from the sentence itself.

UNFINISHED SENTENCE
The fast driver, the slow driver, and the good driver. [What are you saying about those drivers?]
FINISHED SENTENCE
There are three types of drivers: the fast driver, the slow driver, and the good driver.

UNFINISHED SENTENCE
The second son of a naval officer. [What are you saying about the second son of a naval officer?]
FINISHED SENTENCE
He was from a military family, the second son of a naval officer.

Notice how the finished and unfinished sentences are combined. Usually you can put a comma or a colon (:) instead of a period after the finished sentence and join the extra subject or the words describing the subject to the finished sentence. If the extra subject or the words describing the subject come before the finished sentence, often a comma or a dash can be used to join the unfinished and finished sentences.

UNFINISHED SENTENCE
A phone call from his father. That was something Paul was dreading.
FINISHED SENTENCE
A phone call from his father—that was something Paul was dreading.

## EXERCISE 7

Finish all unfinished sentences. Write *F* next to each sentence that is finished.

1. In every state there is an institution for lawbreakers. A reform school for teenagers and a jail for adults. Believe me.
2. There are three main types of fishing boats: rowboats, runabouts, and cabin cruisers.
3. The coming of the Emotions and Earth, Wind, and Fire to the Frank D. Lawrence Stadium. That was a big event. People waited in long lines for tickets.

4. There were no more happy times. No more baseball games. No more children laughing and playing.
5. The beautiful decorations that brought happiness to so many. They have been put away for the winter.

**2e**    **Finish an unfinished sentence that serves as the object of the verb.**

When you write that the subject is doing something, that something is the *object*.

> Joe loves fried chicken.   [*Fried chicken* is the object—the something that Joe is eating.]
> My mother had six children.   [*Six children* is the object—they are what my mother had.]
> I know why you are late.   [*Why you are late* is the object—the something that I know.]

When you write about more than one object or when you describe the object, you accidentally may separate the second object or the words describing the object from the finished sentence. This is especially true if the second object begins with words like *why*, *when*, and *where*.

> SEPARATED
> And why he left in such a hurry.   [What are you saying about why he left in such a hurry?]
> JOINED TO THE FINISHED SENTENCE
> We wondered why he got so angry and why he left in such a hurry.

> SEPARATED
> A wonderful job, plenty of money, and a nice apartment.
> JOINED TO THE FINISHED SENTENCE
> I now have all the things I always dreamed of: a wonderful job, plenty of money, and a nice apartment.

As you can see from the examples above, the second object or the words describing the object should be added to the finished sentence next to them.

## EXERCISE 8

Copy the first sentence of each of the following pairs of sentences. Then complete the unfinished sentence below it by joining a finished sentence to it.

**Example**   *We could see many signs of a declining neigh-borhood:* old wooden staircases, clotheslines in all the yards, and garbage all over the place.

*We found many things to worry us* :   poverty, sickness, and squalor.

1. *Our society puts the mentally ill in institutions* and the el-derly in nursing homes.

   _____ and the dishes in the cabinet above.
2. *Try to find a quiet place to meditate:* a spot where you will not be distracted.

   _____: somewhere that of-fers plenty of excitement.
3. *My children often tell me that they enjoy being at home,* that my home is full of warmth and love.

   _____, that they have really been listening.
4. *The Welches' house has a nice, well-equipped kitchen* and a cozy, comfortable family room.

   _____ and a drive-in movie theater.

**2f**   **Finish an unfinished sentence that begins with an expression like *to see, to walk,* or *to give*.**

Such an expression has almost always been left out of the sentence that comes before it.

UNFINISHED SENTENCE
To solder a joint.
FINISHED SENTENCE
My mother showed me how to solder a joint.

## EXERCISE 9

Finish all unfinished sentences.

1. It's always a good idea. To take along an extra diaper. You never know when you'll need it.
2. I can't help wondering. Did Sally ask you. To get the car keys from her mother?
3. Danny always manages. To get a speeding ticket on Saturday night.
4. It is important to know when to pass a hand and just as important. To know when to bluff.

## EXERCISE 10

Finish all unfinished sentences. Write *F* next to each sentence that is finished.

1. Charles makes you smile. When you really don't feel like being bothered. How I admire him!
2. If you think Gloria is thin. You should see my uncle Jim. He has to jog every morning. Before he goes to work.
3. She dresses that way because she wants to clown around.
4. There aren't many people. Who like to watch that show.
5. By 1980. If people don't have a college degree, they won't be able to find jobs. That's why I'm going to college. Aren't you worried about your sister? Who didn't even finish high school?
6. There are many stores in the Suffolk Shopping Center. Which is found in the middle of town.
7. At dinner, everyone looks at my cousin George, the fattest man in the room. I wonder why he eats so much.
8. Frank has his own dance studio. And teaches all kinds of people. Who have never really learned to dance.
9. Jean was caught at her favorite vice. Sleeping in class.
10. I could see only farm land. Long rows of tomatoes and beans. I was home at last. Here in West Virginia.

# 3

# *Run-Together Sentences*

## Separate your run-together sentences.

Read the following sentences aloud.

> I bought a used boat this past summer from a friend at work it
> needed several repairs.
> Horses have one thing in common they all have four legs and a
> long tail.
> Years have passed since I was last here now the windows are
> covered with boards.
> The score was eight to nine, the Mets were ahead.

As you read the sentences aloud, you probably found that
you read each one as if it were two sentences. In each case,
the writer did not show that there were two complete
thoughts or sentences, and ran two sentences together. What
should the writer have done? There are several ways to correct this problem.

**3a**  Separate your sentences by using a period.

Notice that there are two complete sentences in each wrong
example below. In the first sentence, *I* is the subject and
*bought* is the verb; in the second sentence, *it* is the subject
and *needed* is the verb. You can separate the sentences by
placing a period after *work* and starting *it* with a capital letter; then the sentences will be correct.

WRONG    I bought a used boat this past summer from a friend at work it needed several repairs.

RIGHT    I bought a used boat this past summer from a friend at work. *It* needed several repairs.

WRONG    The room is lighted with large fluorescent lights some fixtures have both tubes missing.

RIGHT    The room is lighted with large fluorescent lights. *S*ome fixtures have both tubes missing.

**3b**    Separate your sentences by using a semicolon.

Again, there are two complete sentences run together in each wrong example below. In the first sentence, the subject is *horses* and the verb is *have*. In the second sentence, the subject is *they* and the verb is *have*. Since the thoughts in the sentences are closely related, the sentences can be separated with a semicolon instead of a period. Notice that the word following the semicolon does NOT begin with a capital letter.

WRONG    Horses have two things in common they all have four legs and a long tail.

RIGHT    Horses have two things in common; they all have four legs and a long tail.

WRONG    Years have passed since I was last here now the windows are covered with boards.

RIGHT    Years have passed since I was last here; now the windows are covered with boards.

### EXERCISE 1

Copy the first sentence of each of the following pairs of sentences. After each sentence, write your own sentence, making it similar to the one you just copied.

**Example**    Our neighbors have a beautiful yard. They enjoy taking care of the shrubs and flowers.
Her *kitchen usually looks terrible*. She *hates washing pans and dishes.*

1. The car started up the long hill. Bob and Jinks ran after it.
The boy _____. Mary and Sue _____.

2. We also have fast drivers. Usually the drivers are teenagers.
   They _____. Sometimes _____.
3. Most cars that drag race at race tracks cannot be driven on
   the streets; they have loud mufflers and are too high in the
   back.
   Many boats _____;
   they are _____.
4. Last year Valerie received the school's drama award;
   maybe one day she will be a great actress.
   Last month _____;
   some day _____.

## EXERCISE 2

Correct the following run-together sentences. Use
periods to correct two of them and semicolons to correct
the other two.

1. I enjoy my bedroom it's so bright and cheerful.
2. There were two doors in the room they were made of heavy
   steel and had no windows to peep through.
3. Some cities have very dirty water you can barely drink it.
4. The wind was strong it blew the papers right out of my
   hand.

**3c** Separate your sentences by using a comma and a
joining word such as *and, but, or, nor,* or *for*.

Sometimes you may not be sure what separating mark to
use to separate your sentences, although you can tell that
something is needed. Use a comma only when you also use a

joining word such as $\begin{Bmatrix} and \\ but \\ or \\ nor \\ for \end{Bmatrix}$ after the comma.

WRONG  The score was eight to nine, the Mets were ahead.
RIGHT  The score was eight to nine, *and* the Mets were
ahead.

WRONG   I want to go home, I have to stay at school.
RIGHT   I want to go home, *but* I have to stay at school.

WRONG   He had trouble driving, the visibility was poor.
RIGHT   He had trouble driving, *for* the visibility was poor.

Notice that all of these sentences are really two complete sentences. If a comma is used between the two complete thoughts or sentences, a joining word must also be used.

## EXERCISE 3

Correct the following run-together sentences, using joining words. Remember that the comma and the joining word must both be used.

1. The sky was bright blue with a few white clouds in it it was a beautiful day for the picnic.   (Use a comma and *and*.)
2. Rain came down in torrents the people in the car were dry.   (Use a comma and *but*.)
3. Do not have the oven too hot the cake will be dry and crumbly.   (Use a comma and *or*.)
4. Sue waited until the last day to register all of the classes were full.   (Use a comma and *and*.)

## EXERCISE 4

Correct the following run-together sentences. Correct three with periods, three with semicolons, and four with commas and the joining words *and, but, or, nor, for*.

1. A college education is very important you need preparation for most jobs.
2. The chair was turned over in the middle of the floor the lamp was in the corner of the room.
3. My car wouldn't start this morning the battery was dead.
4. Jim is a good long-distance runner he has many trophies and medals.
5. The piano needed tuning it sounded like a bunch of tin cans.
6. John lost his books, Bill found them under the desk.
7. The dog ran out growling the man ran after him.

8. I don't know where to go for my vacation, I'll decide by June.
9. Jill can go to college she can start to work with her uncle.
10. The boys did not want to go out in the rain they did not want to stay in the house any longer.

**3d** Separate your sentences by using a joining word such as *before, after, when, because,* and *since.*

When you use this method of separating sentences, you are turning one of the complete sentences into an unfinished, or incomplete, sentence.

If the thing being talked about in one sentence happens before or after or at the same time as the thing being talked about in the other sentence, then the joining words *before, after,* and *when* may be used.

WRONG  Steve and Pete ran along the street and reached the building, the man saw them.
RIGHT  Steve and Pete ran along the street and reached the building *before* the man saw them.

WRONG  He picked up the ball, it fell from the table.
RIGHT  He picked up the ball *after* it fell from the table.

WRONG  The car turned over another car hit it.
RIGHT  The car turned over *when* another car hit it.

If the thing being talked about in one sentence happens because of the thing being talked about in the other sentence, the joining words *because* or *since* may be used.

WRONG  The rubber raft sank it hit a sharp rock.
RIGHT  The rubber raft sank *because* it hit a sharp rock.

WRONG  I am finishing school, without an education I cannot reach my goal.
RIGHT  I am finishing school *since* without an education I cannot reach my goal.

There are several other commonly used joining words. Some of these words are *although, as, if, unless, until,* and *where.* You can learn more about how these words are used by reading Section **24.**

## EXERCISE 5

Copy the first sentence of each of the following pairs of sentences. After each sentence, write your own sentence, making it similar to the one you just copied.

**Example**   Becky baked a cake when Mrs. Collins ate dinner with us.

Helena *made a good grade* when *Mr. Jason gave us a test* .

1. Ronnie heard strange noises when he went into the house.
   Darlene _____ when _____ .
2. The mouse nibbled at the cheese for several minutes before the cat woke up.
   The dog _____ before _____ _____ .
3. Jeanne can always find a summer job because she is a good typist.
   Mr. Ricks _____ because _____ _____ .
4. The sun came out after the storm had cooled the air.
   The wind _____ after _____ _____ .
5. The education I received in 1952 is a bit out of date since the schools have changed in many ways.
   The music _____ since _____ _____ .

You have learned four ways to correct run-together sentences. Read the example of a run-together sentence and study the ways to correct it. If one of the methods still gives you trouble, go back to the section that explains it.

Only a few leaves could be seen the earth was covered with a blanket of snow.

1. Separate the sentences by using a period.

Only a few leaves could be seen. *T*he earth was covered with a blanket of snow.

2. Separate the sentences by using a semicolon.

Only a few leaves could be seen; the earth was covered with a blanket of snow.

3. Separate the sentences by using a comma and a joining word such as *and, but, or, nor,* or *for.*

Only a few leaves could be seen, *for* the earth was covered with a blanket of snow.

4. Separate the sentences by using a joining word such as *before, after, when, because,* or *since.*

Only a few leaves could be seen *because* the earth was covered with a blanket of snow.

## EXERCISE 6

Copy the following paragraph, but separate any run-together sentences. Use any of the ways you have learned from the examples you have just studied.

Your trip can be a happy experience just remember to plan ahead. The car should be checked the tires should be in good condition. Take along any sports equipment you may need select comfortable clothes that do not wrinkle easily. Be sure that you have enough money or travelers' checks to take care of your expenses. Credit cards are very convenient, be careful with them because they are as valuable as money. It is important to allow time to rest a tired and sleepy driver is a dangerous driver. Drive carefully; have a nice trip.

# 4

# *Descriptive Words*

**Learn to recognize words that
describe persons and things and
words that tell how, when, and where.**

When you write a sentence, you are telling about someone
doing something or about something happening. You might
write:

> The woman enters.
> OR
> The clock fell.

As you know, not many sentences are so short. You will usually want to say something more about the woman or the
clock. One of the ways you can do that is to use words that
describe. You can say:

> The *tall* woman enters.
> The *tall, mysterious* woman enters.
> *One tall, mysterious, dark-haired* woman enters.

You can say:

> The *large* clock fell.
> The *large cuckoo* clock fell.
> The *large, white, antique cuckoo* clock fell.

The words *one, tall, mysterious, dark-haired, large, white, antique,* and *cuckoo* describe persons and things. Words like these usually tell:

>          which one     (the *tall* woman)
>                        AND
>                        (the *antique* clock)
>    how many or how much   (*one* woman)

The italicized words below all tell which one, how many, or how much about the things they describe.

>    WHICH ONE   *first* mile
>                *singing* bird
>    HOW MANY    *four* movies
>                *few* friends
>    HOW MUCH    *great* success
>                *little* food

In addition to describing people and things, you will want to say something about how, when, and where something is happening. You might write:

>    HOW     The woman enters *suddenly.*
>    WHEN    The woman enters *early.*
>    WHERE   The woman enters *below.*
>                        OR
>    HOW     The clock fell *noisily.*
>    WHEN    The clock fell *yesterday.*
>    WHERE   The clock fell *there.*

Words that describe verbs and other descriptive words usually tell how, when, and where about the words they describe.

>    HOW     It is *strangely* quiet.
>            She works *really* hard.
>            I will act *quickly.*
>    WHEN    We left *early.*
>            I moved *soon.*
>            You arrived *late.*
>    WHERE   They ran *far.*
>            I lived *nearby.*
>            I went *there.*

Notice that words that tell how, when, and where often end in -*ly* (sudden*ly*, occasional*ly*, sharp*ly*, rude*ly*, happi*ly*).

## EXERCISE 1

In the following sentences, underline all words that describe persons and things.

1. If you work very hard, you can finish two papers in class.
2. The frightened child cried for her mother.
3. Liz has black hair.
4. Suddenly there was a dark cloud in the sky.
5. Tom quickly refused John's kind offer.
6. If you should sneeze in the quiet library, do it as unobtrusively as possible.
7. Her youngest and laziest daughter has a job that pays well.
8. The singing birds disturbed us.
9. An egg-shaped ball is used to play football.
10. That poor dog has no juicy bones to chew on.

## EXERCISE 2

In the following sentences, underline all words that tell how, when, or where something is happening.

1. The frightened cat moved very cautiously.
2. Suddenly, the rain began.
3. The sleepy students entered the room slowly.
4. My older brother has always done his job well.
5. The crackling fire soon cheered us up.

**4a** Use descriptive words ending in *-ed* and *-ing* correctly.

Many words ending in *-ed* or *-ing* describe persons or things.

> *Mimeographed* copies are available. [copies that have been mimeographed]
> This is an *aged* cheese. [a cheese that has been aged]
> Don't open any *closed* doors. [doors that have been closed]
> My *sewing* box is on the desk. [a box used in sewing]
> We have no more *washing* powder. [powder used for washing]
> She saw a *purring* cat. [a cat who was purring]

Do not omit the *-d* or *-ed* at the end of a descriptive word.

| | |
|---|---|
| WRONG | a love one |
| RIGHT | a love*d* one |
| WRONG | a load gun |
| RIGHT | a load*ed* gun |
| WRONG | a frighten child |
| RIGHT | a frighten*ed* child |

Do not omit the *-ing* at the end of a descriptive word.

| | |
|---|---|
| WRONG | a change opinion |
| RIGHT | a chang*ing* opinion |
| WRONG | a gather storm |
| RIGHT | a gather*ing* storm |
| WRONG | a work girl |
| RIGHT | a work*ing* girl |

Descriptive words ending in *-ed* or *-ing* come from verbs.

| | |
|---|---|
| The girls *work*. | They are *working* girls. |
| Movies like *Jaws frighten* children. | The children are *frightened*. |
| They *load* their guns. | They carry *loaded* guns. |
| We *hassle* our mother. | Our mother is *hassled*. |

When words like *work, frighten, load,* and *hassle* are used to describe persons or things, remember to add *-ed* or *-ing* to them.

**EXERCISE 3**

Copy the examples below. Then make a descriptive word from each of the following verbs, and use it in a sentence: *help, admire, work, shout,* and *finish.*

**Examples**  *burn*
The *burned* child dreads the fire.

*wish*
I need a *wishing* well to make my front yard complete.

## EXERCISE 4

In the following sentences, underline the correct word in parentheses.

1. Cher is popular with middle- (age, aged) men.
2. Who is the (injure, injured) party in this case?
3. Thinking of you is a (comfort, comforted) to me.
4. Everyone had to bring a (cover, covered) dish to the picnic.
5. Low (cook, cooking) temperature softens the tissues and makes meat tender.
6. You need the (follow, following) items: scissors, a pattern, pins, and fabric.
7. A successful football team needs a good (pass, passing) attack.
8. You have to be on your guard when buying a (use, used) car.
9. Parents who show (concern, concerned) will worry when their children stay out late.
10. (Fish, Fishing) tackle should be available at any store in that area.

**4b**   **Use the correct words to tell how, when, and where something happens.**

| WRONG | That horse runs good. |
| RIGHT | That horse runs *well*. |

| WRONG | That happened too quick. |
| RIGHT | That happened too *quickly*. |

| WRONG | He is breathing normal. |
| RIGHT | He is breathing *normally*. |

| WRONG | My father dresses conservative. |
| RIGHT | My father dresses *conservatively*. |

Remember that many words that tell how, when, and where end in *-ly*.

**EXERCISE 5**

Correct the incorrect descriptive words in the following sentences by adding *-ly* to words that tell how, when, and where.

1. David is a real good friend of mine.
2. The furniture in my room fits my personality perfect.
3. Renee wears glasses, and all day long she is constant pulling them off and putting them on again.
4. The game started off slow, but after the first quarter the Cowboys made a touchdown.
5. You will need a larger pot than that one almost immediate.
6. After I wash my hair, I rinse the shampoo out very careful and slow.
7. I recently visited my home town and found it changed considerable.

**4c** **Use descriptive words correctly after verbs like** *look, feel, seem, appear, taste,* **and** *sound.*

Often these verbs mean the same as *is, are, was, were,* or some other form of *be.*

> I *feel* restless.   [OR I *am* restless.]
> Strawberry shortcake *tastes* delicious.   [OR Strawberry shortcake *is* delicious.]

Whenever a verb like *look, feel, seem,* or *taste* means the same as *is, are, was,* or *were,* use a describing word like *restless, delicious,* or *angry* after it. Do not use a word like *restlessly, deliciously,* or *angrily.*

> The teacher looked *angry.*   [*Was* can stand for *looked.*]
> The teacher looked *angrily* at me.   [*Was* cannot stand for *looked.*]

Note that after the verbs *feel* or *look, good* and *well* both describe persons and things.

> I look *good* (pretty) today.
> I look *well* (healthy) today.

*Well* is always used instead of *good* to tell how something is done.

> Look *well* before you tell me you can't find my book!

## EXERCISE 6

In the following sentences, underline the correct word in parentheses.

1. Your decision seems (hasty, hastily) to me.
2. With all you ate, I'm not surprised you feel (bad, badly).
3. She looked (good, well) at that dress before she bought it.
4. Homemade ice cream always tastes (good, well).
5. Rock music always sounds (noisy, noisily) to me.
6. My sister appeared (sudden, suddenly) in the doorway.
7. I'm afraid that that flounder doesn't smell very (fresh, freshly).

**4d**   **Use a describing word correctly when comparing two or more persons or things.**

**4d(1)**   **Many descriptive words end in *-er* or *-est* when they compare persons or things.**

> Today is *hotter* than yesterday.
> This is the *hottest* climate of all.
>
> Herb is *lazier* than Jim.
> Herb is the *laziest* person I know.
>
> Ed snores *louder* than Joe does.
> Ed snores *loudest* of all.
>
> Lisa talks *longer* than Julie does.
> Lisa talks the *longest* of any of us.

**4d(2)**   **The word *more* comes before some descriptive words that compare two persons or things. The word *most* comes before some descriptive words that compare more than two persons or things.**

> Ted is *more* interesting than Lee.
> Ted is the *most* interesting person I know.
>
> I talk *more* freely when Sue is not around.
> I talk *most* freely when no one else is listening.

Do not use *more* or *most* before a descriptive word that ends in *-er* or *-est*.

> WRONG    more prettier
> RIGHT    prettier
>
> WRONG    most loveliest
> RIGHT    loveliest

If *more* or *most* comes before a descriptive word, do not put *-er* or *-est* at the end of that word.

> WRONG    more likelier
> RIGHT    more likely
>
> WRONG    most wonderfulest
> RIGHT    most wonderful

## EXERCISE 7

Correct the incorrect descriptive words in the following sentences by using the right form of the descriptive word to compare the persons or things. Write *C* next to any sentences that are correct.

1. The ten-speed is one of the most fastest bikes.
2. A house is more safer than a trailer.
3. Mosquitoes are becoming a bigger problem than ever.
4. One of the loveliest places to visit in the fall is the mountains.
5. Friday is the most greatest day of the week.
6. My father hit me the hardest I had ever been hit.
7. My pastor spoke more longer this Sunday than he did last Sunday.
8. I think my hands are stronger than my little brother's.
9. We jumped off the porch and ran the most fastest we had ever run in our lives.
10. Bill is the most funniest person I know.

**4e** Learn the special forms of *good* and *well,* and *bad* and *badly* used to describe and compare.

### *Words that describe or compare persons and things*

Janice is a *good* daughter.
Janice is a *better* daughter than Sarah.
Janice is the *best* daughter.

I have a *bad* hangover.
I have a *worse* hangover than Earl.
I have the *worst* hangover.

### *Words that describe or compare verbs*

Janice obeys *well.*
Janice obeys *better* than Sarah.
Janice obeys *best* of all.

I drive *badly* when I am tired.
I drive *worse* when I am tired than when I am rested.
I drive *worst* of all when I drink.

### EXERCISE 8

Underline the correct descriptive word or words in parentheses.

1. My father cooks (better, more better) than my mother does.
2. The lectures we get at orientation are (worse, worst) than you can imagine.
3. My girlfriend is the (best, bestest) listener I know.
4. At boot camp we were treated (worse, worser) than animals.
5. Irene drives (better, best) than Frank does.

## EXERCISE 9

Correct any incorrect descriptive words in the following sentences. Write *C* next to each sentence that is correct.

1. All my brothers have jobs that pay good.
2. When you're doing bad in high school, you're called to the counseling office.
3. It is now time for Hank to think serious about his life.
4. When I was inducted into the army, I thought it was the worse thing that could happen to me.
5. Amy seems to have a more bigger writing problem than ever.
6. An F lead is the softer of all the leads.
7. Drafting paper will not tear easily.
8. When you get married, it is for better or worst.
9. My aunt is a middle-age woman who loves to eat.
10. The expressway traffic situation is looking well today.
11. Turn left at the next flash red light.
12. Who was the most admire of all Presidents?

# 5

# *Subject Words, Words That Show Ownership, and Object Words*

## Learn to recognize subject words, words that show ownership, and object words.

The following table shows the different forms of subject words, words that show ownership, and object words:

| SUBJECT WORDS | WORDS THAT SHOW OWNERSHIP | OBJECT WORDS |
|---|---|---|
| I | my | me |
| you | your | you |
| he | his | him |
| she | her | her |
| it | its | it |
| we | our | us |
| they | their | them |
| Mary | Mary's | Mary |

What do the words *I, you, he, she, it, we,* and *they* have in common? They all replace words that name someone or something.

> Mary is usually late. [*I* could replace *Mary.*]
> *I* am usually late.

> The upholstery is stained and torn. [*It* could replace *the upholstery.*]
> *It* is stained and torn.

Words like *Mary* and *upholstery* do not change their form, except when they show ownership, but words like *I*, *he*, and *they* do change.

|            |                     |
|-----------:|---------------------|
| SUBJECT    | John is happy.      |
| OWNERSHIP  | I saw John's book.  |
| OBJECT     | I saw John.         |

|            |                     |
|-----------:|---------------------|
| SUBJECT    | *He* is happy.      |
| OWNERSHIP  | I saw *his* book.   |
| OBJECT     | I saw *him*.        |

*I, you, he, she, it, we*, and *they* are used as the subject of a sentence (the person or thing that is being written about in the sentence).

> *I* rolled into a slimy ditch.
> *You* rolled into a slimy ditch.
> *He* rolled into a slimy ditch.
> *She* rolled into a slimy ditch.
> *It* rolled into a slimy ditch.
> *We* rolled into a slimy ditch.
> *They* rolled into a slimy ditch.

The subject of each of the above sentences tells who or what rolled into a slimy ditch.

*My, your, his, her, its, our*, and *their* show belonging, or ownership. These words cannot be used as the subject of a sentence. You would not say:

> My rolled into a slimy ditch.
> OR
> Their rolled into a slimy ditch.

Instead, *my, your, his, her, its, our*, and *their* tell who or what owns a particular thing. If you wanted to say: "I own a garbage can, and it rolled into a slimy ditch," you would probably say:

> *My* garbage can rolled into a slimy ditch.

If you wanted to say that the top belonging to a garbage can rolled into a slimy ditch, you could say:

> *Its* top rolled into a slimy ditch.

*Me, you, him, her, it, us*, and *them* are object words. They help you tell what the subject is doing. When you say that a garbage can rolled into someone or something, you cannot use *I* or *my* to describe what it rolled into. You would not say:

> A garbage can rolled into I.
>                OR
> A garbage can rolled into my.

But you can use the words *me, you, him, her, it, us,* and *them* to describe what the garbage can rolled into.

> A garbage can rolled into *me.*
> A garbage can rolled into *you.*
> A garbage can rolled into *him.*
> A garbage can rolled into *her.*
> A garbage can rolled into *it.*
> A garbage can rolled into *us.*
> A garbage can rolled into *them.*

**5a**   Use *I, he, she, we,* and *they* only as subjects (persons or things being talked about).

Do not confuse
- *I* with *me*
- *he* with *him*
- *she* with *her*
- *we* with *us*
- *they* with *them*

when your sentence has two subjects.

> WRONG   Me and Althea always come home late.
> RIGHT   Althea and *I* always come home late.

> WRONG   Him and me lost a bet.
> RIGHT   *He* and *I* lost a bet.

> WRONG   Her and Joe are really close.
> RIGHT   *She* and Joe are really close.

When a sentence has a double subject, there is a simple test that you can use to see whether you have used the right word. Try using each subject by itself as the subject of the sentence. In the sentence

> Me and Althea always come home late.

you would not say

> Me always come home late.

because *I*, not *me*, is the subject of the sentence. Therefore, if it is correct to say

I always come home late.

it is also correct to say

Althea and *I* always come home late.

Do not use *us* instead of *we* as the subject of a sentence.

WRONG   Us girls go bowling every Friday.
RIGHT   *We* girls go bowling every Friday.

Since *we* is the subject of the sentence, if you want to show that you are one of the girls, you have to say, "We [girls] go bowling."

*Them* cannot be used to describe persons and things. If you want to say that certain persons or things are in a particular place, use the words *these* or *those* to express that idea.

WRONG   Them books are on the table.
RIGHT   *Those* books are on the table.

Use *me* instead of *I* as an object word. *I* can only be used as a subject. In sentences like

Sally gave the tickets to Jim and *me*.
OR
Mrs. Hodges invited Joan and *me* to the party.

remember that *me* is used as an object word even though it does not directly follow the verb.

WRONG   She called to Ed and I to come in.
RIGHT   She called to Ed and *me* to come in.


## EXERCISE 1

For each of the following four groups of words, write two sentences that use the words correctly.

1. He and I
2. We brothers
3. Those children
4. Nancy and me

## EXERCISE 2

In the following sentences, underline the correct word in parentheses.

1. That gift brought happiness to my husband and (I, me).
2. I told him that (we, us) ex-Marines would have to stick together.
3. When I was in the Army, (my friends and I, me and my friends) saved enough money to start a business.
4. Everyone left except (my brother and me, my brother and I).
5. (Them, These) carrots don't look very fresh to me.
6. (He and I, Him and me) went downstairs to see what was going on.
7. My mother took (Janet and I, Janet and me) to the playground.
8. I just told you that (those, them) glasses have already been washed.
9. (She and Lou, Her and Lou) were already in line when we got to the theater.
10. Matt called to my sister and (I, me) across the street.

**5b**  Show ownership clearly by using the correct forms.

**5b(1)**  Be sure that you change *you* to *your* and *it* to *its* to show ownership.

WRONG  In an emergency you know who you friends are.
RIGHT  In an emergency you know who *your* friends are.

WRONG  Every nation has it secrets.
RIGHT  Every nation has *its* secrets.

**5b(2)**  Remember the two common ways to show ownership.

This is *my* cover.      This cover is *mine*.
This is *your* cover.    This cover is *yours*.

| | |
|---|---|
| This is *his* cover. | This cover is *his*. |
| This is *her* cover. | This cover is *hers*. |
| This is *our* cover. | This cover is *ours*. |
| This is *their* cover. | This cover is *theirs*. |

Notice that *yours, his, hers, ours,* and *theirs* do not have an apostrophe (') before the *s. Mine* does not have an apostrophe (') or an *s.*

| | |
|---|---|
| WRONG | This book is your's. |
| RIGHT | This book is *yours*. |
| WRONG | This book is hi's. |
| RIGHT | This book is *his*. |
| WRONG | This book is her's. |
| RIGHT | This book is *hers*. |
| WRONG | This book is our's. |
| RIGHT | This book is *ours*. |
| WRONG | This book is their's. |
| RIGHT | This book is *theirs*. |
| WRONG | This book is mine's (mines). |
| RIGHT | This book is *mine*. |

**5b(3)**   **Be sure to add an apostrophe (') and *s* to a word naming a person or thing to show ownership.**

| | |
|---|---|
| the book belonging to John ⟶ | John's book |
| the playground for the ⟶ children | the children's playground |
| the health of a person ⟶ | a person's health |

Do not carelessly omit the ending that shows ownership.

| | |
|---|---|
| WRONG | John book |
| RIGHT | John's book |
| WRONG | Children playground |
| RIGHT | Children's playground |

**5b(4)**   Do not confuse a word that shows ownership with another word ending in *s*.

Put an apostrophe before the *s* only when it is needed to show ownership. In particular, do not put an apostrophe before an *s* used to indicate the plural of a word.

WRONG   Sue is alway's in the way.
RIGHT   Sue is *always* in the way.

WRONG   The owner's were often wrong.
RIGHT   The *owners* were often wrong.   [*Owners* is simply the plural of *owner*. An apostrophe is not needed.]

## EXERCISE 3

Underline the word groups that are correctly written.

1. you raincoat; your raincoat
2. This is mines. This is mine. This is mine's.
3. its story; it story; it's story
4. they house; their house
5. What's mine is yours. What's mine's is your's. What's mine is your's.
6. That bar is theirs. That bar is their's.
7. Is it ours or his? Is it our's or hi's? Is it ours or hi's?

## EXERCISE 4

Correct all errors in words showing ownership. Write *C* next to each sentence that is correct.

1. I think that patience and understanding are your greatest strengths.
2. Tom is a dear friend of mine's.
3. Some baggers don't care how they handle you groceries.
4. I didn't like the idea of their going away to school.
5. Several coaches want him to attend they school.
6. My TV set has definitely reached the end of its useful life.
7. Get you equipment ready.
8. They are only giving their opinion.
9. I remember hi's saying he would never let a smaller man beat him.
10. Every marriage has it ups and downs.

## EXERCISE 5

Copy the following sentences, using an apostrophe and *s* when needed to show ownership. Remove the apostrophe when it is not needed.

1. All the women are waiting for the fishermen return.
2. Some people homes are large enough to have laundry room's.
3. The employer's always wanted more than a high-school diploma.
4. Getting into someone business can cause a lot of trouble.
5. He was always right by his father side.
6. To the right of the jewelry counter is the children department.
7. Harry Reasoner broadcast's on Watergate were very interesting.
8. The walls in Larry room were filled with hubcaps.
9. He ought not to play around with another person feelings.

## EXERCISE 6

Put a check mark next to any of the following word groups that show ownership correctly. Rewrite any of the word groups that do not show ownership correctly.

1. from Joe point of view
2. in today world
3. the student name
4. a citizen's property
5. today's time's

**5c** *Myself, yourself, himself, herself, itself, ourselves, yourselves,* **and** *themselves* **never are used alone.**

Use these words with subject and object words to give emphasis to the subject or object words.

> I walked by *myself.*
> Charles thinks for *himself.*
> We *ourselves* want to get the job finished.
> The lesson *itself* is not difficult.

**5c(1)**  *Myself, yourself, himself, herself, itself, ourselves, yourselves,* or *themselves* cannot be the subject of a sentence.

> WRONG  Myself and some friends moved all the furniture.
> RIGHT  Some friends and *I* moved all the furniture.

**5c(2)**  Be sure to spell *himself, itself, ourselves,* and *themselves* correctly.

| himself | NOT | hisself |
|---|---|---|
| itself | NOT | its self |
| ourselves | NOT | ourself |
| themselves | NOT | theirself |
| | | theirselves |
| | | themself |

## EXERCISE 7

In the following sentences, underline the correct word or words in parentheses.

1. Most of the time he is by (hisself, himself).
2. (My wife and myself, My wife and I) didn't want our daughter to move into an apartment.
3. We wanted to finish painting the barn by (ourself, ourselves).
4. Jenny and Lynn picked all those strawberries by (theirselves, themselves).
5. I know that mirror didn't get broken all by (its self, itself).

## EXERCISE 8

Correct the incorrect sentences by changing the italicized words to the correct forms. Write *C* next to each sentence that is correct.

1. *Myself and three other people* were participating in the talent show.

2. Robert Kennedy was struck down by an *assassin* bullet.
3. Did he mean to keep that letter a secret from *you and I?*
4. Around the corner *he and George* were waiting for us.
5. Are these children *their's* or *her's?*
6. *Her and I* were planning to go to the dance until you called.
7. *We kids* ought not to get in trouble right before Christmas.
8. That red motorcycle is *mine's;* the other one is *his.*
9. Remember that a sales tax takes money out of *you* pocket.
10. I call what he has on *his* face a *rat* nest, but he thinks it's a beard.
11. I found all of *those* stones in *them* beans I just washed.
12. I thought no one would ever break *Babe Ruth* home-run record.

# 6

# *Going Together*

**Make a subject go with its verb; make singular and plural words go with the words they refer to.**

**6a** **Make each subject go with its verb.**

A sentence is made up of two parts: a subject (the person or thing you are writing about) and a verb (the word telling what the subject is doing or what is happening to the subject). It is important that these two parts go together smoothly.

**6a(1)** **When you have a choice to make, singular (*he, she, it*) subjects go with verbs that end in *s*, and plural (*they*) subjects go with verbs that do not end in *s*.**

*Some subjects and verbs that do **not** go together*

| | |
|---|---|
| (*he* subject) | Bob write letters to his friends. |
| (*she* subject) | Lisa smile and look happy. |
| (*it* subject) | The party last all night. |
| (*they* subject) | Sal and Syl skates together. |
| (*they* subject) | Her eyelashes curls beautifully. |
| (*they* subject) | The weird noises of the night keeps us awake. |

56

### Some subjects and verbs that **do** go together

| | |
|---|---|
| (*he* subject) | Bob *writes* letters to his friends. |
| (*she* subject) | Lisa *smiles* and *looks* happy. |
| (*it* subject) | The party *lasts* all night. |
| (*they* subject) | Sal and Syl *skate* together. |
| (*they* subject) | Her eyelashes *curl* beautifully. |
| (*they* subject) | The weird noises of the night *keep* us awake. |

*Caution:* Words sometimes come between a singular subject and the verb that goes with it. When this happens, be very careful to make the verb end in *s* to go with its subject.

WRONG   One of my best friends sing off key.

RIGHT   One of my best friends *sings* off key.   [*One* is the subject of the sentence, not *friends*. Since *one* is singular, *sings* should end in *s* to go with it.]

The following singular (*he, she, it*) subjects go with verbs that end in *s:*

| | |
|---|---|
| one | *One* of the children *plays* quietly by himself. |
| everyone | *Everyone tries* to get her attention. |
| someone | *Someone waits* for Jane after class every day. |
| something | *Something falls* in the attic every night. |
| everything | *Everything happens* to me. |
| each | *Each* of the policemen *guards* one section of the mall. |
| kind | This *kind* of jewelry *costs* a lot. |
| either | *Either* drink *tastes* good to me. |
| neither | *Neither works* very hard. |

The following plural (*they*) subjects go with verbs that do not end in *s:*

| | |
|---|---|
| lots | *Lots* of my friends *attend* this school. |
| all | *All* of the salesmen *smile* at Carolyn when she comes in. |
| kinds | Many *kinds* of clothes *cost* a lot. |
| both | *Both* of the boys *study* a lot. |
| many | *Many* of us *worry* about the future. |
| several | *Several* members of the club always *come* late to the meetings. |

## EXERCISE 1

In the following sentences, underline the verb in parentheses that goes with its subject.

1. Vernon will talk from the time he (start, starts) cutting your hair until the time he is finished.
2. Sometimes she (dresses, dress) that way to clown around.
3. Every time he has some extra money he always (spend, spends) it.
4. Those children (makes, make) you smile when you really don't feel like it.
5. My cousins (sings, sing) in the church choir.

## EXERCISE 2

In the following sentences, underline the verb in parentheses that goes with its subject.

1. One of my cousins (play, plays) the piano beautifully.
2. The mall has several kinds of stores which (stays, stay) open late.
3. Lots of my friends (spends, spend) their evenings in that bar.
4. Everything (bother, bothers) me today.
5. Either of the plans (sounds, sound) good to me.

## EXERCISE 3

Correct the incorrect italicized verbs in the following sentences so that they go with their subjects. Write *C* next to each sentence that is correct.

1. The hallway *look* like a race track.
2. He always *want* me to invest my money in something.
3. Bill usually *sing* in the chorus.
4. Sandra and Herman *dances* well together.
5. Becky always *look* her best.
6. Each of the classrooms *fill* with water when it rains.
7. Sammy told me about the parts of the movie that *scares* everybody.
8. Everyone *enjoys* a good laugh.

9. He *drive* a 1977 Buick.
10. Not one of the students *come* to class the first night.

**6a(2)** When you have a choice to make, *I*, *we*, and *you* subjects go with verbs that do not end in *s*.

### Some subjects and verbs that do **not** go together

I likes to visit him.
You always finishes first.
I works every day from 8:00 to 4:30.
We understands your problem.
You treats John like trash.

### Some subjects and verbs that **do** go together

I *like* to visit him.
You always *finish* first.
I *work* every day from 8:00 to 4:30.
We *understand* your problem.
You *treat* John like trash.

### EXERCISE 4

Copy the first sentence of each of the following pairs of sentences. Then write a sentence of your own using the subject given. Do not use the verbs used in the sentences you copy.

1. I need to leave early tonight.
   I _____.
2. You look tired.
   You _____.
3. You smile too much.
   You _____.
4. I know the truth.
   I _____.
5. I never please my father.
   I _____.

6. Mack and I spend too much money. (Mack and I = *we* subject; We spend too much money.)
   Joe and I _____.
   We _____.

## EXERCISE 5

Correct the incorrect verbs in the following sentences so that the subjects and verbs go together. Write *C* next to each sentence that is correct.

1. I cries during sad movies.
2. You always thinks of others.
3. You eats too much junk food.
4. I read the directions carefully.
5. You never seem to care about other people.
6. I wishes you would come.
7. We dances to the music.
8. Bill and I never see each other.

**6a(3)** **Learn the forms of the verb *be* that go with their subjects.**

| PRESENT | | PAST | |
|---|---|---|---|
| *Subject* | *Verb* | *Subject* | *Verb* |
| I | am | I | was |
| you | are | you | were |
| he, she, it | is | he, she, it | was |
| we | are | we | were |
| you | are | you | were |
| they | are | they | were |

*Caution:* In *here is (are)*, *there is (are)*, and *where is (are)* sentences, the subject comes after the verb. Be sure to look after the verb for its subject in such sentences, and make the verb go with its subject.

Here is the key you have been looking for.   [*Is* is singular to go with the subject *key*.]
There are definitely mice in this attic.   [*Are* is plural to go with the subject *mice*.]

Where <u>were</u> those <u>shoes</u> when you found them?   [*Were* is plural to go with the subject *shoes*.]

## EXERCISE 6

In the following sentences, underline the correct verb form in parentheses.

1. Empty beer cans and wine bottles (was, were) all over the yard.
2. I (am, is) taking a make-up test on Wednesday.
3. There (is, are) only a few days of vacation left.
4. Teenage boys (is, are) always getting into trouble.
5. I never suspected that you (was, were) the one who called.
6. There (was, were) about fifteen men in my section.
7. On that shelf there (is, are) several of my favorite knick-knacks.
8. There (is, are) about twenty-five seats in our classroom.
9. Where (is, are) the mountains you said would be covered with snow?
10. Here (is, are) the books and tapes the language lab supplies to help you.

**6a(4)**   Singular (*he, she, it*) subjects go with the verb form *has;* all other subjects go with the verb form *have.*

| Subject | Verb |
|---|---|
| I | have |
| you | have |
| he, she, it | has |
| we | have |
| you | have |
| they | have |

## EXERCISE 7

In the following sentences, underline the correct verb form in parentheses.

1. My high school (has, have) its first game of the season this weekend.

2. The boat (have, has) a tall mast with sails flying.
3. You (has, have) to jog every morning to keep your weight under control.
4. My uncle (have, has) things pretty well organized.
5. Tina and Carol (has, have) to be in bed by 9 P.M.

**6a(5)** Singular (*he*, *she*, *it*) subjects go with the verb forms *does* and *goes*; all other subjects go with the verb forms *do* and *go*.

| *Subject* | *Verb* |  | *Subject* | *Verb* |
|-----------|--------|--|-----------|--------|
| I | do |  | I | go |
| you | do |  | you | go |
| he, she, it | does |  | he, she, it | goes |
| we | do |  | we | go |
| you | do |  | you | go |
| they | do |  | they | go |

### EXERCISE 8

In the following sentences, underline the correct verb form in parentheses.

1. My best friend (do, does) better in math than I (do, does).
2. It looks as though they (go, goes) to all the school activities.
3. Many young parents today (does, do) seem too busy to take care of their babies.
4. Ann will see that everything (go, goes) well.
5. It just (go, goes) to show you that a daughter (do, does) not always do what you would have done in her place.

**6a(6)** Learn the subjects that go with the contracted forms of the verb + *not*.

*I* subjects go with the verbs *don't, wasn't, haven't.*
*He, she, it* subjects go with the verbs *isn't, doesn't, wasn't, hasn't.*
*We, you, they* subjects go with the verbs *aren't, don't, weren't, haven't.*

## Some subjects and verbs that do **not** go together

| | |
|---|---|
| (*I* subject) | I doesn't understand you. |
| (*he* subject) | Dennis don't like Janis. |
| (*she* subject) | Rhonda haven't heard the news. |
| (*it* subject) | My car don't start on cold days. |
| (*we* subject) | We wasn't going to tell him. |
| (*they* subject) | Joe and Richard wasn't always friends. |
| (*they* subject) | His teeth isn't straight. |

## Some subjects and verbs that **do** go together

| | |
|---|---|
| (*I* subject) | I *don't* understand you. |
| (*he* subject) | Dennis *doesn't* like Janis. |
| (*she* subject) | Rhonda *hasn't* heard the news. |
| (*it* subject) | My car *doesn't* start on cold days. |
| (*we* subject) | We *weren't* going to tell him. |
| (*they* subject) | Joe and Richard *weren't* always friends. |
| (*they* subject) | His teeth *aren't* straight. |

Spell these verbs correctly. The apostrophe goes between the *n* and the *t* because the *o* has been left out.

isn't NOT is'nt
are't NOT are'nt

wasn't NOT was'nt
weren't NOT were'nt

doesn't NOT does'nt
don't NOT do'nt

hasn't NOT has'nt
haven't NOT have'nt

## EXERCISE 9

Correct the incorrect italicized verbs in the following sentences so that they go with their subjects. Write *C* next to each sentence that is correct.

1. Larry *don't* ever catch any fish.
2. Lucy *wasn't* very friendly yesterday.
3. David and Josephine *aren't* going together anymore.
4. This book *haven't* a very good ending.

5. You *wasn't* very fair in your decision.
6. I *wasn't* very happy about getting that teacher.
7. People *isn't* likely to watch that show.

## EXERCISE 10

Using the verbs *doesn't*, *wasn't*, *haven't*, and *aren't*, write four sentences of your own, making sure that the subjects and verbs go together.

1. _____ doesn't _____.
2. _____ wasn't _____.
3. _____ haven't _____.
4. _____ aren't _____.

## 6b    Make subject words, words that show ownership, and object words go with the words they refer to.

You wouldn't expect to read a sentence like

> Joe reads Joe's book.
>
> **OR**
>
> The children took the children's places in the classroom.

To keep from using the same word over and over again, sometimes you may want to use another word to refer to that word. When you do this, it is important that the two words go together smoothly.

## 6b(1)    Use *he, she, it, its, his, him, her,* or *hers* to go with a word that names only one person or thing.

$$\text{Use} \begin{cases} \text{he} \\ \text{him} \\ \text{his} \end{cases} \text{to go with } Sam.$$

Sam hides *his* beer cans when *his* father comes into the room.

$$\text{Use} \begin{cases} \text{she} \\ \text{her} \\ \text{hers} \end{cases} \text{to go with } \textit{mother.}$$

Mother said *she* would see *her* lawyer on Thursday.

$$\text{Use} \begin{cases} \text{it} \\ \text{its} \end{cases} \text{to go with } \textit{beer.}$$

I poured the beer slowly, but *it* still has a head on *it*.

**6b(2)**  Use *they, them, their, theirs* to go with a word that names more than one person or thing.

$$\text{Use} \begin{cases} \text{they} \\ \text{them} \\ \text{their} \\ \text{theirs} \end{cases} \text{to go with} \begin{cases} \text{students} \\ \text{desks} \end{cases}.$$

Students shouldn't write on *their* desks or leave *their* gum stuck to *them.*

### *Some words that do* **not** *go together*

A boy who prepares carefully for class will probably pass their exams.
Since a school desk is used by so many students, they always lose their shine.

### *Some words that* **do** *go together*

A boy who prepares carefully for class will probably pass *his* exams.
Since a school desk is used by so many students, *it* always loses *its* shine.

### EXERCISE 11

· Correct the incorrect sentences by changing the italicized words to go with the words they refer to. If you have to change any verbs to correct the sentences, change them also. Write *C* next to each sentence that is correct.

1. Bob sold *his* books for more than *it* was worth.
2. A hungry kitten will cry for *their* mother.
3. A student's life isn't *their* own.
4. Vicky's eyebrows are very thin, but *it* suits her face.
5. Draftsmen have to be particular about the type of eraser *they* use.
6. Most high-class customers read the menu and decide *he* will take the usual.
7. A coward uses other people to send messages to people *they* can't face.
8. The old desk had writing on *their* top.
9. Most young people I know don't want to work unless *they* really have to.
10. The working student has to budget *their* time carefully.

## 6b(3) Use words like *he, she, it,* and *his* to go with singular words like *one, everyone, each, everything, neither,* and *kind.*

### Some words that do **not** go together

Neither of the men left their name with the secretary.
What else can someone ask of their mother?
They are the kind of class I like best.

### Some words that **do** go together

*Neither* of the men left *his* name with the secretary.
What else can *someone* ask of *his* mother?
*It* is the *kind* of class I like best.

## 6b(4) Use words like *they, their,* and *them* to go with plural words like *all, kinds,* and *both.*

### Some words that do **not** go together

All of the workers have to take care of her own tools.
It is the kinds of clothes I like best.

### Some words that **do** go together

*All* of the workers have to take care of *their* own tools.
*They* are the *kinds* of clothes I like best.

### EXERCISE 12

In the following sentences, underline the word or words
in parentheses that go with the italicized word.

1. *Each* of my friends gave me (her, their) phone number.
2. *One* of the books had lost (its, their) cover.
3. Bill dropped *something.* Will you pick (it, them) up?
4. (He is, They are) the *kind* of teacher I like.
5. *Everyone* brought (his, their) own beer.
6. (It is, They are) the *types* of exercises all the students do.
7. I babysit so often that when *someone* comes to visit me,
   (they get, he gets) the impression that I am running a nur-
   sery.
8. When the time comes for a football game, *everyone* is excited because each thinks that (his, their) team is going to
   win.

**6b(5)**   Use *he, she, it, its, her, hers, his, him* to go with two or
more singular words joined by *or* or *nor.* Use *they, them,
their, theirs* to go with two or more plural words joined
by *or* or *nor.*

### Some words that do **not** go together

Either Bill or Bob left their own work unfinished.
Neither Jackie nor Susan ever cleans their own room.

### Some words that **do** go together

Either Bill or Bob left *his* own work unfinished.
Neither Jackie nor Susan ever cleans *her* own room.

## EXERCISE 13

In the following sentences, underline the word in parentheses that goes with the italicized words.

1. *Neither Barbara nor Pam* finished (her, their) paper in class.
2. Did *your truck or your trailer* fail (their, its) inspection?
3. *Neither the fathers nor the children* lost (their, his) temper.
4. *Either the rain or the wind* had (its, their) effect on the garden.
5. Will *Bill or Ed* take (their, his) vacation in August?
6. Neither *the trees nor the bushes* kept (their, its) leaves this winter.

## EXERCISE 14

Copy the following paragraph, changing any words necessary to make all subjects and verbs go together and to make all words go with the words they refer to.

The detective will always be a favorite character on American television because people enjoys seeing how police protection work. The TV detective always seem to know the solution to the crime without really thinking the case over. They are a superhuman mastermind, as well as an expert in self-defense, a good citizen, and a hero to all the kids. The TV detective is also so good-looking that all the women wants to kiss them. The real detective, though, are not like this. They has to think over dangerous situations because it could endanger their loved ones.

# 7

# *Verbs*

## Learn to recognize
## the correct forms of verbs.

In a sentence, a verb is a word that tells what the subject is doing or what is happening to the subject. You can usually use verbs correctly if you know how verb forms are spelled and if you understand their purpose in a sentence.

A verb can stand by itself (*love, loves, loved*), or it can appear with another verb — often called a *helping verb* (for example, *is, have, does, can, will*).

VERB BY ITSELF
I *love* money.
He *loves* money.
We *loved* money.

VERB WITH HELPING VERB
Money *is loved* by many.
I *have loved* money.
I *could love* money.
They *do love* money.
We *will love* money.

A verb can be helped by one helping verb or by more than one helping verb.

I *have* loved money.
I *could have* loved money.

69

A verb that is sometimes used as a helping verb can also appear by itself as the main verb of a sentence.

>   I *have* a lot of money.

Most verbs have no more than five basic forms. If you know these forms, you can express any number of ideas by using a form in a sentence either with or without a helping verb. For example, here are the five basic forms of *give:*

| give | gives | giving | gave | given |

These are some of the things you can say when you know these forms:

| *give* | *gives* | *giving* | *gave* | *given* |
|---|---|---|---|---|
| I give | he gives | I was giving | she gave | I have given |
| we will give | she gives | I have been giving | | it was given |
| I like to give | it gives | They are giving | | they are given |
| I can give | | | | |
| I did give | | | | |

**7a**   **Learn the verb forms that express the simple past.**

Each verb except *be* has only one simple past form.

> I  
> you  
> he  
> she  } *gave*  
> it  
> we  
> they

The simple past just says that something happened, and it says it using one verb. No helping verbs are used with the simple past. The italicized verbs in the following sentences all tell about something that happened in the simple past.

>   I *sang* in the choir.
>   You *lost* your way in the woods.
>   We *laughed* on the way home.
>   She *danced* all night long.

**7a(1)**     Simple past forms ending in *-ed*

Most verbs end in *-ed* when they express the simple past. Only a *d* is added when the verb already ends in *e* (*add + ed → added; change + d → changed*). Sometimes the ending is not clearly heard in speech, but it always appears in writing.

> WRONG    I notice that there were some buses full of people.
> RIGHT      I *noticed* that there were some buses full of people.
>
> WRONG    I watch the news last night.
> RIGHT      I *watched* the news last night.

Be sure to add *d* or *ed* to express the simple past of *use, suppose,* and *happen.* If you do not do this, it will sound as if you are talking about something happening now — in the present.

> PRESENT      I use my commuter tickets. [I use them every day.]
> SIMPLE PAST   I *used* my commuter tickets. [I used them all up.]
>
> PRESENT      I happen to be against that plan. [I am against it now.]
> SIMPLE PAST   I *happened* to be against that plan. [I was against it.]

## EXERCISE 1

If any of the following sentences shows that something happened in the past, make the italicized verb simple past by adding *d* or *ed*. If you cannot tell whether the past or present is intended, do not change the verb.

1. Everybody *finish* eating an hour ago.
2. The last time Sid *play* cards was a year ago.
3. The bus *approach* as I saw my father's car.
4. I *realize* that you are right.
5. I *like* this class.
6. We *use* to have plenty of money.
7. We all *decide* to go fishing last Saturday.
8. I *open* the door, and there she was!
9. People with allergies often *use* a special soap.
10. We *happen* to be wrong in this case.

## 7a(2)   Irregular simple past forms

### Simple past forms having the sound *an*

Many verbs end in *-an* or have *an* (as in *and*) as the main sound when they express the simple past. Some common ones are *ran*, *began*, *drank*, *sang*, *sank*, and *shrank*. These verbs are the simple past forms of *run*, *begin*, *drink*, *sing*, *sink*, and *shrink*. They appear without a helping verb.

> Eve *ran* home.
> We *began* to sort the mail.
> Phil *drank* all the beer.
> We *sang* silly songs.
> The leaky boat *sank*.

Do not confuse a simple past form (*ran*, *began*, *drank*, *sang*, *sank*) with the form that must be used with a helping verb.

> WRONG   I have ran.
> RIGHT   I *ran*.
>         I *have run*.

> WRONG   I have began.
> RIGHT   I *began*.
>         I *have begun*.

> WRONG   We had drank water.
> RIGHT   We *drank* water.
>         We *had drunk* water.

### EXERCISE 2

When the simple past is expressed *without* a helping verb, change the italicized verb to *ran*, *began*, *drank*, *sang*, or *shrank*.

1. When we heard that noise, we *run* all the way home.
2. I *begun* to worry about my clothing.
3. I can see that your dress *shrunk* a lot in the wash.
4. Walter had *drunk* a lot before he came.
5. That song was *sung* at the band concert on Saturday.

### *Blew, drew, flew, grew,* and *knew*

*Blew, drew, flew, grew,* and *knew* are the simple past forms of *blow, draw, fly, grow,* and *know.* Notice the contrast between the present (right now) and the simple past.

|  |  |
|---|---|
| PRESENT | Today I blow bubbles. |
| SIMPLE PAST | Yesterday I *blew* bubbles. |
| PRESENT | Today I draw a picture. |
| SIMPLE PAST | Yesterday I *drew* a picture. |
| PRESENT | Today I fly planes. |
| SIMPLE PAST | Yesterday I *flew* planes. |
| PRESENT | Today I grow gardenias. |
| SIMPLE PAST | Yesterday I *grew* gardenias. |
| PRESENT | Today I know everything. |
| SIMPLE PAST | Yesterday I *knew* everything. |

Do not make the mistake of thinking that *blow, draw, fly, grow,* and *know* are regular verbs that add *d* or *ed* to form the past.

| WRONG | RIGHT |
|---|---|
| blowed | blew |
| drawed | drew |
| flied | flew |
| growed | grew |
| knowed | knew |

## EXERCISE 3

Write two sentences using each of the following beginnings: I blew, He drew, We flew, It grew, They knew.

### *Swore, tore,* and *wore*

*Swore, tore,* and *wore* are the simple past forms of *swear, tear,* and *wear.* They cannot be used with helping verbs.

| WRONG | I have tore my dress. |
|---|---|
| RIGHT | I *tore* my dress. |
| WRONG | He has wore out that lawnmower. |
| RIGHT | He *wore* out that lawnmower. |

## EXERCISE 4

Write two sentences using each of the following beginnings: He swore, She tore, They wore.

### *Came* and *became*

Be sure that you know the simple past forms (*came* and *became*) of the verbs *come* and *become*.

| | |
|---|---|
| PRESENT | They all come to our house. [They come every year.] |
| SIMPLE PAST | They all *came* to our house. [They came last week.] |
| PRESENT | I become jealous easily. [I become jealous often.] |
| SIMPLE PAST | I *became* jealous when I saw them. [I became jealous that one time.] |

Do not use *came* or *became* with a helping verb.

| | |
|---|---|
| WRONG | He has often came to our house. |
| RIGHT | He often *came* to our house. |

## EXERCISE 5

Write two sentences using each of the following beginnings: They came, It became.

### *Did, saw,* and other unusual forms

The following lists show some very common verbs that have unusual forms in the simple past.

| PRESENT | SIMPLE PAST |
|---|---|
| go | went |
| do | did |
| eat | ate |
| fall | fell |
| forget | forgot |
| give | gave |
| see | saw |
| shake | shook |
| take | took |

Remember not to use the simple past forms with helping verbs.

WRONG   They have did their English lesson.
RIGHT   They *did* their English lesson.

WRONG   He has already went home.
RIGHT   He already *went* home.

Do not use the incorrect forms *done, seen,* or *seed,* thinking they are simple past forms.

WRONG   I done all that you asked.
RIGHT   I *did* all that you asked.

WRONG   I seen the motorcycle in the rear-view mirror.
RIGHT   I *saw* the motorcycle in the rear-view mirror.

## EXERCISE 6

Write two sentences using each of the following beginnings: We did, It went, They fell, I forgot, You forgave, I gave, They shook, It took, She saw, He ate.

### Simple past forms having the sound *o*

*Arose, broke, chose, drove, froze, rode, spoke, stole,* and *wrote* are all simple past forms. When you say these words, you hear the sound *o* as in *hole.* All these forms end in a silent *e.* Do not use a helping verb with any of these forms.

WRONG   A dispute has arose.
RIGHT   A dispute *arose.*

WRONG   The glass has broke.
RIGHT   The glass *broke.*

WRONG   He has chose a partner.
RIGHT   He *chose* a partner.

WRONG   I have spoke to him about it.
RIGHT   I *spoke* to him about it.

WRONG   You have never wrote to her.
RIGHT   You never *wrote* to her.

## EXERCISE 7

Write two sentences using each of the following simple past forms: *arose, broke, chose, drove, froze, rode, spoke, stole, wrote.*

## EXERCISE 8

If the italicized verbs in each of the following sentences express the simple past correctly, write *C* next to the sentence. If the simple past is not used, change the form of the verb to the simple past.

1. I had friends who *had went* into the Navy.
2. Al often *has rode* up and down the street to catch a glimpse of a pretty girl.
3. Sara *done* a lot for me when I *lived* in the dorm.
4. Many problems *have came* to the surface.
5. There was so much wind my house almost *blowed* away.
6. Leo *has swore* to tell the truth, the whole truth, and nothing but the truth.
7. The men who held me up *took* all my money.
8. I *knowed* it was wrong when I *saw* it.
9. Jo *has wore* my dress three times, and I haven't even had it on.
10. Edna *has gave* that dog all the bones she could find in the house.
11. They *have* all *chose* to stay in the same group.
12. Phil *became* very angry when Ed *told* him the news.
13. They *have drove* that way for years.
14. He *flied* his plane into a mountain.
15. We *seen* him coming.
16. George and Steve *run* all the way home.
17. Eileen and I *had ate* too much that time.

### Burst, caught, dug, led, and passed

The irregular simple past forms of *burst, catch, dig, lead,* and *pass* are often used incorrectly.

| | |
|---|---|
| WRONG | I busted a balloon. |
| RIGHT | I *burst* a balloon. |
| | |
| WRONG | I catched the flu. |
| RIGHT | I *caught* the flu. |

WRONG   I digged a hole.
RIGHT   I *dug* a hole.

WRONG   I lead the list yesterday.
RIGHT   I *led* the list yesterday.

WRONG   I past (OR pasted) the chicken.
RIGHT   I *passed* the chicken.

## EXERCISE 9

Write a sentence using each of the following simple past forms: *burst, caught, dug, led,* and *passed.*

Review **7a** carefully. Then do Exercises 10, 11, and 12.

## EXERCISE 10

Write the simple past form of the verb given in parentheses in the space provided in each sentence.

(do)      1. We all _____ our homework.
(see)     2. I _____ the dog.
(burst)   3. Harvey _____ the bubble.
(take)    4. She _____ a letter.
(run)     5. They _____ down the hill.
(steal)   6. Milly and I _____ some money.
(draw)    7. Joan and Peggy _____ some pictures.
(break)   8. Marty _____ a bottle.
(know)    9. I _____ the answer.
(catch)  10. You _____ a cold.

## EXERCISE 11

Rewrite the following sentences so that each verb is in the simple past form. Follow the pattern given in the examples and begin each of your sentences with *They.*

**Examples**   It was seen as a big problem.
             They *saw it as a big problem.*

> Sugar was used to make a cake.
> They *used sugar to make a cake.*

1. Plenty of examples were given.
   They _____.
2. The escapees were seen in this area.
   They _____.
3. The actor was chosen for the part.
   They _____.
4. The mayor was welcomed.
   They _____.
5. The work was soon done.
   They _____.
6. All the facts were known.
   They _____.
7. The boy's kite was torn.
   They _____.
8. The mirror was accidentally broken.
   They _____.
9. The hamburgers were soon eaten.
   They _____.
10. All the bad memories were forgotten.
    They _____.
11. The letter was written too late.
    They _____.
12. My good advice was not taken.
    They _____.
13. The ice cream was frozen.
    They _____.
14. Many gifts were given.
    They _____.
15. Only one fish was caught.
    They _____.

## EXERCISE 12

If the italicized verb in each of the following sentences expresses the simple past correctly, write *C* next to the sentence. If the simple past is not used, change the form of the verb to the simple past.

1. I *notice* many buses full of people.
2. I *watched* the news that night.
3. My neighbor's dog *digged* a big hole in my yard.
4. They *ask* us what was going on.
5. After an hour *pasted,* I went to look for him.

## IRREGULAR VERBS

| Present | Simple Past | Present | Simple Past |
|---------|-------------|---------|-------------|
| arise | arose | have | had |
| become | became | hear | heard |
| begin | began | hide | hid |
| blow | blew | hit | hit |
| break | broke | hold | held |
| bring | brought | hurt | hurt |
| build | built | keep | kept |
| burst | burst | know | knew |
| buy | bought | lay | laid |
| can | could | lead | led |
| catch | caught | leave | left |
| choose | chose | let | let |
| come | came | lie | lay |
| cut | cut | lose | lost |
| deal | dealt | make | made |
| dig | dug | meet | met |
| dive | dove (dived) | pay | paid |
| do | did | put | put |
| drag | dragged | quit | quit |
| draw | drew | read | read |
| drink | drank | ride | rode |
| drive | drove | ring | rang |
| eat | ate | rise | rose |
| fall | fell | run | ran |
| feed | fed | say | said |
| feel | felt | see | saw |
| fight | fought | seek | sought |
| find | found | sell | sold |
| fly | flew | send | sent |
| forget | forgot | set | set |
| forgive | forgave | shake | shook |
| freeze | froze | shine | shone |
| get | got | show | showed |
| give | gave | shrink | shrank |
| go | went | sink | sank |
| grow | grew | sit | sat |

IRREGULAR VERBS (*continued*)

| Present | Simple Past | Present | Simple Past |
|---------|-------------|---------|-------------|
| sleep | slept | tear | tore |
| speak | spoke | tell | told |
| spend | spent | think | thought |
| spring | sprang | throw | threw |
| stand | stood | understand | understood |
| steal | stole | wake | woke (waked) |
| swim | swam | wear | wore |
| take | took | win | won |
| teach | taught | write | wrote |

**7b** **Learn the verb forms that are used with helping verbs.**

Four of the verbs used with helping verbs (such as *has, have, had, is, was, will be,* and *has been*) are the verbs *loved, given, done,* and *run.* The verb *loved* is regular. It looks just like the simple past and is constructed by adding *d* to the present form (*love* + *d* → *loved*). The others (*given, done,* and *run*) are not regular, and you must learn them separately. Here are some of the different ideas you can express by using these verbs with helping verbs:

> I have loved (given, done, run)
> he has loved (given, done, run)
> I will have loved (given, done, run)
> I would have loved (given, done, run)
> I can have loved (given, done, run)
> I could have loved (given, done, run)
> it is loved (given, done, run)
> it was loved (given, done, run)
> they will be loved (given, done, run)
> they have been loved (given, done, run)

Remember that a verb may be separated from its helping verb by other words in the sentence. Do not let this situation make you forget to use the correct verb form.

> WRONG   I have never love you.
> RIGHT   I *have* never *loved* you.

WRONG   Was her favorite doll gave to her sister?
RIGHT   *Was* her favorite doll *given* to her sister?

**7b(1)**   Forms ending in *-ed*

Regular verb forms ending in *-ed* are often used with helping
verbs like *has, have, had, is, are, was, were,* and *has been.*
Some common examples are *loved, danced, watched, waited,*
and *listened.* Remember that you do not always hear the *d*
ending clearly in speech, but it always appears in writing.

WRONG   Our group was single out for criticism.
RIGHT   Our group *was singled* out for criticism.

WRONG   The air is then push out of the carburetor.
RIGHT   The air *is* then *pushed* out of the carburetor.

Be especially careful to add *d* or *ed* to *use, happen,* and *sup-*
*pose* when these words are used with helping verbs.

WRONG   He is use to hard times.
RIGHT   He *is used* to hard times.

WRONG   We are suppose to be there.
RIGHT   We *are supposed* to be there.

WRONG   It has happen many times.
RIGHT   It *has happened* many times.

**EXERCISE 13**

After adding *d* or *ed* to each verb given in the left-hand
column, write eight sentences. Use the beginnings given
in the right-hand column.

**Example**   change   They have   They have changed their
                                              clothes.

1. finish      Gary had
2. happen      It has
3. start       The engine has been
4. clean       The rug was
5. explode     It will be
6. suppose     We were
7. use         The time has been
8. accustom    Alan and I are

## EXERCISE 14

Write *C* next to each sentence in which *d* or *ed* is correctly added to the end of a verb. Add *d* or *ed* to a verb where it is needed.

1. Have you noticed that some of the buses are already full?
2. Different blades are use for the kind of cut the barber desires.
3. If you walk through that door, you will really be frighten.
4. It is the worst thing that has ever happen to me.
5. The catalog is divided into two sections.

## 7b(2)   Irregular forms

### Forms having the sound *un*

The verbs *run, begun, drunk, sung, sunk, sprung,* and *shrunk* are used with helping verbs such as *has, have, had, is,* and *was.* When you pronounce them, you hear that *un* (as in *under*) is their main sound. Do not confuse these words with the simple past verbs, which are not used with helping verbs.

WRONG   I have just began.
RIGHT   I *have* just *begun.*

WRONG   They are ran by electricity.
RIGHT   They *are run* by electricity.

WRONG   He didn't know you had drank all his beer.
RIGHT   He didn't know you *had drunk* all his beer.

You should not hear an *un* sound when you use *bring* with a helping verb. *Brought,* not *brung,* is the verb used with helping verbs.

WRONG   She has brung her lunch.
RIGHT   She *has brought* her lunch.

## EXERCISE 15

Write at least ten sentences using the verbs *run, begun, sung, sprung,* and *shrunk* with the helping verbs *is, was, has,* and *had.*

## EXERCISE 16

In the following sentences, underline the correct form of the verb in parentheses.

1. Heats are (ran, run) until there is only one racer left.
2. Your troubles with that child have just (begun, began).
3. I couldn't believe that my mother had (shrank, shrunk) my sweatshirt again.
4. I hope that the McDonalds have (brought, brung) the salt.
5. That surprise was (sprung, sprang) on Tim last week.

### Forms ending in -n or -en

Many verbs used with the helping verbs *have, had, is, are, was,* and *were* end in *-n* or *-en*. Some common examples are:

| | | |
|---|---|---|
| arisen | forgiven | stolen |
| beaten | forgotten | sworn |
| broken | given | taken |
| chosen | seen | torn |
| driven | shaken | worn |
| eaten | spoken | written |

Do not confuse these verbs with the simple past forms, which are not used with helping verbs.

WRONG  He had swore to be true.
RIGHT  He *had sworn* to be true.

WRONG  He was beat by $\frac{2}{10}$ of a second.
RIGHT  He *was beaten* by $\frac{2}{10}$ of a second.

## EXERCISE 17

Change the verbs listed in the left-hand column to the correct form ending in *-n* or *-en* so that they can be used with the helping verbs listed in the right-hand column. Then write a sentence using each of the verbs and its helper correctly.

**Example**  shake  has been  Jay has been badly shaken.

1. write   had been
2. beat   should be

3. eat     was
4. take   will be
5. forget  have
6. give   should have been
7. see    has
8. speak  were
9. break  could have been
10. tear   had

## EXERCISE 18

Change the italicized verb in each of the following sentences so that it will go with its helping verb. If any sentence is correct, write *C* next to the sentence.

1. Amy likes to be *seed* in the best places.
2. The policeman has *swore* out a warrant for his arrest.
3. That merchandise is sure to be *stolen*.
4. A student from my high school was *chose* to represent Dayton in the debating finals.
5. I think Ali was definitely *beat* in a fair fight.
6. All first offenders were *given* a warning.
7. Come home; all is *forgave*.
8. Larry has often *spoke* to me about her.
9. It would have *took* even longer if I hadn't called home.
10. My father has to be *driven* to work every morning because our car is still in the shop.

### Forms ending in -*wn*

The verbs *blown, drawn, flown, grown, known,* and *shown,* all of which end in -*wn,* are used with the helping verbs *has, have, had, is, are.* Do not make the mistake of thinking these are regular verbs that end in *d* or *ed.*

WRONG  The wind has blowed us about.
RIGHT    The wind *has blown* us about.

WRONG  You have drawed an accurate picture.
RIGHT    You *have drawn* an accurate picture.

WRONG   She is really growed up.
RIGHT   She *is* really *grown* up.

WRONG   We have knowed this for over a year.
RIGHT   We *have known* this for over a year.


## EXERCISE 19

Using each of the verbs ending in -*wn* that you have just learned, write a sentence beginning "My sister has" and a question beginning "Have you."

**Examples**   My sister has *flown to Chicago.*
Have you *ever flown to Honolulu?*


### *Gone, done, come,* and *become*

Four of the verbs you use very often are *go*, *do*, *come*, and *become*. When they are used with helping verbs,

*go* changes to (have) *gone*
*do* changes to (have) *done*
*come* and *become* do not change:   (have) *come*
(have) *become*

It is important not to confuse *gone, done, come,* and *become* with the simple past forms, which are not used with a helping verb.

WRONG   Many of my friends had went into the Army.
RIGHT   Many of my friends *had gone* into the Army.

WRONG   I have did everything I know how to do.
RIGHT   I *have done* everything I know how to do.

WRONG   This had all came to pass.
RIGHT   This *had* all *come* to pass.

WRONG   In just one more year we all will have became rich.
RIGHT   In just one more year we all *will have become* rich.

## EXERCISE 20

Write a sentence using the correct form of *go*, *do*, *come*, and *become* with the helping verbs *will have* and another sentence with the helping verbs *could have*.

**Examples**   In one year I *will have become* a millionaire.
He *could have become* another Humphrey Bogart.

### *Burst, caught, dug, found*, and *passed*

*Burst, caught, dug, found*, and *passed* are some irregular verb forms used with helping verbs like *has, have, was, were*. If you do not know them well, you will have to study them. They are often used incorrectly.

WRONG   It has bursted.
RIGHT   It *has burst*.

WRONG   He has been catched.
RIGHT   He *has been caught*.

WRONG   We have digged.
RIGHT   We *have dug*.

WRONG   He was founded.
RIGHT   He *was found*.

WRONG   The day has past (OR pasted).
RIGHT   The day *has passed*.

## EXERCISE 21

Using the beginning "It will be" or "We have been," write a sentence using each of the following verbs: *caught, dug, found, passed*.

Review **7b** carefully. Then do Exercises 22, 23, and 24.

### EXERCISE 22

In the following sentences, add *d* or *ed* to the italicized verb only when needed. Correct any incorrect italicized forms. If any sentence is correct, write *C* next to it.

1. Joe Riddick has *retire* from the shipyard.
2. I have *learned* many things in my new job.
3. That would not have *happen* if you had been on time.
4. All of the fishing tackle can be *founded* on the table.
5. None of us was really *suppose* to be there.
6. After an hour had *past*, I went to look for Jack.
7. Clay refused the order and was *fined*.
8. We were *showed* the microfilm section.
9. Only fresh whole eggs are *used* in making an orange dream cake.
10. We have all *knowed* girls like Ava.

### EXERCISE 23

In the following sentences underline the correct form of the verb in parentheses.

1. Bob should have (gave, given) the car more gas.
2. Many problems have (came, come) to the surface.
3. I know I could have (become, became) a long-distance runner.
4. Buck's job was to look for mines that had not (gone, went) off.
5. I sometimes think the government is (ran, run) by idiots!
6. Have they (did, done) everything possible to find my records?
7. My sister has (worn, wore) every dress I own.
8. In spite of all my letters of inquiry, that company has never (wrote, written) me.
9. Fried chicken is often (ate, eaten) with the fingers.
10. That ship was (sank, sunk) in the Atlantic about twenty-five years ago.

## EXERCISE 24

Write ten sentences using the correct form of the verb given in the left-hand column to go with the helping verb given in the right-hand column.

**Examples**   finish   has   It looks as if everyone has fin-
                                ished eating.
               steal    were   The hubcaps on my new Monza
                                were stolen.

1. do       have
2. write    has been
3. go       is
4. give     will be
5. come     had
6. forget   are
7. begin    were
8. take     has
9. run      had
10. eat     could have

### IRREGULAR VERBS

| Present | Form Used with Helping Verbs | Present | Form Used with Helping Verbs |
|---|---|---|---|
| arise | arisen | choose | chosen |
| become | become | come | come |
| begin | begun | cut | cut |
| blow | blown | deal | dealt |
| break | broken | dig | dug |
| bring | brought | dive | dived |
| build | built | do | done |
| burst | burst | drag | dragged |
| buy | bought | draw | drawn |
| can | could | drink | drunk |
| catch | caught | drive | driven |

| Present | Form Used with Helping Verbs | Present | Form Used with Helping Verbs |
|---------|------------------------------|---------|------------------------------|
| eat | eaten | ride | ridden |
| fall | fallen | ring | rung |
| feed | fed | rise | risen |
| feel | felt | run | run |
| fight | fought | say | said |
| find | found | see | seen |
| fly | flown | seek | sought |
| forget | forgotten | sell | sold |
| forgive | forgiven | send | sent |
| freeze | frozen | set | set |
| get | got | shake | shaken |
| give | given | shine | shone |
| go | gone | show | shown |
| grow | grown | shrink | shrunk |
| have | had | sink | sunk |
| hear | heard | sit | sat |
| hide | hidden | sleep | slept |
| hit | hit | speak | spoken |
| hold | held | spend | spent |
| hurt | hurt | spring | sprung |
| keep | kept | stand | stood |
| know | known | steal | stolen |
| lay | laid | swim | swum |
| lead | led | take | taken |
| leave | left | teach | taught |
| let | let | tear | torn |
| lie | lain | tell | told |
| lose | lost | think | thought |
| make | made | throw | thrown |
| meet | met | understand | understood |
| pay | paid | wake | woken (waked) |
| put | put | wear | worn |
| quit | quit | win | won |
| read | read | write | written |

**7c**   **Add the *-ing* ending to a verb that tells that something is continuing.**

In addition to saying that something is happening now,

> He *bothers* me.
> He *is bothered* by a fly.

or that something happened in the past,

> He *bothered* me.
> He *has bothered* me.
> He *was bothered* by a fly.

or that something will happen,

> That fly *will bother* him.
> He *will* not *want* to *be bothered*.

verbs also say that something happens all at once or over a period of time. Verbs that end in *-ing* (*bothering, saying, doing, wanting, loving*) tell the reader that something is, was, or will be going on or continuing. They appear with helping verbs like *am, is, are, was, were,* and *will be.*

> ALL AT ONCE   I *said* something suspicious.   [I said it at one time.]
>
> CONTINUING   I *am saying* something suspicious.   [I am continuing to say it.]
>
> ALL AT ONCE   I *have said* something suspicious.   [I have already said it.]
>
> CONTINUING   I *was saying* something suspicious.   [I was saying it over a period of time.]
>
> ALL AT ONCE   I *will say* something suspicious.   [I will say it at some one time in the future.]
>
> CONTINUING   I *will be saying* something suspicious.   [I will be saying it for a while.]

Sometimes a word ending in *-ing* appears without a helping verb, yet it still tells about something that is going on or continuing.

> Betsy ran down the street, *calling* my name.
> You can get more food than George can by *eating* fast.

*Calling* and *eating* come from verbs and express continuing action as verbs do. Do not forget to add *ing* to these words that tell something is going on or continuing, even though they do not appear with helping verbs.

WRONG  Carl had a sign on his door say "Do not enter."
RIGHT  Carl had a sign on his door *saying* "Do not enter."

WRONG  He made a sharp U-turn, bring the ambulance to a complete stop.
RIGHT  He made a sharp U-turn, *bringing* the ambulance to a complete stop.

For more information about these *ing* words that look like verbs, see **7h(I)**.

### EXERCISE 25

Copy the first sentence of each of the following pairs of sentences. Then complete the second sentence, beginning the part you write with an *-ing* word.

**Example**   Sam wrote a good composition, *following the suggestions of his teacher.*
Ida wrote a funny letter, _____ .

1. I find out many things by *listening to my sister talk.*
I learn a lot by _____ .
2. The students are still *playing cards in the lounge.*
My father is always _____ .
3. I worked the dough on the counter, always *rolling it from the center toward the sides.*
Sue finished the chores assigned, always _____ .
4. My solution is *adding another room and calling this room the lounge.*
My suggestion is _____ .
5. My buddies and I were late as usual, *giving excuses you wouldn't believe.*
My daughter forgot my birthday as usual, _____ .

**7d**    **Learn to use the verb *be* correctly.**

*Be* is the most useful verb in English. A form of *be* can appear either by itself or with other verbs.

It appears by itself to tell what is happening.

I *am*
You *are*
He *is*
She *is*  } very silly.
It *is*
We *are*
They *are*

It appears by itself to tell what was happening.

I *was*
You *were*
He *was*
She *was*  } very silly.
It *was*
We *were*
They *were*

It appears with another verb as a helping verb — to help the verb say something about the subject.

It helps the verb say what the subject is doing.

I *am* bouncing along.
It *is* bounced along.

It helps the verb say what the subject was doing.

I *was* bouncing along.
They *were* bounced along.

It helps the verb say what the subject will be doing.

I *will* bounce along.

Sometimes it appears with other helping verbs to tell what the subject is doing.

I *have been* bounced along.
They *could have been* bouncing along.
I *am being* bounced along.
They *will be* bouncing along.

**7d(1)** *Is* and *are* are used more than any other forms of the verb *be*.

Be sure to use the verbs *is* and *are* or their contractions (*'s*) and (*'re*) to complete the meaning of a sentence.

| | |
|---|---|
| WRONG | My roommate snores sometimes, but otherwise he great. |
| RIGHT | My roommate snores sometimes, but otherwise he *is* great. |
| WRONG | It not often that teenagers are on time. |
| RIGHT | It *is* not often that teenagers are on time. |
| WRONG | What happening? |
| RIGHT | What*'s* happening? |
| WRONG | They gone! |
| RIGHT | They*'re* gone! |

Do not use *be* in place of *is* or *are* to complete the meaning of a sentence.

| | |
|---|---|
| WRONG | He be waiting here. |
| RIGHT | He *is* waiting here. |
| WRONG | These children be very happy. |
| RIGHT | These children *are* very happy. |

**7d(2)** *Being* and *been* are used with helping verbs.

He *is being* hassled.
We *have been* worried.

Be sure to remember that a helping verb is needed to complete the meaning of such sentences.

| | |
|---|---|
| WRONG | He being stubborn. |
| RIGHT | He *is* being stubborn. |
| WRONG | We been here a long time. |
| RIGHT | We *have* been here a long time. |

Review **7d** carefully. Then do Exercises 26, 27, and 28.

### EXERCISE 26

Insert *is* or *are* when needed to complete the meaning of the sentence. Write *C* next to any sentence that is correct.

1. If it not her head that hurts, it is her back.
2. This is a description of my brother.
3. Marty very slim and handsome.
4. The noise of the pool hall is still ringing in my ears.
5. They supposed to be here by 5:30.

### EXERCISE 27

Write two sentences using *being* and two sentences using *been* with helping verbs.

### EXERCISE 28

In the following sentences, underline the correct verb forms in parentheses.

1. They (being, are being) foolish about those children.
2. The child cried a lot, but otherwise he (been, has been) great.
3. If those girls (be, are) any later, they won't find any barbecue left.
4. I know Judy (been, has been) putting me on.
5. The whole time it (is, be) so noisy, you can't hear yourself talk.

**7e**  **Change the form of a verb only when necessary.**

You may find that you are occasionally confused about how to spell a verb form. You cannot always depend on what you hear because the verb ending does not always have a distinct sound. You remember that the verb changes when used with a helping verb like *has, have, had, is, are, was,* and *were:*

NO HELPING VERB   They *dance.*
HELPING VERB   They *have danced.*

NO HELPING VERB    We *sing.*
HELPING VERB    We *are singing.*

But *has, have, is, was,* and the others are not the only helping verbs. Verbs like *do, did, can, could, will,* and *would* are also helping verbs. They affect the spelling of the words they help differently from the helping verbs you learned about in **7b**.

**7e(1)**    **Learn how to spell the verb forms that are used directly after the helping verbs *will, would, do, did, can, could, should, may,* and *might* and their negative forms (*won't, wouldn't,* and so on).**

These helping verbs (unlike *has, have, is, are,* and so on) do not change the spelling of the verbs they help.

   WRONG    You did needed to study.
   RIGHT    You *did need* to study.

   WRONG    They would reacted badly.
   RIGHT    They *would react* badly.

   WRONG    He will tries to jump over the fence.
   RIGHT    He *will try* to jump over the fence.

   WRONG    A roofer can used both sides at once.
   RIGHT    A roofer *can use* both sides at once.

   WRONG    Alice won't wanted to be too early.
   RIGHT    Alice *won't want* to be too early.

**7e(2)**    **When there are two helpers (*will be, could have, can be,* and so on), the one directly before the verb controls the spelling of the verb.**

   will be visited    [*Be* controls the spelling of *visited.*]
   could have gone    [*Have* controls the spelling of *gone.*]

The helping verbs *be* and *have* change the spelling of the verbs that follow them.

   WRONG    In time, I would have react better.
   RIGHT    In time, I *would have reacted* better. [*Have* comes before the verb, so you must add *ed* to react.]

WRONG    Meanwhile, I can be use the book.
RIGHT    Meanwhile, I *can be using* the book. [*Be* comes before the verb, so you must add *ing* to *use*.]

**7e(3)**   Use *have* (not *had*) after other helping verbs, such as *will*, *would*, *should*, *could*, *can*, *may*, and *might*.

WRONG    They might had encountered some problems while looking for a job.
RIGHT    They might *have* encountered some problems while looking for a job.

WRONG    I should had given up my old habits.
RIGHT    I should *have* given up my old habits.

### EXERCISE 29

Correct any errors in the italicized verbs in the following sentences. Do not change any verb forms that are already correct.

1. When she did *arrived*, everyone was ready to go.
2. If children are forced to do what does not *interests* them, they will put forth little effort.
3. If I had known Lisa was going to be at the dance, I might *had* gone somewhere else.
4. I can still *heard* Daddy going up the creaking steps.
5. The car won't *rolled* down the hill.
6. Jimmy does *wants* some rock candy.
7. My mother-in-law did *come* early, as usual.
8. I could only *see* and *believed* in him.
9. Julie figured they needed help, but she didn't *figured* they would *refuse* it.
10. If you get overtired, you can *began* to lose your patience with others.

**7f**   Use the correct forms of *lay* and *lie*, and *set* and *sit*.

The verbs *lay* and *lie* and *set* and *sit* have been bothering students for a long time. Here are the guidelines you need to remember to use these verbs correctly.

**7f(1)**  Be sure to use the correct forms of *lay* and *lie*.

### Present

*Lay* (or *laying*) in the present means "place" or "put." When you lay something or someone down, you are doing something to that thing or person.

> We *lay* the packages down on the table.
> They *are laying* aside their prejudices.
> She *lays* the sleeping baby on his bed.

*Lie* (or *lying*) in the present means "stretch out and rest." When you lie down, you are doing something yourself.

> We often *lie* on the beach for hours.
> The alligators *are lying* in the sun.
> She *lies* in bed too long every morning.

### Past

*Laid* (or *laying*) in the past means "placed" or "put." When you laid something or someone down, you did something to that thing or person.

> We *laid* our brushes down.
> They *laid* their sleeping children on the mattress.
> The workers *were laying* brick.

*Lay* (or *lying*) in the past means "stretched out." When you lay down last night, you were not doing anything to anyone else; you were just resting.

> Yesterday we *lay* on our backs in the calm water.
> A jellyfish *was lying* near the shore.

### Laid and *lain* with helping verbs

*Laid* with a helping verb means "put down."

> I *have laid* my work aside.
> Our fears *will* all *be laid* to rest.

*Lain* with a helping verb means "stretched out."

> The dog *has lain* under the rosebush for a long time.  [This
> form is not often used. Most writers prefer to write: "The
> dog *has been lying* under the rosebush."]

## EXERCISE 30

In the following sentences, underline the correct form of *lay* and *lie* in parentheses.

1. A bank employee who was (laying, lying) in the corner got a look at both of the robbers.
2. He ordered me to (lay, lie) face-down on the floor.
3. Engine parts are (laying, lying) in huge piles in the garage.
4. Henry was (laying, lying) the groundwork for the talk.
5. Our Christmas packages were so heavy, we (laid, lay) them down as soon as we entered the house.

**7f(2)**   **Be sure to use the correct forms of *set* and *sit*.**

### Present

*Set* (or *setting*) in the present means "arrange in place." When you set something down, you are doing something to that thing.

> We *set* down certain rules each year.
> The girls *are setting* their hair.
> She *sets* the timer for the roast.
> *Set* your priorities.

*Sit* (or *sitting*) in the present means "rest in a sitting position" or "occupy a place." When you sit, you do not do something with anything else.

> Are you going to *sit* around and do nothing?
> She *is* always *sitting* in the same spot.

### Past

*Set* (or *setting*) in the past means "arranged" or "put into place." When you set something down, you were doing something to that thing.

> Last week we *set* up a summer schedule.
> My mother and sister *were setting* out tomato plants.

*Sat* (or *sitting*) in the past means "rested" or "occupied a seat."

> My grandmother often *sat* for hours, rocking back and forth.

My boyfriend and I *were sitting* on the sofa when my father entered the room.

*Set* **and** *sat* **with helping verbs**

*Set* with a helping verb means "arranged."

I *have set* the alarm for 6:00 A.M.
The time *is set* for the match.

*Sat* with a helping verb means "occupied a seat."

How long *have* you *sat* in that position?

## EXERCISE 31

In the following sentences, underline the correct form of *set* and *sit* in parentheses.

1. While I was (setting, sitting) on the porch, I was trying to figure out what happened.
2. There is a house (sitting, setting) on that land across the river.
3. You should have (set, sat) down and drawn the object you wanted to build.
4. Paul often comes over and (sits, sets) awhile with me.
5. (Set, Sit) that package down over there on the table.

*Lay* means "place" or "put something down."

| *When writing about* | *Use* | *Examples* |
|---|---|---|
| the present: | lay | They *lay* canvas over it each night. |
| with a helping verb: | laying | She *is laying* it on the counter. |
| the past: | laid | He *laid* the book on the table. |
| with a helping verb: | laying | They *were laying* the bricks too far apart. |
| | laid | We *have laid* boards over the muddy spots. |

*Lie* means "rest" or "be in a horizontal position."

| When writing about | Use | Examples |
|---|---|---|
| the present: | lie | They *lie* on the grass every afternoon. |
| with a helping verb: | lying | The pen *is lying* on the desk. |
| the past: | lay | He *lay* there for an hour. |
| with a helping verb: | lying | The muddy dog *was lying* on our new chair. |
| | lain | It *has lain* there for an hour. |

*Set* means "arrange" or "put in place."

| When writing about | Use | Examples |
|---|---|---|
| the present: | set | Please *set* the flowers here. |
| with a helping verb: | setting | The committee *is setting* guidelines. |
| the past: | set | He *set* the time for the meeting. |
| with a helping verb: | setting | They *were setting* the chairs in a row. |
| | set | She *has set* the books down. |

*Sit* means "rest in a sitting position" or "occupy a place."

| When writing about | Use | Examples |
|---|---|---|
| the present: | sit | They *sit* here every day for lunch. |
| with a helping verb: | sitting | He *is sitting* in the car. |
| the past: | sat | The cat *sat* in the warm sunshine. |
| with a helping verb: | sitting | The boys *were sitting* on the fence. |
| | sat | They *have sat* there each evening. |

**7g**    **Use verbs to help you tell time.**

Whenever you use a verb, you are telling time. This is true because verbs give you an idea of when something is happening. They can tell you that something is happening now.

> I *surrender.*
> He *surrenders.*
> We *are surrendering.*
> They *do surrender.*
> It *is being surrendered.*

They can tell you that something happened in the past.

> I *surrendered.*
> We *did surrender.*
> We *have surrendered.*
> It *was surrendered.*
> They *had* all *surrendered.* [before the fighting stopped]
> It *had been surrendered.* [before we realized it]

They can tell you that something will happen in the future.

> I *will surrender.*
> He *is going to surrender.*
> We *are surrendering.* [tomorrow]
> They *will* all *have surrendered.*

There is another way that verbs tell time. They tell you

whether something happens all at once or continues to happen.

| | |
|---|---|
| ALL AT ONCE | I *hid* from the pirates. |
| ALL AT ONCE | He *has hidden* all his money. |
| CONTINUING | We *are hiding* from the pirates. |
| CONTINUING | We *would hide* whenever the pirates approached. |

**7g(1)** **Be accurate in telling your reader when something happened.**

As you know, a sentence can be very simple:

My raccoon bit me.

or it can be involved:

When he became frightened, my raccoon bit me.

In the first sentence, time is no problem. (My raccoon bit me at some time in the past.) In the second sentence, there are two verbs (*became* and *bit*). When you write a sentence with more than one verb, it is important to be accurate in telling time—that is, in telling the reader whether something has happened, is happening now, will happen in the future, or happened before something else that has already happened. Otherwise you will confuse the reader.

It is confusing to write:

When he becomes frightened, my raccoon bit me.   [Does he bite you whenever he becomes frightened, or did he bite you that one time?]

It is better to write:

When he *becomes* frightened, my raccoon *bites* me.
OR
When he *became* frightened, my raccoon *bit* me.

Here are some other examples that show how important it is to tell time correctly.

CONFUSING I notice there were some buses full of people.
   [Do you notice now that there are buses full of
   people?

        **OR**

   Did you notice yesterday that there were buses
   full of people?]

 CLEAR I *noticed* that there *were* some buses full of
   people.

        **OR**

   I *notice* that there *are* some buses full of people.

CONFUSING I knew I would not be able to get the job I want.
   [Did you know you would not be able to get the
   job you wanted?

        **OR**

   Do you know now that you will not be able to get
   the job you want?]

 CLEAR I *knew* I *would* not *be able* to get the job I *wanted*.

When you are telling a story, don't get so caught up in the experience of telling it that you think something is really happening while you tell it.

 WRONG I saw him cross the street. I knew he wanted to talk
   to me, so I stop right in front of him.

 RIGHT I *saw* him cross the street. I *knew* he *wanted* to talk to
   me, so I *stopped* right in front of him.

## EXERCISE 32

Clear up your reader's confusion. Change one of the verbs in each of the following sentences to make clear whether you are talking about past, present, or future time.

1. Blow into the victim's mouth or nose until you see his chest began to rise.
2. Howard doesn't like to take orders because he wants to live as a free man, able to do what he wanted.
3. I saw a red light flashing behind me, so I pull my car to the side of the road.
4. After they locked me up for two hours, my lawyer comes to get me.

5. When Carl was away from home for a week, he starts to get homesick.
6. If Nancy told him to stop seeing a girl he likes very much, he will do it.
7. The reason I enjoy the job so much was that I could make fifty dollars a day.

**7g(2)**  Use the word *would* correctly in telling time.

*Would* is often used to suggest that something was done often or regularly.

> After church we *would* visit my grandmother.
> On Saturday mornings, my father and I *would* pick up our fishing rods and head for the lake.

Do not use *would* instead of *will* to describe something that is going to happen in the future.

> WRONG   Next Sunday Joe would definitely be at her house.
> RIGHT   Next Sunday Joe *will* definitely be at her house.

Use *would* to suggest that it is possible for something to happen. Often when you write *would,* you want to say that something would happen if something else happened.

> If I saw him, I *would* tell him the truth.

Notice that the above example has two parts:

1. *If* something happened,
2. something else *would* happen.

Be sure not to use *would* in part 1 after *If.*

> WRONG   If they would be able, they would visit him.  [You want to say that if they *really were* able, they would visit him.]
> RIGHT   If they *were* able, they would visit him.

> WRONG   If they would have known that he was sick, they would have visited him.  [You want to say that if they *had really known* that he was sick, they would have visited him.]
> RIGHT   If they *had* known that he was sick, they would have visited him.

Sometimes part 2 comes before part 1.

> The *would* visit him *if* they were able.
> They *would* have visited him *if* they had known that he was sick.

## EXERCISE 33

Copy the first sentence of each of the following pairs of sentences. Then complete the second sentence with words of your own, using *if* and the part of the sentence you are given.

**Examples**   If *we touched the dog's bowl while he was eating*, he would really snap at us.

If _____ , she would be furious.

We would have told you the answer if *we had known it.*

We would have called you last week if _____

_____ .

1. If Ed *played the game at all*, he would try to do his best.
   If Ed _____ , he would always follow through on his promise.
2. If you *had worn your safety belt*, you would not have been thrown against the windshield.
   If you _____ , you would not have gotten into trouble.
3. If I *had a free throw right now*, I would probably make it.
   If I _____ , I would find one somewhere.
4. I would have done better on my finals if *I had just relaxed.*
   I would have made a million dollars if _____ .
5. If I *had called my brother*, he wouldn't have heard me.
   If I _____ , they wouldn't have listened.

*Would* is often used with the helping verb *have* to suggest something you wanted to do or thought about doing.

> I *would have* liked to see her.

Be sure to express this idea clearly. Don't make the mistake of writing:

> I would have liked to have seen her.

That sentence suggests that you would have liked yesterday to have seen her a month ago. What you mean is that you would have liked yesterday to see her yesterday.

Here is another example.

WRONG    I would have wanted to have gone.
RIGHT    I *would have* wanted to *go*.


## EXERCISE 34

In the following sentences, change the italicized verbs if they are incorrectly used. Write *C* next to any sentence in which the verb is used correctly.

1. If I *wouldn't have known* what to do, it would have been a tragic accident.
2. We knew you would have wanted *to have visited* Elaine then.
3. Whenever I *called* her, she always found an excuse.
4. If you *had studied* the map, you would have known what trails to take.
5. Use great caution in working underneath your car, so you *would* not let it fall on you.
6. If I had known you were going to be there, I would have wanted *to have gone* too.
7. Roger certainly would not have been able *to have known* my address.


## EXERCISE 35

Copy the first sentence of each of the following pairs of sentences. Then complete the second one, using the beginning given and following the italicized pattern.

1. I would not have been able *to work that day.*
   I would not have been willing to _____ .
2. Sara and Robert would have wanted *to be there.*
   Joe and Arlene would have decided to _____ .

3. My sister would have liked *to be invited.*
   My brother would have liked to _____ .
4. We would have been afraid *to swim that far.*
   We would have been pleased to _____ .
5. If I *had thought about it,* I would have tried to get there early.
   If I _____ , I would have torn up that letter.

**7h**  **Recognize words that only look like verbs.**

Some words masquerade as verbs. They come from verbs, and they look like verbs, but these words have other important uses.

**7h(1)**  **Use *-ing* words correctly.**

Words like *buying, being, singing,* and *running* can be verbs. They end in *-ing,* and when they appear with helping verbs, they say something about a subject.

> She *is buying* a new car.
> He *is being* stubborn.

Sometimes, however, they only masquerade as verbs. Besides appearing with helping verbs to say something about the subject, words ending in *-ing* have other uses.

A word ending in *-ing* can be the subject of a sentence:

> *Eating* is my uncle's favorite pastime.   [*Eating* tells what my uncle's favorite pastime is.]

or the object of a verb:

> Unhappiness can cause *overeating.*   [*Overeating* tells what unhappiness can cause.]

or a describing word:

> My brother Billy reminds me of a *laughing* hyena.   [*Laughing* tells what kind of hyena my brother reminds me of.]
> *Being stubborn,* my father wouldn't listen to my explanations.   [*Being stubborn* describes my father.]

There are some things to remember about *-ing* words when they are not used as verbs.

1. Do not separate an *-ing* expression from the rest of the sentence.

WRONG   Driving carefully.
            [Is *driving* being used as a subject, as an object, or as a describing word?]
RIGHT   *Driving carefully* is always important.   [*Driving* is the subject.]
RIGHT   My mother always stresses *careful driving.*   [*Driving* is the object.]
RIGHT   *Driving carefully,* I make my way home.   [*Driving* is a describing word.]

2. The *-ing* ending suggests that something is going on or continuing. (See **7c.**) Be sure to add this ending to a word expressing continuing action.

WRONG   She often eats a snack while watch the news on TV.
RIGHT   She often eats a snack while *watching* the news on TV.

WRONG   Charlie finally went home, have no other place to go.
RIGHT   Charlie finally went home, *having* no other place to go.

**7h(2)**   **Use expressions like *to swim*, *to walk*, or *to find* correctly.**

A word used with *to* in an expression like *to swim, to walk,* or *to find* also masquerades as a verb. It looks like a verb, but it usually serves as the subject or object of a verb.

*To swim* well demands much practice.   [*To swim* is the subject of the sentence.]
A baby tries *to walk* at the age of six months.   [*To walk* is the object; it tells what the baby tries to do.]

Sometimes an expression like *to swim, to walk,* or *to find* appears first in a sentence. Do not separate this expression from the rest of the sentence; since it is not a sentence, it cannot stand by itself.

WRONG   To find your errors.
RIGHT   *To find* your errors, read over your paper carefully.

Be sure not to add an *-s* or an *-ed* ending to an expression like *to swim, to walk,* or *to find.*

WRONG   In basketball, you need four people to assists you in a fast-break execution.
RIGHT   In basketball, you need four people *to assist* you in a fast-break execution.

## EXERCISE 36

In the following sentences, decide whether the italicized word is a verb or a word masquerading as a verb. Write *v* above all verbs and *m* above all words masquerading as verbs.

**Examples**

                    v
Everyone is always *talking* about the good old days.

        m
To *forget* my lines during the play would be a great embarrassment.

1. You are just *being* modest about your accomplishments.
2. *Wishing* for the telephone to ring is no way to *spend* your life.
3. To *have* all the money in the world is my fondest desire.
4. All of us are *going* to my grandmother's house tomorrow.
5. It is impossible to *find* a clean shirt in that closet.
6. *Slamming* the garage door, my brother ran toward the car.
7. Our dog Trixie, *barking* constantly, followed the mailman back to his truck.

## EXERCISE 37

In the following sentences, underline the correct form in parentheses.

1. I have to (use, used) a good shampoo.
2. Children don't always (wash, washing) carefully when they are in a hurry to see a good TV program.

3. Just to (show, showed) how well educated Clyde is, I will give an example.
4. I felt that all those parades and street lights only helped to (commercialize, commercialized) Christmas.
5. My sister (use, used) up all her free movie coupons last week.
6. Inflation has caused prices to just about (double, doubled) in the last five years.
7. The first thing Ellen does is to (mark, marks) the card to show how long she has (work, worked).
8. By (read, reading) the directions carefully, you will be less likely to make a mistake.
9. (Go, Going) to school on time is a good idea.

# *Making Sense of Sentences*

## Learn to recognize and correct mixed-up and non-sense sentences.

**8a**    Avoid the mixed-up sentence.

Sometimes you know that something is wrong with a sentence, but you cannot figure out what it is. In this section we are going to look at some sentences that are mixed up and try to see how they can be corrected. You will see several kinds of sentence mistakes that you will not find explained anywhere else in this handbook.

**8a(1)**    Avoid falling into the *in which, for which,* or *of which* trap.

Suppose you write:

> He had been told to obey the last orders from his superiors in which he had received that morning.

If you were trying to say that he obeyed the orders *which* he received, the *in* has no place in the sentence. You probably also had in the back of your mind that he had been told to

111

obey orders *in which* certain instructions appeared. You meant to say, then,

> He had been told to obey the last orders from his superiors, *which* he had received that morning.
>
> OR
>
> He had been told to obey the last orders from his superiors, *in which* he had been instructed to prepare for an invasion.

Here are other examples of sentences in which the writer needlessly uses *in, on, for,* or *of* and, therefore, writes a mixed-up sentence.

> WRONG   I have had plenty of experience in that type of job in which you will see in my personal data sheet.
>
> RIGHT   I have had plenty of experience in that type of job, *which* you will see in my personal data sheet.

> WRONG   Love is a feeling of which is developed from a friendship into a meaningful and happy affection.
>
> RIGHT   Love is a feeling *which* is developed from a friendship into a meaningful and happy affection.

## EXERCISE 1

Combine each of the following pairs of sentences by putting *which* between them and omitting any words that you do not need.

**Example**   This is the chocolate cake.
You told me not to eat it.   (*which*)
This is the chocolate cake *which you told me not to eat.*

1. A new wallet was the only gift.
   I received it this Christmas.   (*which*)
2. That is a job.
   I have always wanted that job.   (*which*)
3. Laziness is a habit.
   It is easy to acquire.   (*which*)
4. Bobby finally caught the basketball.
   He was trying to get his hands on it during the whole second quarter.   (*which*)

## EXERCISE 2

Correct the following sentences, crossing out *in, on,* and *of* when they are not needed.

1. There is a rabbit pen in which is located near the dog house.
2. A dealer will give you a price in which is more than the true value of the car.
3. Jealousy is an emotion of which many people feel.
4. The handle is the wooden part on which the blade is attached to.
5. Eddie likes the school in which he is enrolled.

**8a(2)** **Avoid using *who* or *which* when it serves no purpose in the sentence.**

The words *who* and *which* are commonly used to refer to words which you have just used. It is correct to say:

> This is the actress *who* broke a million hearts in the movies of the 1930s. [*Who* refers to the actress.]

It is also correct to say:

> Here are the keys *which* I have been looking for all day. [*Which* refers to the keys.]

*Who* or *which* cannot be used as a joining word in place of *and.* When you write:

> He is very bright which he is always telling me about his accomplishments.

you probably meant to use *and* instead of *which* because you have joined two complete thoughts or finished sentences. You should have written:

> He is very bright, *and* he is always telling me about his accomplishments. [*And* used as a joining word]
>
> OR
>
> He is very bright, a fact *which* I never realized. [*Which* used as a referring word]

Here are some other mixed-up sentences in which the writer should have decided whether to use *and* as a joining word or *who* or *which* as a referring word.

WRONG   I have a friend who I enjoy everything he does.
RIGHT   I have a friend, *and* I enjoy everything he does.
                      OR
        I have a friend *who* does things that I enjoy.

WRONG   The men have been drinking which they knew they
        were not supposed to drink.
RIGHT   The men have been drinking, *and* they knew they
        were not supposed to drink.
                      OR
        The men have been drinking something *which* they
        were not supposed to drink.


## EXERCISE 3

If the word *which* is incorrectly used as a joining word in
any of the following sentences, change it to a comma
plus *and*. Do not change any correct sentences.

**Example**   I found his notebook which I carefully put it
              away for him.
              I found his notebook, *and* I carefully put it away
              for him.

1. We have to stop the children from leaving school early
   *which* I now believe they are doing so.
2. There is a black-and-white clock to the right of the sign
   *which* the time on it says ten minutes to three.
3. I looked through the rack until I found a dress *which* I really
   liked.
4. The cabinets are brown *which* we keep our glasses, cups,
   toothpicks, hot sauce, sugar dish, and other things we need
   there.


**8a(3)**   **Avoid mixing up a statement and a question in the same
sentence without meaning to do so.**

When you say:

    He asked me did I want to go.

you are mixing two things. You meant to say:

He asked me if I wanted to go.
**OR**
He asked me, "Do you want to go?"

WRONG   I asked him one day how does it feel to be his size.
RIGHT   I asked him one day how it feels to be his size.
**OR**
I asked him one day, "How does it feel to be your size?"

WRONG   The mechanic asked me did I keep my car tuned up nicely.
RIGHT   The mechanic asked me whether I kept my car tuned up nicely.

Notice that each of these sentences contains two parts: (1) the asking or wondering part and (2) the thing the person asked or wondered or wanted to know. When both of these parts are written in statement form, the subject should come before the verb in both parts.

She wondered if I would wear my new ring.
He asked her where she had put the extra cookies.

## EXERCISE 4

Change the following direct questions to statements by following these five steps.

1. Put the asker or wonderer first.
2. Write *if* or *whether*.
3. Write the thing being asked.
4. Make sure you put the subject before the verb in step 3.
5. You may need to change the second verb. For example, *will* may become *would*.

**Example**   My brother asked me, "Will you be home at four?"
My brother asked me *if I would be home at four.*

1. John asked my sisters, "Are you going home?"
2. Lisa asked, "Will he be at the party?"
3. Sarah wondered, "Will there be a meeting at the recreation center?"
4. We all wondered, "Will we get home in time for dinner?"
5. I asked her, "Did you have to go to court on Tuesday?"

**EXERCISE 5**

Correct the following sentences by putting the subject before the verb in each of the two parts. Add *if* or *whether* and change the verb form when necessary. Take out any unnecessary words.

**Example**  She wanted to know why was I always giving her a smart answer.
She wanted to know why *I was always giving her a smart answer.*

1. Her aunt asked her what was she really looking for in life.
2. They will soon see do you have the qualifications for the job.
3. I asked her could we study together.
4. I asked my friend when was the last time this place had been raided.
5. They wanted to know which room did we see the fire in and how bad was it.

**8a(4)**  **Avoid writing a mixed-up sentence when you are trying to give someone a definition of a word you are using.**

It is hard to define something, so instead of telling the reader what a word means, you may give an example of when or where it happens. When you say:

A *hassle* is when a policeman searches someone for no real reason.

you are forgetting that a *hassle* is not *when* a person gives another a hard time; it is the hard time itself. You should have said:

A *hassle* is a hard time or run-around one person gives another.
                                    OR
When a policeman searches someone for no real reason, he is hassling him.

Often the best way to define a word is to decide what class or general category the word belongs to and to make that class the first part of the definition.

| WORD | CLASS | DEFINITION |
|------|-------|------------|
| clutch | device | A *clutch* is a device used for holding an object firmly. |
| home run | hit in baseball | A *home run* is a hit in baseball that allows the batter to touch all the bases and score. |

## EXERCISE 6

Copy the following sentences. Under each sentence, write one of your own, giving a definition of something. Remember to make the class the first part of the definition.

1. The *four corners* is a strategy used by some college basketball teams when they are ahead in a game, to keep the basketball out of the hands of their opponents.
2. *Cool* is a word that describes people who run their affairs in a very capable way.
3. A *pop rivet tool* is a device used to fasten together parts made of thin metal.
4. *Jealousy* is a feeling that makes you dislike someone who has something you would like to have yourself.

## EXERCISE 7

Correct the following definitions by saying *what* something is, not when or where it is.

1. *Greed* is when you want something that you don't need.
2. *Love* is when two people want to be together.
3. A *carburetor* is where you mix air and gasoline.
4. A *field goal* is where a team tries to score three points by kicking the football between the opponents' uprights.

**8a(5)**    **Avoid writing a mixed-up sentence that has no subject.**

If you are trying to say two different things in the same sentence, you sometimes write a sentence without a subject (the person or thing you are talking about in the sentence). For example, suppose you say:

> After finishing your education will assure you of a job in the future.

What will assure you of a job in the future? You have not answered that question. You meant to say:

> After finishing your education, *you* will be assured of a job in the future.
>
> OR
>
> *Finishing* your education will assure you of a job in the future.

Here is another example:

> WRONG    To pull a cart needs twice the strength of a pony.
> RIGHT    To pull a cart, a *person* needs twice the strength of a pony.

## EXERCISE 8

Copy the first sentence of each of the following pairs of sentences. Then write one of your own, using the beginning you are given. Be sure that each sentence has a subject.

1. When driving a new car, be careful not to damage the upholstery.
   When sitting on a bus, _____ .
2. After getting your certificate, you will be able to get a good job in data processing.
   After going to a ballgame, _____ .
3. To help a team win a championship, a player must cooperate with other members on the team.
   To have a perfect evening with your family, _____ .
4. Singing in a church choir helped Bessie Smith become a great blues singer.
   Living in England _____ .
5. When a person is wrong, he ought to admit his mistake.
   When someone goes to school on a scholarship, _____ .

**EXERCISE 9**

Correct the following sentences by giving the sentence a subject.

1. After knowing policemen in Portsmouth and Suffolk agree they are very different.
2. For students living away from home have to decide what kind of housing is best suited to them.
3. When people feel that everything they say or do is right because of what they believe or have been taught is a wrong attitude to take.
4. Underneath the hood consists of many parts.
5. In the typing class has enough machines for all the students to use.

**8a(6)**    **Avoid mixing two thoughts so completely that the reader cannot tell which of the two ideas you are trying to get across.**

Sometimes your problem is not the absence of a subject. Suppose you write:

> Once you get used to driving, the hard part is over except for when you get on the highway with other cars you feel as if you can't cope with it.

You have two ideas here. One idea is:

> Once you get used to driving, the hard part is over except for the period when you have to get on the highway with other cars.

The other idea is:

> When you get on the highway with other cars, you will feel as if you can't cope with the situation.

Here are some other examples of this problem.

WRONG    The first thing to do in order to bake a cake you will need two 8-inch cake pans.

RIGHT    The first thing to do in order to bake a cake is to get out two 8-inch cake pans.

OR

In order to bake a cake, you will need two 8-inch cake pans.

WRONG   She is too nice a person until people like to take ad-
              vantage of her.

RIGHT   She is such a nice person that people like to take ad-
              vantage of her.

OR

              She is a nice person until people take advantage of
              her.

## EXERCISE 10

Copy the first sentence of each of the following pairs of
sentences. Then finish the second one with words of
your own, using the beginning you are given and following the italicized pattern.

1. The first thing to do when *changing a tire is to place a
   concrete block behind each tire so that the car will not roll
   backward.*
   The first thing to do when _____.
2. My father has such a bad temper that *you have to be careful
   when he is angry.*
   My teacher has such a bad memory that _____.
3. In order to *bathe a baby correctly, you will need several
   things.*
   In order to _____.
4. By washing my hair in such cold weather, *I did a foolish
   thing.*
   By forgetting to lock my front door, _____.
5. In the laundry room there is *a clothesline that you can use
   to dry your socks.*
   In my closet there are _____.
6. After my teacher saw my paper, *she threw up her hands in
   horror.*
   After I waited five days, _____.
7. When my baby was born, *her length was only twenty-two
   inches.*
   When I measured the length, _____.
8. Our farm was near a lake, a fact that *made our summers very
   pleasant.*
   My English class is near the library, a fact that _____
   _____.

## EXERCISE 11

Correct the following sentences by rewriting them, after deciding which idea you want to emphasize.

1. The way to make a jumper is first you have to lay your pattern out.
2. After about an hour had passed before he decided to let me go.
3. In the other corner there is a closet where you can put your clothes in it.
4. Football games last anywhere from a half-hour to three or four hours long.

## EXERCISE 12

This exercise contains all of the types of mixed-up sentences described in **8a.** Correct each of the sentences.

1. Turn the engine off, turn the emergency flasher on, and apply the emergency brake are the next three things to do.
2. A lazy person is when you always wait for other people to do your work for you.
3. After Burt finished, I asked him how did it taste.
4. Jack the car up according to the side you wish to change the tire.
5. To be a maid she seems to be head of the house all the time.
6. Rudeness is a trait in which everyone needs to think about.
7. My cousin Stella is one of the most ignorant girls of which I have ever met.
8. Then I just thought about it was payday and I had just been paid.
9. Ann's letter was very well written which I feel it showed much planning.
10. When you see the happy look on the face of someone you have just given a gift is a very good feeling.

**8b**  Cure your seriously mixed-up sentences.

Be your own doctor. *Diagnose the illness in your mixed-up sentences, and cure them by saying what you meant to say.* In the last section, you looked at some mixed-up sentences and saw how easy it is to mix two thoughts in the same sentence so that neither thought comes across clearly. Sometimes a mixed-up sentence can so get out of hand that it is hard to do just one single thing to correct it. When that happens, about the only thing you can do is resort to drastic surgery. Look at the sentence again, decide what you wanted to say, and say it. Then cut out everything that does not have anything to do with your main point.

> MIXED-UP   You try to be alert for additional game, whether it be rabbit, quail, or squirrel, not so much to bag it, but to acquaint ourselves with what the natures of many woodland creatures look like for the purpose of passing this knowledge on to our children.

There are at least five different things the writer might have been saying in this sentence:

1. You need to be alert for game.
2. We need to be alert for game.
3. We need to acquaint ourselves with the natures of woodland creatures.
4. We need to acquaint ourselves with what woodland creatures look like.
5. You (or we) need to pass on the knowledge of woodland creatures to your (our) children.

It is best to start over with this sentence. Its main point seems to be the importance of gaining and passing on the knowledge of wildlife.

> BETTER   We try to acquaint ourselves with rabbit, quail, and squirrel so we can pass on our knowledge of these creatures to our children.

> MIXED-UP   Not like soul, which is slow and meaningful, rock is a fast-moving age in the years before me, the present years and the years to come.

It is difficult to be sure, but the writer might have been saying one of three things:

1. Unlike soul, rock is fast-moving.
2. Rock is part of a fast-moving age.
3. Rock has its own place in history.

Let us say that the writer is talking about the place of rock in this age.

> BETTER  Unlike soul, which is a slow, meaningful form of music, rock is part of a fast-moving age.

You can see that it is impossible to give a prescription to cure all mixed-up sentences. You must be your own doctor. Make a diagnosis of why the sentence is mixed up, and cure it. It will be easier to make this diagnosis if you ask yourself what one thing you meant to say in the sentence and eliminate anything that gets in the way of saying it.

## EXERCISE 13

Cure the following sentences. Decide what the writer meant to say. Then rewrite the sentence, eliminating anything that does not help the writer make the point.

1. The beach is very beautiful with its light-blue water floating with large and small waves are seen from afar.
2. I feel that since I am the first of all my brothers who really had a hard time, I should be the first of which to get ahead, but I learned that's not true.
3. The students of today will have to run this country one day, and it's going to be in bad shape when the student who breaks his back to pass the exam and others break theirs to see the other's paper.
4. The Midway Shopping Center which is found in the middle of town, and there you will find several stores that may be convenient to anybody that likes to shop can shop there.
5. Behind that man was a tree on shore with grass, bark, and is split with a tree stump.
6. There are several vines hanging from this tree in which there is one on the man's left side of the boat.
7. That's another example of how visual aids and other communication forms he uses, stating that they are a cause of violence.

**8c**  Think about what you are saying. Make your sentences make sense.

Some sentences seem to make sense, but the more you think about them, the more you realize that they don't. A group of words may have a subject and a verb and it may sound like a sentence, but unless it says something, it is not really a sentence. The words

> I am going to ambition a muskrat

contain a subject and a verb, but the resulting sentence does not mean anything. Although you have probably never written anything that silly, it is easy to write a sentence which sounds all right technically, but which does not say anything. You need to consider both the way a sentence is put together and what it says.

> NON-SENSE   I believe the views of society are that a woman is not liberated and she should not work because she should slave at home and should not own her own business.

The writer has not really made a clear statement about the views of society on women's liberation. Slaving at home and owning a business do not *cause* a woman to be liberated or not liberated. They do not *cause* a woman to work or not to work. Writers are entitled to express any opinion they wish, but they must make sure that their readers understand what that opinion is. After thinking about what he wanted to say, this writer might have written:

> BETTER   In our society, no woman is truly liberated.

Another type of non-sense sentence is this:

> Women's liberation is widely known among Americans.

This sentence makes sense from the standpoint of structure, but the writer is not saying anything. He is simply stating an obvious truth like "Bread is a type of food" or "Lollipops taste good." Once you have said these things, you have not contributed anything to the world's storehouse of knowledge. The writer should have thought about what statement he wanted to make about women's liberation. Perhaps he wanted to say:

> Women's liberation has gained respectability among Americans during the last ten years.

## EXERCISE 14

Rewrite the following non-sense sentences so that they make sense.

1. Night driving takes place after the sun goes down.
2. Although my wife and I do not need to agree on every issue, her opinions should be the same as mine.
3. When a woman marries, she should take care of her home and children if she has children.
4. Even though women act as if they are liberated, they are not really liberated, and they do accept responsibilities with great pride.
5. We are not aware of what our dreams mean when we're not asleep because of the existence of day-to-day living.
6. Nobody can do anything about the high cost of living because the problem hasn't been found. Maybe one day everything will come to an end, but until then, we'll have to take life as it comes.
7. She's short and stocky, which to me makes her age unbelievable.
8. No honor or responsibility conferred on the students by the faculty excels that which the National Honor Society represents.

# PART TWO

# More About Sentences

# 9

# *Sentences with Misplaced and Hanging Parts*

## Improve your sentences by eliminating misplaced and hanging parts.

**9a** Relocate the misplaced parts in your sentences.

Sometimes a sentence will sound awkward because one or more words are out of place. These words have to be relocated or placed next to the person or thing they are describing.

OUT OF PLACE   I see a boat beside this man that is green and looks as if it is tied to a tree.  [The man is not green or tied to a tree; to make this sentence clear, put the words describing the boat next to the word *boat*.]

BACK IN PLACE   Beside this man I see a boat *that is green and looks as if it is tied to a tree.*

OUT OF PLACE   Television coverage puts the president on the air any time he suggests which includes all available channels.  [It is the television coverage that includes all available channels.]

BACK IN PLACE   Television coverage, *which includes all available channels*, puts the president on the air any time he suggests.

## EXERCISE 1

Relocate the italicized misplaced parts so that the following sentences will be clear.

**Example**   My aunt bought an antique clock at the auction last week *and an old steamer trunk.*

My aunt bought an antique clock and an old steamer trunk at the auction last week.

1. Most of the time when a team is playing on TV *that we like,* we watch the game together.
2. I saw your advertisement in the *Times-Picayune* of November 28, 1975 *for a clerk-typist.*
3. I would describe this place as being very warm and cozy *which is my bedroom.*
4. One thing you can do in your home is to keep all lights turned off *that are not necessary.*
5. Love of money has gotten people killed *such as robbers and gamblers* over the years.
6. In the 1930s she became chief clerk and knew all the farmers in our county by name *and most of the businessmen.*
7. Have you tried recently to buy gasoline for your car *that isn't sixty cents?*
8. Remove all the equipment from the trunk *that was mentioned in the previous paragraph.*

**9b**   Give any hanging part in your sentences something to hang on.

Sometimes, without really wanting to, you can make your reader laugh. Suppose you had written the sentence:

When thoroughly stewed, the patients will enjoy our prunes.

A reader would probably have found this sentence funny because it certainly doesn't mean what it seems to mean. You do not want to suggest that the patients have to be stewed in order to enjoy the prunes. The words *when thoroughly stewed* are hanging in the sentence like a loose part. Make it clear that they refer to the prunes instead of to the patients by giving them a subject to describe. The sentence should read:

> *When the prunes are thoroughly stewed*, the patients will enjoy them.

Here are some other sentences with hanging parts. Notice in each case that the corrected sentence supplies a clear subject for the hanging part to describe.

| | |
|---|---|
| HANGING | Driving to the lodge, the car's transmission started acting up. [Who is doing the driving?] |
| CLEAR SUBJECT | *When we were driving to the lodge*, the car's transmission started acting up. |
| HANGING | In order to clean, the bathroom door must stand open. [Who is doing the cleaning?] |
| CLEAR SUBJECT | *When you are cleaning*, the bathroom door must stand open. |
| HANGING | Passing through the door on my right, psychedelic posters showing a lion, the Taj Mahal, a dog with suitcases, and a sign saying "I Won't Stay in a World Without Love" can be seen. [Who is passing through the door?] |
| CLEAR SUBJECT | *A person passing through the door on my right* can see psychedelic posters showing a lion, the Taj Mahal, a dog with suitcases, and a sign saying "I Won't Stay in a World Without Love." |

Be careful not to allow a group of words to hang loose without a subject for them to describe.

## EXERCISE 2

In each of the following sentences the hanging part is italicized. Correct the sentences so that there is no longer a hanging part by supplying a clear subject for that part to describe.

**Example**    *Hoping to keep awake in class,* plenty of coffee was consumed.

Hoping to keep awake in class, we consumed plenty of coffee.

1. *By trying to remember my speech,* some of the contents were twisted.
2. The new oil filter needs oil around the gasket *before putting it on.*
3. Check to see that the jack is on solid ground *to avoid sinking from the car's weight.*
4. *Desiring to have a perfect evening,* how can it turn out any other way?
5. *By doing this,* it will avoid an argument later on.
6. Louis feels that *by flying,* a person's fate is planned for him.
7. *After searching over an hour for a used separator,* the snow began to pile up on the ground.
8. Similarities between the two cars come in handy *when trying to get parts.*

## EXERCISE 3

Pick out the hanging part in each sentence. Then rewrite the sentence, giving the part something to hang on.

1. By having this extra room, kitchen cabinets can be easily installed.
2. Driving to California, the roads were crowded with noisy tourists.
3. By trying to get started on time, it will avoid a later argument in the event that they miss out on something.
4. After leaving the highway at the Effingham Street off-ramp, the street is brightly lit.
5. By using government enforcement of gasoline rationing regulations, gasoline can be conserved and distributed evenly to all citizens.

# 10

# *Unbalanced and Rambling Sentences*

## Write balanced sentences and sentences that go somewhere.

**10a** **Give your sentences balance.**

An unbalanced sentence doesn't say exactly what you want it to say. For example, a student wrote about trick-or-treating:

> Parents don't want to see their children robbed of candy bags, hit by cars, and consumption of doped candy by their children.

You can easily see that the above sentence is unbalanced. In the list of the hazards of trick-or-treating, the third item is clearly not the same as the others. The writer should have balanced the sentence by making the third item like the other two. A verb form was needed to balance the other verbs.

UNBALANCED
Parents don't want to see their children
: robbed of candy bags
hit by cars
consumption of doped candy by their children

BALANCED
Parents don't want to see their children
: robbed of candy bags
hit by cars
given doped candy

Parents don't want to see their children *robbed* of candy bags, *hit* by cars, and *given* doped candy.

In the following sentences, two or more things are out of balance. In each case, making the things like one another helps the writer say what he or she wants to say.

> The park is a place where everyone can have a good time or just to be sitting around doing nothing.

UNBALANCED

| The park is a place where everyone can | have a good time<br>just to be sitting around<br>    doing nothing |

BALANCED

| The park is a place where everyone can | have a good time<br>sit around doing nothing |

> The park is a place where everyone can *have* a good time or just *sit* around doing nothing.

> You can use landmarks such as houses, streams, or even cutting notches on trees.

UNBALANCED

| You can use landmarks such as | houses<br>streams<br>cutting notches on trees |

BALANCED

| You can use landmarks such as | houses<br>streams<br>notches cut on trees |

> You can use landmarks such as *houses*, *streams*, or even *notches* cut on trees.

> The more options a car has and the larger it is, it will cost more and its maintenance will be greater.

UNBALANCED

| The more options a car has | the larger it is<br>it will cost more<br>its maintenance will be greater |

BALANCED

| The more options a car has | the larger it is<br>the more it will cost<br>the more maintenance it will<br>    require |

> The *more* options a car has and the *larger* it is, the *more* it will cost and the *more* maintenance it will require.

Sometimes you will have to eliminate one or two items from your sentence because they cannot be made like the others. If you want to mention these items, you will have to put them into a new sentence.

> She is medium-sized, 5′5″ tall, wears glasses, dresses neatly, and very attractive.

UNBALANCED
She is | medium-sized
5′5″ tall
wears glasses
dresses neatly
very attractive

BALANCED
She is | medium-sized
5′5″ tall
[eliminate item]
always neatly dressed
very attractive

> She is *medium-sized, 5′5″ tall, always neatly dressed,* and *very attractive.*

Sometimes, just correcting an item on a list is not enough to make the sentence make sense. In the example

> Her eyes are dark brown, thin eyebrows, a smooth complexion, and a thin mouth.

not all the things listed describe that person's eyes. In this case, the items themselves are balanced, but the writer has to decide what he or she is listing. In this case, the writer is really describing a person's features.

CONFUSING
Her eyes are | dark brown
thin eyebrows
a smooth complexion
a thin mouth

CLEAR AND BALANCED
She has | dark brown eyes
thin eyebrows
a smooth complexion
a thin mouth

> She has *dark brown eyes, thin eyebrows, a smooth complexion,* and *a thin mouth.*

## EXERCISE 1

Balance the items in each of the following sentences. Decide what you are listing, and make a chart like the one in the example. Change wording if necessary.

**Example**   He has thick eyebrows, long eyelashes, sideburns, and has a few strands of hair under his chin.

He has | (1) thick eyebrows
       | (2) long eyelashes
       | (3) sideburns
       | (4) a few strands of hair under his chin.

1. If you are careless when you work with electricity, you may get shocked, burned badly, or loss of life.
2. Some people go to college to play football, get married, and for many other reasons.
3. Cities and towns have more teenagers roaming the streets, people have diseases, more deaths, and more people in institutions than ever before.
4. The first thing Mrs. Johnson did was to introduce herself and that she is the librarian.
5. The acetylene torch is used to heat metals, free bolts, bend steel pipes, and numerous other things in workshops.

## EXERCISE 2

Rewrite each of the following sentences, being sure that the items in them are balanced.

**Example**   I'm glad I am young, handsome, and never been married.

I'm glad I am young, handsome, and *unmarried.*

1. Ann tells everybody she has an apartment of her own and what she does every night.
2. I told him I had just arrived in town and to call and ask my mother.
3. Mike is 5'11", broad shoulders like a football player, a big fat stomach, and is rough in his actions.
4. Tom has complete control over his emotions, whether love, friendship, or even someone he dislikes.

5. A husband forgets that there are bills to pay, food to buy, and that the rent has to be paid.
6. Life is going to dances, to football games, wrestling matches, and going to track meets.
7. We talk about things like buying clothes, shoes, what style someone is going to wear, and how to make clothes.
8. When you vote, consider the candidate's political background, his point of view on different issues, and if you think he will get the job done.

## EXERCISE 3

Copy the first sentence of the following pairs of sentences. Write your own sentences, using the pattern of the words in italics and the beginning given.

1. A prospective employer is usually looking for an employee who is *neat, intelligent,* and *reliable.*
   A prospective husband is usually looking for a wife who is
   _____ , _____ , and _____ .
2. A good pitcher often ends up with *tired muscles, sagging spirits,* and *a very sore arm.*
   A good race-car driver usually has _____ , _____ , and _____ .
3. If you want to be a good carpenter, you have to learn *to judge correctly, to measure accurately,* and *to saw carefully.*
   If you want to make money at the races, you have to learn
   _____ , _____ , and _____ .
4. I told my son that *I was tired of his hanging around the house doing nothing* and *that I expected him to get a job.*
   She told her mother that _____ and
   _____ .

**10b**   **Make your sentences go somewhere.**

A rambling sentence seems to go nowhere. Perhaps you have forgotten what you wanted to say, yet you feel the need to fill up space on the paper. When you find a rambling sentence in your writing, rewrite it so that it takes you somewhere. Decide what you meant to tell the reader in the first place.

> Carelessness is shown when children leave their toys on a stairway or sidewalk where others can trip over them and be seriously injured, which may result in a tremendous loss of income.

This sentence does not go anywhere because it is difficult to decide whether the writer is listing the results of carelessness, worrying about a possible lawsuit, or warning a potential victim. The writer has to decide where the sentence is going, and then eliminate what is not needed or put it into another sentence.

> Carelessness is shown when children leave their toys on a stairway or sidewalk where others can trip over them. (An injury resulting from such carelessness can lead to disability and possible loss of income.)

The following sentence has too much unnecessary information at the beginning.

> As I was a technical consultant on diesel electric power plants to the Turkish Air Force, which had fifteen radar sites and thirty air force bases with this type of equipment, I traveled most of the time.

The writer does not need all the information about radar sites and bases to make the point.

> As I was a technical consultant to the Turkish Air Force on their many diesel electric power plants, I had to travel most of the time.

## EXERCISE 4

Make these sentences go somewhere. Decide what the writer is telling you, and eliminate all unnecessary information or put it into another sentence.

1. It may have been a busy day or my uncle may have gotten on his nerves, but sometimes my father can be an understanding man as long as nothing goes wrong.
2. For a woman who is already neglected because she is the wife of a successful businessman and the member of a prominent family and has many family problems, the time spent playing golf when he could be at home would make the situation even worse.

3. In the area of the house where my son's bedroom is, the wall sticks out, making a corner on the house where the wall changes levels, making the wall wider where my son's and my mother's rooms connect.
4. I don't allow anybody to sit on my bed because after I finish making it up and putting my stuffed animals in place, I don't want people sitting up here because they may knock things out of place.

# 11

# *Guiding Readers*

## Guide your readers so that they will not feel puzzled.

Your readers should not have any doubts about when things are taking place or whether what you have written is intended to be serious, funny, sad, or exciting. You, the writer, should be clear in your own thinking and should make it clear to the reader:

*when* things are happening,

*who* is telling about events,

*what* emotion, or feeling, is expressed, and

*who* is referred to when short substitute words are used.

**11a**  Guide your readers so that they will know when events are happening.

If you are writing about things that are happening now, the verbs you use should tell about the present. If you are writing about things that happened at some time in the past, let the reader know. Do not confuse the reader by mixing the time of the verbs, or action words.

140

CONFUSING   Liz has a nice personality, and she wore makeup and clothes that suit her. [The writer has not made it clear whether he is telling about Liz as she is now or Liz as she used to be.]

BETTER   Liz *had* a nice personality, and she *wore* makeup and clothes that suited her. [The writer is telling about Liz as she was in some past time.]

OR

Liz *has* a nice personality, and she *wears* makeup and clothes that suit her. [The writer is telling about Liz as she is now.]

CONFUSING   As I stroll through the supermarket, my nose came upon many smells. [The writer has not made it clear whether the time is the present or the past.]

BETTER   As I *stroll* through the supermarket, my nose *comes* upon many smells. [Everything is happening now.]

OR

As I *strolled* through the supermarket, my nose *came* upon many smells. [Everything happened in the past.]

CONFUSING   It will be a beautiful day tomorrow; we went to the beach early.

BETTER   It *will* be a beautiful day tomorrow; we *will go* to the beach early.

Some sentences may tell about something that is happening now but also refer to something that happened in the past. The verb tells the reader when each part of the sentence takes place.

CONFUSING   If we think back five or six years and recall what we are wearing then, we can realize the change in our style of dress. [All verbs tell about the present, but *what we are wearing then* should refer to a time in the past.]

BETTER   If we think back five or six years and recall what we *were* wearing then, we can realize the change in our style of dress. [The speaker is now thinking about and recalling what was done at some past time.]

## EXERCISE 1

Read the following sentences. In each sentence, one verb should be changed so that the time of the action is clear. Decide on the changes to be made and correct the sentences.

1. She raised many foster children but never has any of her own.
2. The wind was blowing, and the sun was shining; the children are digging in the sand while I played volleyball with my friends.
3. As Eileen entered the shop, she sees the different colors of wax and the various sizes and shapes of candles.
4. I remember the good times I have as a child, but I am happy to be old enough now to decide things for myself.

**11b**  **Guide your readers so that they will know who is telling about events and to whom the writer is speaking.**

Many of your papers will be about personal experiences, and you will make frequent use of the words *I* and *we*. Some papers may give directions for doing something or may ask for some action and will be directed to *you*. Other papers may be stories, or narratives, which are about someone else, and you will use the words *he*, *she*, *it*, or *they*. Before beginning, decide which type of paper or paragraph you are writing and write in the same way throughout the paper.

> CONFUSING  I went to the mountains for my vacation. You certainly learn to drive carefully on the steep roads.
>
> BETTER  *I* went to the mountains for my vacation. *I* certainly learned to drive carefully on the steep roads. [The reader sees the experiences through the eyes of the writer (*I*).]
>
> CONFUSING  Remove the globe or shade before you take out the bulb that doesn't work. Then he screws the new bulb firmly in place.
>
> BETTER  Remove the globe or shade before *you* take out the bulb that doesn't work. Then screw the new bulb firmly in place.  [The reader (*you*) is receiving directions from the writer.]

CONFUSING John and Toby went down the river in a canoe. You need to pull the canoe up on the grass at your campsite.

BETTER *John and Toby* went down the river in a canoe. *They* remembered to pull the canoe up on the grass at the campsite. [The writer and the reader are watching what happens to others (*they*).]

## EXERCISE 2

Read the first sentence of the following pairs of sentences. Write three sentences of your own: an *I* sentence, a *you* sentence, and a *he* or *they* sentence. Use the beginning words given and follow the pattern of the words in italics.

1. While *I was on my way to the store yesterday*, I *stumbled upon the most horrible sight that I have ever seen.*
   When I _____ , I _____.
2. You should *take proper care of your dog;* give *him food, fresh water, and exercise.*
   You must _____; take _____.
3. The three *boys were usually together;* they *went to the same school, and they all enjoyed fishing and playing baseball.*
   The five _____; all of them _____.

**11c** Guide your readers so that they will know whether your writing is serious, funny, sad, or exciting.

Do not confuse your reader by mixing two writing styles.

CONFUSING In the corner of the room stood an elegant velvet-upholstered sofa with a bunch of funny-looking pillows at one end. [The reader probably doesn't know whether the writer is admiring or making fun of the sofa.]

BETTER In the corner of the room stood an elegant velvet-upholstered sofa with *several unusual pillows* at one end.

CONFUSING    The smoke drifted gently from the chimney;
             there was a warm haze of sunlight, and it was
             cool, man, cool.    [The slang expression at the
             end of the sentence is not in the same style as
             the dignified description at the beginning.]

BETTER    The smoke drifted gently from the chimney;
          there was a warm haze of sunlight, and *every-
          one felt calm and relaxed.*

Don't confuse your reader. Before you begin to write, decide
on the feeling you wish to express and be sure that each sentence contributes to it.

## EXERCISE 3

Rewrite the following paragraph so that the reader will
not be confused about the ideas and feelings.

The beach is a happy place. The sand is as warm as a
blanket on a cool night, and the air was fresh and clean. The
children are jumping and screaming; the adults are running
around playing touch football. You feel slow and lazy as I run
down the beach.

## 11d  Guide your readers so that references are clear.

Most of the time, when writers want to refer to a person or
thing they have just named, they use a short word to avoid
using the same word or group of words again. For example,
writers would not say:

My friends laughed because my friends thought I was cute.

Writers would almost certainly use the word *they* in place of
the second *my friends.* When words like *they, he, she, it,* and
*this* are used in place of other words, it is important that they
refer clearly to definite persons or things coming before
them.

UNCLEAR  Several teachers complained about those noisy students. We thought they were being unreasonable.  [Did we think the teachers or the students were being unreasonable?]

CLEAR  Several teachers complained about those noisy students. We thought *those teachers* were being unreasonable.

UNCLEAR  Snow on a highway gives drivers steering problems. This can be a major cause of accidents.  [What can be a cause of accidents? Snow? Bad steering? The dangerous situation itself?]

CLEAR  Snow on a highway gives drivers steering problems. *These problems* can be a major cause of accidents.

**11d(1)**  Be sure that when you use a word like *it,* *they,* *them,* or *that,* you have already given your readers a clear reference for this word.

Do not expect your readers to guess something that you have not told them.

UNCLEAR  My paper looks OK, but my teacher with her 20/20 vision will spot them every time.  [You know that *them* refers to the mistakes in your paper, but you should not expect your readers to guess this fact.]

CLEAR  My paper looks OK, but my teacher with her 20/20 vision will spot *my mistakes* every time.

UNCLEAR  In high school, they want a note for every day you are late or absent.  [Tell your readers who *they* are.]

CLEAR  In high school, *the principal's staff* wants a note for every day you are late or absent.

UNCLEAR  The steering wheel is small, but it is easy to steer.  [*It* cannot refer to the steering wheel; it must be the unnamed car.]

CLEAR  The steering wheel is small, but *the car* is easy to steer.

Do not use the words *this* and *that* when you mean *a, an,* or *the.* When you are describing or referring to a person or thing

that you have not previously mentioned to the reader, write
*a* boy or *the* boy instead of *this* boy. Never use the incorrect
expressions *this here* or *that there*.

WRONG   I met this here girl I liked in Knoxville.
RIGHT   I met *a* girl I liked in Knoxville.

WRONG   I walked into this store, and I saw this really great
        bargain.
RIGHT   I walked into *a* store, and I saw *a* really great
        bargain.

**11d(2)**   Be sure to give no more than one possible reference for a
word.

Sometimes *this, it, they, he, she, his, her, them,* or *their* can
refer to more than one person or thing that comes before it.
Do not force your reader to guess which reference you intend. When necessary, rewrite the sentence, removing the
incorrect reference.

UNCLEAR   Citizens need to conserve their coupons so that
          they will last through a long and difficult ration-
          ing period.   [It is not entirely clear whether the
          citizens or the coupons will have trouble lasting
          through the rationing period.]
CLEAR     *Coupons* need to be conserved so that *they* will last
          through a long and difficult rationing period.

UNCLEAR   I don't need music to start dancing that step. I can
          feel it in my bones.   [Can I feel the music or the
          step?]
CLEAR     I don't need music to start dancing that step. I can
          feel *the music* in my bones.

## EXERCISE 4

In each of the following sentences, the italicized word
should refer to a person or thing already named. If there
is no clear reference for the italicized word or if the word
could refer to more than one person or thing, correct the
sentence to clear up the confusion.

**Example**    This is a badly written article. Instead of giving the readers more specifics, *they* avoid the issue.

This is a badly written article. Instead of giving the readers more specifics, the authors avoid the issue.

1. Nowadays people buy new appliances as if *it* were no more than writing a check.
2. The carburetor is not very large. *It* has power steering and power brakes.
3. It is dangerous at night because *they* have not turned on the street lights.
4. The first thing you notice about the roads is the gravel. *This* can be a hazardous situation.
5. We could only see the rice paddies move as *they* got close to us.
6. We were shown the microfilm section and the order in which *they* were filed.
7. If you were in one of those large cities in Germany, it would remind you of New York because of *their* fast driving and walking.
8. There are many ruts and holes in the road. *This* makes it impossible to stay on your side of the road.
9. The doctor told Mr. Nelson that until his fever went down, he should stay away from *his* son.
10. When a policeman stopped us, this was the third time *they* had stopped us that night.

**11d(3)**    Use a singular word like *he, she, his, its,* or *him* to refer to one person or thing. Use a plural word like *we, they, their,* or *them* to refer to more than one person or thing.

WRONG    The wise shopper looks inside the garment to see that they have adequate seams.

RIGHT    The wise shopper looks inside the garment to see that *it* has adequate seams.

In guiding your readers, remember to

1. be sure you have already given a clear reference for words like *it, they,* and *them.*
2. be sure that words like *he, she,* and *their* have only one possible reference.

3. use a singular word to refer to one person or thing; use a plural word to refer to more than one person or thing.

## EXERCISE 5

Rewrite the following sentences so that the italicized words refer clearly and correctly to one particular word coming before it.

1. Every viewer of pay TV receives a TV guide so *they* don't need previews to keep the viewers informed of upcoming programs.
2. We became familiar with the play index. *They* listed books and plays and their location.
3. Ed should find it easy to locate Harry's house since *he* understands the importance of giving and getting good directions.
4. Time schedules should be posted at bus stops. *It* should be protected from the elements and the graffiti artists.
5. A person must be able to use *their* hand to signal if *they* are going to turn right.
6. In Washington I saw a really pretty girl from the West Indies. There were many of *them* walking around.
7. High-class people eat as though *he* does not care whether *he* is eating his dinner or not.

# PART THREE

# Spelling
# and Punctuation

# 12

# *Spelling*

**Spell the words in your papers correctly.
Learn to use hyphens when needed.**

**12a**   Learn the simple rules of spelling.

To write acceptable papers, you must spell the words in them
correctly. If you have trouble with spelling, the words that
give you the most trouble are probably not particularly long
or unusual, but actually short and familiar — so familiar that
you don't think you have to look them up in your dictionary.
But use a dictionary whenever you are in doubt about the
spelling of a word. There are some rules you can use to help
you remember the spelling of some of the familiar words that
might cause you trouble.

**12a(1)**   Change the *y* at the end of a word to *i* before you add an
ending, except when you add the ending *-ing.*

| | |
|---|---|
| happy + ness = happiness | pretty + est = prettiest |
| study + es = studies | party + es = parties |
| study + ed = studied | party + ed = partied |
| study + ing = studying | party + ing = partying |

*Exceptions*

| | |
|---|---|
| enjoy + able = enjoyable | employ + er = employer |
| enjoy + s = enjoys | employ + s = employs |
| enjoy + ed = enjoyed | employ + ed = employed |

## EXERCISE 1

Add the endings indicated to the following words and write the words correctly with the added endings.

| | | |
|---|---|---|
| 1. sloppy + ness | 5. vary + es | 9. happy + er |
| 2. marry + ing | 6. marry + ed | 10. enjoy + ing |
| 3. easy + est | 7. duty + ful | 11. vary + ed |
| 4. employ + able | 8. carry + ed | 12. greedy + est |

**12a(2)**   Write *i* before *e*

field       *gr*i*ef*       bel*ief*
rel*ieve*     *n*i*ece*       fr*ien*d

**except after *c.***

c*ei*ling     dec*ei*ve   rec*ei*pt
rec*ei*ve     conc*ei*t   conc*ei*ve

*Exceptions*   seize       neither     height
            weird       either      neighbor

*Note:* These are not the only exceptions to this rule. Look in your dictionary if you are not sure about the spelling of a word.

## EXERCISE 2

Fill in the blanks with *ie* or *ei* to complete the following words.

1. p _ _ ce
2. th _ _ f
3. bes _ _ ge
4. dec _ _ t
5. w _ _ ght
6. perc _ _ ve
7. s _ _ ge
8. rel _ _ f
9. ch _ _ f
10. bel _ _ ve

**12a(3)** **Learn the different ways to make words plural.**

You usually add *s* to a singular word naming a person or thing to make it plural.

> fence + s = fences      girl + s = girls

If a singular word naming a person or thing ends in *-s, -ch, -sh,* or *-x,* add *es* to make the word plural.

> class + es = classes      brush + es = brushes
> church + es = churches     box + es = boxes

If a singular word naming a person or thing ends in *y* preceded by a consonant, change the *y* to *i* and add *es* to make the word plural.

> baby + es = babies
> party + es = parties

If a singular word naming a person or thing ends in *y* preceded by a vowel, keep the *y* and *s* to make the word plural.

> joy + s = joys
> boy + s = boys

If a singular word naming a person or thing ends in *-fe,* change the *fe* to *ve* and add *s* to make the word plural.

> life + s = lives
> wife + s = wives

*Exceptions*    safe + s = safes
              café + s = cafés

If a singular word naming a person or thing ends in *f*, change the *f* to *v* and add *es* to make the word plural.

> half + es = halves
> calf + es = calves

*Exceptions*    belief + s = beliefs
dwarf + s = dwarfs
OR
dwarf + es = dwarves

Add *es* to some singular words naming persons or things that end in *o* to make them plural.

> hero + es = heroes
> potato + es = potatoes

*Note:* Not all singular words that end in *o* take *es* to make them plural. Look in your dictionary if you are not sure about the plural form of a word.

Add *s* to the first word of singular combination words to make them plural.

> mother-in-law + s = mothers-in-law
> head of state + s = heads of state

Some singular words naming persons or things change their spelling without adding *s* to make them plural.

> woman = women
> child = children

Some singular words naming persons or things do not change at all in the plural.

> A *deer* jumped into the clearing.
> I saw three *deer* beside the road.

**EXERCISE 3**

Make the following singular words plural.

| | |
|---|---|
| 1. study | 9. industry |
| 2. noise | 10. business |
| 3. man | 11. tomato |
| 4. pass | 12. mix |
| 5. valley | 13. foot |
| 6. match | 14. child |
| 7. piano | 15. belief |
| 8. sister-in-law | 16. sheep |

**12a(4)** **Learn the difference between words ending in *-ent* and *-ence*, and between words ending in *-ant* and *-ance*.**

Some words may sound the same when you say them quickly, but they do not mean the same thing.

| DESCRIBING WORDS | DESCRIBING WORDS USED WITH WORDS NAMING PERSONS OR THINGS |
|---|---|
| different | That is a *different* idea. |
| important | This is an *important* letter. |
| convenient | That is a *convenient* restaurant. |
| patient | He is a *patient* teacher. |

| WORDS NAMING PERSONS OR THINGS | WORDS NAMING PERSONS OR THINGS USED BY THEMSELVES |
|---|---|
| difference | That is the *difference*. |
| importance | This letter has *importance*. |
| convenience | A dishwasher is a kitchen *convenience*. |
| patience | He has very little *patience*. |
| patients | The emergency room was full of *patients*. |

| | |
|---|---|
| WRONG WORD | Another different between these two restaurants is the hours they are open. |
| RIGHT WORD | Another *difference* between these two restaurants is the hours they are open. |
| WRONG WORD | J. J. is a very intelligence dog. |
| RIGHT WORD | J. J. is a very *intelligent* dog. |
| WRONG WORD | Don has more patient than I have. |
| RIGHT WORD | Don has more *patience* than I have. |

*Note:* If you are in doubt about the way to spell the form of the word you need, it is best to look up the word in your dictionary. For example, your dictionary can show you that *evident* and *evidence* are two different words.

ev·i·dence (ev ə den[t]s)   an outward sign; something that furnishes proof

ev·i·dent (ev ə dent)   clear to the vision or understanding

## EXERCISE 4

Correct the following sentences by changing the spelling of any word forms spelled incorrectly.

1. No one is going to strike my neighbor in J. J.'s present.
2. Probably the main different between Mary and Elmer is their personalities.
3. The detective has found no evident to support his suspicions.
4. A nurse's aide has to be patience.
5. They are from two difference faiths.
6. The new shopping center in the middle of town is the most convenience place to shop.
7. I don't understand the significant of what you are saying.
8. Living in Germany is much difference from living in the United States.
9. It takes a lot of intelligent to get a college degree.
10. In the nursing home there are many patience to help.

**12b**   Use a hyphen (-) to join words and numbers.

**12b(1)**   Use a hyphen to join two or more words that work together as one word to describe another word, except when the words come after the word they describe.

middle-aged woman     The woman was middle aged.
well-known writer        The writer was well known.

If you are in doubt, look in your dictionary to find out when to use a hyphen between two words joined to describe another word.

**12b(2)** Use a hyphen when you spell out compound numbers from twenty-one to ninety-nine.

>   sixty-eight
>   seventy-three

**12b(3)** Use a hyphen with fractions.

>   one-fourth
>   three-fifths

**12b(4)** Use a hyphen to join *self-*, *all-*, and *ex-* to a word in order to make a single word.

>   self-control
>   all-powerful
>   ex-husband

### EXERCISE 5

Add hyphens if they are needed in the following sentences.

1. All night study sessions soon become a way of life for many students.
2. I will be twenty seven on my next birthday.
3. All new employees have six weeks of on the job training before they are expected to work alone.
4. Rick is a very self conscious man, probably because he's only five feet tall.
5. Three fourths of my paycheck is spent before I even get it.
6. The surprisingly mild mannered nurse was a relief after the quick tempered doctor.
7. Many gas stations now have self service only.
8. We used to live in a five room apartment with orange shag wall to wall carpeting.
9. George Forman is a well known boxer.
10. The middle class neighborhood has changed a lot since I moved away.

**12c**   Learn these fifty frequently misspelled words.

| | | | |
|---|---|---|---|
| accommodate | definite | necessary | themselves |
| all right | describe | occurred | together |
| a lot | dining | paid | truly |
| always | does | perform | until |
| attempt | experience | potato | usually |
| basically | explanation | prepare | weigh |
| believe | field | probably | were |
| business | fifties | receive | whatever |
| cannot | forty | referring | where |
| category | height | separate | woman |
| cigarette | hospital | shining | writer |
| clothes | interest | studying | |
| convenience | lose | than | |

# 13

# *Commas and No Commas*

## Use a comma when you need it.

Some students feel that the comma was invented only to cause problems in writing. Others decide where commas go in a sentence by reading the sentence aloud and placing commas wherever they pause or vary their tone of voice. Both groups of students could manage the comma correctly and easily if they would learn the reasons for using commas and use commas only when there is a reason.

**13a** Use commas and the joining words *and, but, or, nor,* and *for* to join two complete, or finished, sentences.

If the sentences are short and are about the same thing or are closely related, they can be joined to make a longer sentence.

| | |
|---|---|
| TWO SENTENCES | It was a small shop between two other stores. It was a nice place. |
| JOINED SENTENCE | It was a small shop between two other stores, *and* it was a nice place. |
| TWO SENTENCES | The gym is located on Main Street. It is a large building with a green lawn around it. |
| JOINED SENTENCE | The gym is located on Main Street, *and* it is a large building with a green lawn around it. |

159

TWO SENTENCES   We thought that Jean would be hard to get along with. We found out that this was not true.

JOINED SENTENCE   We thought that Jean would be hard to get along with**,** *but* we found out that this was not true.

Remember to use the comma *before* the joining word.

## EXERCISE 1

Join the following pairs of sentences with commas and the joining words *and, but, or, nor,* or *for.*

**Example**   Some of us enjoyed the fashion show. Others thought it was foolish and boring.
Some of us enjoyed the fashion show**,** *but* others thought it was foolish and boring.

1. The food was brought out. There was music for dancing.
2. All the girls were frightened. The noise finally stopped.
3. The books can go on the top shelf. They can go in a box.
4. The children walked to school last year. This year they ride the school bus.
5. There have been many changes. New buildings have been put up everywhere.

**13b**   Use commas to join unfinished sentences containing subjects and verbs that begin with words like *after, although, because, if, when,* and *while* to complete, or finished, sentences.

The comma is used only when the unfinished sentence comes first and is followed by the finished sentence.

UNFINISHED SENTENCE   Because it rained every day for a week

FINISHED SENTENCE   We could not go on the camping trip.

JOINED WITH COMMA   *Because* it rained every day for a week**,** we could not go on the camping trip.

Notice that if the unfinished portion comes last, a comma is *not* used.

| | |
|---|---|
| JOINED WITHOUT COMMA | We could not go on the camping trip because it rained every day for a week. |
| UNFINISHED SENTENCE | When the wind blows from the north |
| FINISHED SENTENCE | The house creaks and groans. |
| JOINED WITH COMMA | *When* the wind blows from the north, the house creaks and groans. |
| JOINED WITHOUT COMMA | The house creaks and groans when the wind blows from the north. |

## EXERCISE 2

Copy the first sentence of each of the following pairs of sentences. Then write your own sentence, using the pattern of the one you have just copied and the word given.

**Example**   Because we didn't follow the directions, we lost our way.

Because *she didn't read the assignment, she failed the quiz today* .

1. After *the school term ended,* the *brothers returned to their home in Vermont.*
   After _____ , the _____ .
2. *Marianne was hurt in the accident* because *she was careless.*
   _____ because _____ .
3. As *the phone rang in the next room,* the *baby started to cry.*
   As _____ , the _____ .
4. When *the cherry trees are in bloom,* the *yard is a beautiful place.*
   When _____ , the _____ .
5. Although *she had met him at a party last year,* she did not recognize him.
   Although _____ , he _____ .

**13c** Use commas between the words or groups of words in a series or list. (See also **14b**.)

Notice how the commas are used in the following sentences.

> The room was small, dingy, and cold.
> Make your breakfast table beautiful with a bowl of apples, oranges, bananas, and pears.
> Pearl ran down the stairs, threw her books on the table, grabbed her coat, and started toward the door.

If you are not sure about the use of the comma in the last sentence, look at the series or list of things that Pearl did:

> Pearl $\left\{ \begin{array}{l} \text{ran down the stairs,} \\ \text{threw her books on the table,} \\ \text{grabbed her coat,} \\ \text{and} \\ \text{started toward the door.} \end{array} \right.$

**13d** Use commas between descriptive words such as *large, small, dark, beautiful, exciting,* and *noisy* in place of the word *and*. If *and* cannot be used, a comma is not needed.

Either the comma or *and* shows that both of the descriptive words refer to the person or thing being described.

Study the following sentences, which use either a comma or the word *and* between the descriptive words.

> She came running into the large, empty room.
> She came running into the large and empty room.
>
> It was a noisy, exciting race.
> It was a noisy and exciting race.
>
> The only clue was a small, dark stain on the carpet.
> The only clue was a small and dark stain on the carpet. [The words *small* and *dark* both describe *stain*. The word *and* can substitute for the comma.]

Study the following sentences, which do not need either a comma or the word *and* between the descriptive words.

> He wore a bright blue sweater.
> He wore a bright and blue sweater. [*Blue* describes *sweater,*

and *bright* describes the color *blue*. Neither a comma nor *and* is needed.]

Both of the girls had dark brown hair.
Both of the girls had dark and brown hair. [*Dark* describes *brown*, and *brown* describes *hair*. Neither a comma nor *and* is needed.]

**13e** Use commas to set off, or separate, the name of a person to whom you are speaking.

If the name of a person is simply mentioned in the sentence, the commas are not needed.

Jim, take the books to the library. [A comma is used because someone is speaking *to* Jim.]
Jim will take the books to the library. [Someone is speaking *about* Jim, and no comma is needed.]

Wait, Angie, and I will go with you. [Angie is spoken *to*.]
The two girls asked Angie to wait for them. [Angie is spoken *about*.]

**13f** Use commas to separate the names of speakers from their exact, or quoted, words.

Earlene said, "The books must go to the library before Tuesday."
"The books," Earlene said, "must go to the library before Tuesday."
"The books must go to the library before Tuesday," Earlene said.

See Section **16a** for a more complete discussion.

**EXERCISE 3**

Add commas where they are needed in the following sentences. Look back at **13c, 13d, 13e,** and **13f** if you need help.

1. You will need a bowl two spoons a cup and a plate.

2. A twisted rotten tree crashed through the porch roof.
3. Melinda had small delicate hands and narrow feet.
4. Did you see Sylvia last night?
5. Catch the ball Sally.
6. Joe's car had a flat tire a broken headlight two dented fenders and a cracked windshield.
7. The boys ran and jumped and yelled all afternoon.
8. Wilbur asked "Where are the papers and cans for collection?"
9. Irene wore a beautiful emerald bracelet.
10. "The meeting will be held tomorrow" said Mr. Mason.

## 13g   Use commas to separate the parts of names of places, dates, and addresses.

If only one item in a place name, date, or address is used, it is not separated by commas from the rest of the sentence.

Norfolk, Virginia, is the location of the famous Azalea Gardens.
The Azalea Gardens are located in Norfolk.   [Name of city only]
Virginia has many beautiful flowers in the spring.   [Name of state only]

Please send the package to Mrs. C. R. Chesterton, Lyman, Wyoming   82937.   [The zip code number is not separated by a comma from the name of the state.]
Please send the package to Mrs. C. R. Chesterton in Wyoming.   [Only the name of the state is given. A comma is not needed.]

We will arrive on Sunday, July 17, 1977.

If the day of the month is not given, or if the day of the month is given before the name of the month, the comma may be left out.

He will start his new job in August 1977.
He will start his new job on Monday, 8 August 1977.   [Letters and information from military offices and government services often use this form.]

The main office is located at 317 Palm Avenue, Summerfield, Oklahoma   74966.

**EXERCISE 4**

Add commas where they are needed in the following sentences.

1. My sister moved to Lewisville Texas in June 1969.
2. Dave's new address is 21786 Hallwood Drive Walnut Creek California 94595.
3. The celebration was scheduled for the last Friday in September.
4. Plainfield Kansas is a small town where all of the people know each other.

**13h** Use commas to separate a word or a group of words that may add information but are not necessary to the meaning of the sentence.

**3h(1)** Use commas around a word or words that describe a person or thing that you have already mentioned.

Sometimes a person or thing is renamed or described, but the word or group of words that is used is not necessary to the meaning of the sentence.

Mary, *the girl in the red dress,* will be the first one in the talent show.

The words *the girl in the red dress* help to describe Mary, but the meaning of the sentence does not depend on them. The group of words is properly separated from the rest of the sentence by commas.

Mary will be the first one in the talent show.

Barbara has a wonderful job as a model.
Barbara, *my sister,* has a wonderful job as a model. [The words *Barbara* and *my sister* describe the same person, but the fact that Barbara is someone's sister is not a necessary part of the sentence.]

My neighbor's dog needs obedience training.
My neighbor's dog, *which howls at night,* needs obedience training. [The howling may not be part of the problem.]

Notice what happens when the particular problem is identified.

> A dog that jumps up on people needs obedience training. [The thing that the dog does *is necessary* to the idea that obedience training is needed; commas, therefore, are not used.]

**13h(2)**   Use commas to separate words such as *however, therefore, for example, as a result, in fact,* and *in that case* from the rest of the sentence.

These words may be used at the beginning, in the middle, or at the end of the sentence.

> *As a result,* air and water pollution are increasing every day.
> The tire, *however,* will need to be balanced before it is used.
> They knew, *in fact,* that a mistake had been made.
> Not all dogs get along with small children, *for example.*

When words such as *however, therefore, for example, as a result, in fact,* and *in that case* are used to begin a sentence that is joined to another sentence, a semicolon is used before the word or words, and a comma is used after them. (See also **3b** and **14a.**)

> The score was forty-two to six at the half; *therefore,* the coach gave everyone on our team a chance to play.

The semicolon is needed because the word *therefore* is not the same as a joining word like *and* or *but*. The word *therefore* may be used in another place in the sentence without changing the meaning.

> The score was forty-two to six at the half; the coach gave everyone on our team, *therefore,* a chance to play.

**13h(3)**   Use commas to separate introductory expressions containing *-ing* words or beginning with words such as *to run, to walk,* or *to remove* from the rest of the sentence.

> *Moving rapidly,* the last runner began to catch up with the rest of the group.   [The words *moving rapidly* describe the last

runner, but need to be separated from the rest of the sentence because of the *-ing* word.]

The last runner began to catch up with the rest of the group.

*After selecting the lettuce and radishes,* wash them carefully and cool them before it is time to make the salad.

*To remove any lint,* go over each windowpane with a paper towel.

**13h(4)** Use commas after words such as *yes, no, well,* and *oh* when these words begin a sentence.

*Yes,* I think I knew Charlie's brother when I was in school.

*Well,* where did you find that horrible pink hat?

*Oh,* what a rainy day this has been.

*No,* they could not find the package.

**13h(5)** Expressions such as *I hope, I believe, I say,* and *she says* are separated from the rest of the sentence by commas when they are *not* used at the beginning of the sentence.

This is, *I hope,* the last time it will happen.

The money, *she says,* must last for the rest of the month.

Notice that when the expression is used at the beginning of the sentence, the rest of the sentence tells what is hoped or said. In this case, a comma should *not* be used.

I hope this is the last time it will happen.

She says the money must last for the rest of the month.

**13i** Use commas to make your meaning clear.

You may have to think carefully about what you mean to say. The following sentences use the same words in the same order, but notice that the meaning of the sentence is reversed when commas are added.

Women say the men are more suitable for that work.

Women, say the men, are more suitable for that work.

In the first sentence, women are speaking, and they say that men are better for a particular job. In the second sentence, men are speaking, and the men say that the women are better for the job.

### EXERCISE 5

Add commas and semicolons where they are needed in the following sentences.

1. Mr. Jenkins our neighbor won a new car last week.
2. There are however some very good reasons for not smoking.
3. The boy who wrecked the car was not even scratched I believe.
4. We are Matt thinks part of a nationwide experiment.
5. We had three great days to enjoy our vacation at the beach as a result we all had terrible sunburns.
6. I say that we need a larger student recreation room.
7. Yes Ruth is in my history class.
8. Putting aside all doubts the people should move ahead with the plans.
9. George believes we will win the election therefore he has stopped trying to get votes.

Commas are used in the following ways. Read this list before doing Exercise 6.

1. Commas are used with joining words $\left\{\begin{array}{l} and \\ but \\ or \\ nor \\ for \end{array}\right\}$ to join two complete sentences.

2. Commas are used to join an unfinished sentence to a complete sentence when the unfinished part comes first.

3. Commas are used between the words or groups of words in a series or list.

4. Commas are used between descriptive words in place of *and*.

5. Commas are used to set off, or separate, the name of the person to whom you are speaking.

6. Commas are used to separate the names of speakers from their exact words.

7. Commas are used to separate the parts of names of places, dates, and addresses.
8. Commas are used to separate words or groups of words that may add information but are not necessary to the meaning of the sentence.

**EXERCISE 6**

Add commas where they are needed in the following sentences.

1. A good driver pays attention to the driving regulations and he is aware of other drivers on the road.
2. When Gail went to class yesterday she forgot to take some of her books with her.
3. The counter was stacked with dishes pots glasses cups and towels.
4. The old wrinkled man jumped up and threw the ball.
5. Here Martha is the recipe for the chocolate cake.
6. Mike said "The team will never win without Gill in the line."
7. May 21 1914 is an important date in that little town.
8. She lives in Norton Iowa at 2115 Graham Street.
9. Yes there will be two more field trips this summer.
10. Bob Jamison one of my classmates wrote the article.

**13j** Do not use a comma by itself to join two complete, or finished, sentences. (See also **14a.**)

Use one of the following correct ways to join sentences:

1. Use a comma with a joining word such as *and, but, or, nor,* or *for.*
2. Use a semicolon.
3. Leave the sentences separated, and begin each with a capital letter and end with a period, a question mark, or an exclamation point.

See **13a** for additional help if you are not sure how to use the comma and a joining word to connect two finished sentences.

**13k**  **Do not use a comma to separate the subject from its verb.**

|  | (subject) | (verb) |
| --- | --- | --- |

WRONG  Many people with dogs, never train them properly.

RIGHT  Many people with dogs never train them properly.

WRONG  The boy with the basketball, was my brother.

RIGHT  The boy with the basketball was my brother.

**13l**  **Do not use a comma to separate the verb from its object.**

(verb)          (object)

WRONG  The two women brought, great bunches of flowers to the hospital every week.

(verb)          (object)

RIGHT  The two women brought great bunches of flowers to the hospital every week.

(verb)          (object)

WRONG  Johnson carried, *Gulliver's Travels* around for three weeks before he started to read it.

(verb)          (object)

RIGHT  Johnson carried *Gulliver's Travels* around for three weeks before he started to read it.

Notice that in the last sentence the title of the book is not separated in any way from the rest of the sentence because it is simply the object of the verb *carried*.

**EXERCISE 7**

Copy the following sentences. Leave out any commas that are not needed. Add any joining words that are needed.

1. Marianne always makes very good grades, her sister usually gets the lowest grades in the class.

2. All of the students with green sweaters, went up to the platform.
3. Three of the boys found, boxes from the wreck.
4. The girl with red hair, was the best dancer at the party.
5. Sally's mother usually cooked, spaghetti with meatballs on
   Thursday.

**13m**   **Do not use a comma with the word *and* when *and*
is used between words or groups of words in a
series or list, or when *and* is used between two
subjects, verbs, or objects.**

WRONG   He carried a book, and a basket, and a hat, and three
coats.

RIGHT   He carried a book, a basket, a hat, and three coats.
                              OR
He carried a book and a basket and a hat and three
coats.

WRONG   Jenny, and Evelyn went across the yard to the
gate.   [*Jenny* and *Evelyn* are both subjects of the
verb *went* and should not be separated by a
comma.]

RIGHT   Jenny and Evelyn went across the yard to the gate.

WRONG   Simpson tripped on the rock, and dropped the
bag.   [Simpson did two things: he *tripped on the
rock; dropped the bag.* The word *Simpson* is the
subject of the *two* verbs *tripped* and *dropped.* The
two verbs should not be separated by a comma.]

RIGHT   Simpson tripped on the rock and dropped the bag.

WRONG   The dog would not pick up the paper, or come back
to Laurie.   [The two actions of the dog should not
be separated by a comma.]

RIGHT   The dog would not pick up the paper or come back to
Laurie.

**13n**   **Do not use a comma before the first word or after
the last word in a list or series.**

WRONG   We planted, beets, peas, beans, and potatoes, in the
garden.

RIGHT   We planted beets, peas, beans, and potatoes in the
garden.

WRONG   Hard work, dedication, and many hours, will be needed to complete that job.

RIGHT   Hard work**,** dedication**,** and many hours will be needed to complete that job.

**13o** **Do not use a comma between descriptive words if *and* cannot substitute for the comma.**

WRONG   The team wore pale, green shirts and dark, green pants. [The shirts were pale green, not pale and green; the pants were dark green, not dark and green.]

RIGHT   The team wore pale green shirts and dark green pants.

WRONG   The noisy, jet plane ruined the music. [The jet plane was noisy.]

RIGHT   The noisy jet plane ruined the music.

**EXERCISE 8**

Copy the following sentences. Leave out any commas that are not needed.

1. Homer, and Kelly went to Pleasant Hill Community College for two years.
2. Robert picked up the bat, and hit the ball over the high fence.
3. Some people may own five suits, and only one shirt.
4. Each desk held books, paper, and pencils.
5. The bright, blue van had a dark, red stripe around the top.

**13p** **Do not use a comma when adding an unfinished sentence to a finished sentence if the unfinished part is very short (two or three words) or if the unfinished part comes last in the sentence.**

SHORT UNFINISHED PART   *If it rains* we will go next week.
LONG UNFINISHED PART   *If it rains on Tuesday and Wednesday***,** we will go next week.
UNFINISHED PART LAST IN SENTENCE   We will go next week *if it rains on Tuesday and Wednesday.*

**13q**  Do not use a comma between the name of a state and the zip code.

> WRONG   He lives at 809 Bernau Avenue, Greensboro, North Carolina,   27407.
>
> RIGHT   He lives at 809 Bernau Avenue, Greensboro, North Carolina   27407.

**13r**  Do not use a comma unless there is a reason.

It is usually better to leave out needed commas than to add unnecessary commas. Read the following sentences and avoid similar mistakes.

> WRONG   The music sounded, like thunder.
> RIGHT   The music sounded like thunder.
>
> WRONG   The resolution passed, by one vote.
> RIGHT   The resolution passed by one vote.
>
> WRONG   When traveling, by back roads, be sure to have a full gas tank.
> RIGHT   When traveling by back roads, be sure to have a full gas tank.

You have studied the following rules about commas. Reread them before doing Exercise 9.

1. Do not use a comma by itself to join two complete sentences.
2. Do not use a comma to separate the subject from its verb.
3. Do not use a comma to separate the verb from its object.
4. Do not use a comma if the word *and* is used between words or groups of words in a series or list.
5. Do not use a comma before the first word or after the last word in a series or list.
6. Do not use a comma between descriptive words if *and* cannot substitute for the comma.
7. When adding an unfinished sentence to a complete, or finished, sentence, the comma is not needed if the

unfinished part is very short or if it comes last in the sentence.
8. Do not use a comma between the name of a state and the zip code.
9. Do not use a comma without having a reason.

## EXERCISE 9

Add commas where they are needed in the following sentences. If any sentence is correct, write *C* next to it.

1. Garnet ran around the block twice but Jim only laughed and shook his head.
2. The boy with red hair can play a guitar sing and tapdance.
3. The newspaper reported three serious traffic accidents yesterday.
4. You will need pencil paper and eraser.
5. Graham had three dogs and two cats.
6. The marchers carried a large American flag.
7. The winter has been a cold snowy one.
8. If the delivery truck from Eason's comes before noon I will be there to pick up my materials.
9. The reporter was not there when the crowd came down the street.
10. Send the package to Mr. Harding in Jewett Illinois 62436.

# 14

# *The Semicolon*

**Use the semicolon between closely related sentences and between groups of words that already contain commas. Use the semicolon only when the parts to be joined are equal in importance.**

**14a** Use a semicolon to join two complete, or finished, sentences that are closely related.

The semicolon is sometimes called a weak period; when it is used between two complete, or finished, sentences, it takes the place of a period at the end of the first sentence. Notice that the second sentence does not begin with a capital letter because it has been joined to the first sentence by the semicolon.

> John did not know what to do; he stood in the middle of the room and tried to decide how to move the boxes.

The above sentence is made up of two complete, or finished, sentences which have been joined by a semicolon. The sentences could be written separately:

> John did not know what to do. He stood in the middle of the room and tried to decide how to move the boxes.

The sentences can also be correctly joined with a semicolon because they are closely related and because they are equal in importance. The choice is up to you, the writer. Because you have a choice, you can vary the length of sentences and make your papers more interesting than they would be with only short, choppy sentences. Read the following examples.

Jim has never played football. He doesn't enjoy the game.
Jim has never played football; he doesn't enjoy the game.

The rain poured down. Mud ran into the street.
The rain poured down; mud ran into the street.

Some words or groups of words help the reader move smoothly from one thought or sentence to another; these words are called *transitional words,* and they tell something about when or how the action of the sentence is taking place. These words are different from the joining words *and, but, or, nor,* and *for,* which can be used with a comma to connect two finished sentences. (See also **13a.**) The transitional words have a semicolon in front of them and are usually followed by a comma. Some of these words are:

| | | |
|---|---|---|
| also | however | nevertheless |
| as a result | in addition | on the other hand |
| besides | in fact | still |
| for example | instead | then |
| furthermore | meanwhile | therefore |

The people were tired and hungry; *as a result,* no progress was made.
Love is a universal emotion; *still,* some people never know love.
Billie pushed all of the chairs and tables out of the room; *then* she started cleaning the dirty floor.

When words such as *also* and *however* are not used to begin a sentence, they are usually set off from the rest of the sentence by commas.

TWO JOINED SENTENCES   It is my book; however, you are welcome to use it.
ONE SENTENCE   Sally needs the book, *however,* by tomorrow.

**EXERCISE 1**

Join each pair of sentences. Use semicolons to join sentence pairs 1 and 2; use semicolons and transitional words to join sentence pairs 3, 4, and 5.

1. My brother went to school in Colorado.
   He enjoyed skiing and hiking while he was there.
2. Sheltie dogs are intelligent and obedient.
   They make very good pets.
3. The paint on the car door was badly scraped.
   The metal rusted in a month.
4. The house has shutters on the windows and a huge chimney at each end.
   All of the wood needs to be painted.
5. Taxes keep going up and up.
   Personal property taxes have doubled in only three years.

**14b**   **Use semicolons between groups of words that already contain commas.**

This use of the semicolon helps the reader find the main divisions of the sentence and makes the ideas clear.

> Mr. Howard bought a pot, knives, and bowls; two folding tables; and three kinds of bread from Graham's Bakery.
> Some drivers seem to count every fence post; examine, discuss, and reject every side road; and enjoy delaying traffic.

**14c**   **Do not carelessly use a semicolon instead of a comma.**

**14c(1)**   **Do not use a semicolon to join an unfinished sentence to a complete sentence. (See also 13b.)**

> WRONG   When cold weather comes; many of the birds fly south. [The first part of the sentence is not complete. It should be joined to the complete portion by a comma.]
>
> RIGHT   When cold weather comes, many of the birds fly south.

WRONG   While we watched with amazement; five men came running out of the house.

RIGHT   While we watched with amazement, five men came running out of the house.

**14c(2)**   **Do not use a semicolon with the joining words *and, but, or, nor,* and *for*. A comma is the correct mark to use. (See also 13a.)**

WRONG   All of my friends like baseball; but I just can't get excited about the game.

RIGHT   All of my friends like baseball, *but* I just can't get excited about the game.

WRONG   Everyone talks about the need for good management in government; and no one does anything about it.

RIGHT   Everyone talks about the need for good management in government, *and* no one does anything about it.

**14d**   **Do not confuse the semicolon and the colon.**

The semicolon joins two sentences, but the colon calls attention to what follows. (See also **17d.**)

SEMICOLON   Pick up your supplies tomorrow; be sure to have everything with you on Friday.

COLON   On Friday, bring the following supplies: a tack hammer, large tacks, a yard of burlap, and two yards of denim.

SEMICOLON   The provost talked about student government; the entire student body listened with interest.

COLON   The provost called for two things: more active participation in student government and involvement in community affairs.

### EXERCISE 2

Use semicolons and commas correctly in the following sentences.

1. When Ruby found the lost dog she took it home with her.

2. All the books are here pick the ones you need.
3. Most people want good jobs however some people don't want to work.
4. Freedom isn't free it must be earned and guarded.
5. The car hit two trees a fence and Mr. Adams's bicycle.
6. Everyone went to the beach for a picnic as a result the package was not delivered.
7. After the mayor spoke there was a beautiful display of fireworks.
8. Ten families live on that block and they all have dogs.
9. Education is very important but not everyone should study the same things.
10. Our new neighbors were very critical of small cars nevertheless they gladly accepted one as a gift.

# 15

# *The Apostrophe*

**The apostrophe (') is used to show ownership or omission and to form some plural words.**

The apostrophe is placed near the top of the written word in which it is used.

**15a** **The apostrophe shows that something belongs to or is related to something else.**

The ideas of ownership or relationship can be expressed in other ways, but the apostrophe makes it possible to write those ideas in fewer words.

| WITH APOSTROPHE | WITHOUT APOSTROPHE |
|---|---|
| Jamie's book | the book that belongs to Jamie |
| everyone's hope | the hope of everyone |
| the cat's favorite food | the favorite food of the cat |
| a day's work | the work accomplished in a day |
| tomorrow's class | the class for tomorrow |
| a dollar's worth of gas | the amount of gas that is worth a dollar |

Notice that the **'s** is not the same as an *s* that is added to the name of a person or thing to make it plural.

I saw the boy**'s** car.   [The car belongs to the boy.]
The boys saw the car.   [Several boys saw the car.]

She slept in the girl**s'** cabin.
She slept with the girls in their cabin.

For things which are not alive, the **'s** is frequently dropped or replaced by the words *of* or *in*.

the table leg     the leg of the table
the kitchen stove    the stove in the kitchen

There are certain ways to add the **'s** to words to show possession, as in the following examples.

**15a(1)**    **If the name of a person or thing does not end in *s*, add the 's.**

Mary**'s** dog was hit by a car.
Wind blew down the store**'s** sign.

**15a(2)**    **Use either 's or only ' after a word that ends in s.**

If the extra *s* makes pronunciation difficult, the apostrophe by itself is acceptable.

Mr. Hopkins**'s** car was stolen.
Mr. Hopkins**'** car was stolen.

**15a(3)**    **If the word is plural (meaning more than one), use 's if the word does not end in s and only ' if the word does end in s.**

The children**'s** feet made muddy tracks on the floor.
The men**'s** hats were on the table.
[*Children* and *men* are plural words which do not end in *s*. Add **'s**.]

The little girls**'** toys were scattered over the yard.
The boys**'** jackets had disappeared.
[*Girls* and *boys* are plural words which do end in *s*. Add **'** only.]

### EXERCISE 1

Copy the following sentences. Add apostrophes where they are needed.

1. The happiness on Carols face was enough of a reward for them.

2. Will you take Selmas jacket to her?
3. The birds nests were empty.
4. Mrs. Hargis party was talked about for a week.
5. The children and the dogs ran up and down the playground.

**15b**   When words are used in place of the names of people or things, there are special rules for the use of the apostrophe.

**15b(1)**   Do not use ' with *his, hers, its, ours, yours, theirs,* or *whose.*

These special words already show ownership.

| WRONG | | RIGHT | |
|---|---|---|---|
| hi's | her's | his | hers |
| it's | our's | its | ours |
| your's | their's | yours | theirs |
| who'se | | whose | |

Here is John's sweater.
Here is *his* sweater.

That book belongs to Sally.
That book is *hers.*

**15b(2)**   Words such as *anybody* or *everyone* should have **'s** added.

Everyone**'s** house was damaged by the bad storm.
Have you seen anybody**'s** jacket?

### EXERCISE 2

Copy the following sentences. Select the correct word to complete each one.

1. Has _____ book been re-turned? (everybody's, everybodies)
2. It could have been _____ mistake. (anybody's, anybodys)

3. The car lost _____ muffler when we hit a bump. (it's, its)
4. Do you know _____ painting won the prize? (who'se, whose)
5. She dropped _____ coat in the fish pond. (her's, her)

**15c**   **If something belongs to two or more people, use 's with only the last of the names.**

> I went to Jane and Sally**'s** apartment.   [Two people live in one apartment.]
> I went to Jane**'s** and Sally**'s** apartments.   [Two people each have their own apartment.]
>
> The new coffee shop is named Mike and Ed**'s.**   [Two people own the business.]

Words with hyphens have **'s** added to the last word only.

> Jack drove his brother-in-law**'s** car.
> The governor-elect**'s** speech was very boring.

**EXERCISE 3**

Add *'s* where needed in the following sentences.

1. The neighbor dog and our cat are always fighting.
2. Did you hear that John and Bill car was completely wrecked?
3. We saw Nita and Gina new stereos yesterday.
4. The man was wearing my father-in-law new hat.
5. He was quite impressed by the senator-elect article on tax reform.

**15d**   **The apostrophe is used to show omission.**

**15d(1)**   **Use an apostrophe to show that a word has been shortened or that two words have been made into one by the omission of one or more letters.**

This shortening is called a *contraction*.

| CONTRACTED FORMS | LONG FORMS |
|---|---|
| o'clock | of the clock |
| we'll | we will |
| don't | do not |
| Class of '75 | Class of 1975 |
| rock 'n' roll | rock and roll |
| they're | they are |

Remember to spell contractions correctly by placing the apostrophe where the letter has been omitted.

isn't NOT is'nt
aren't NOT are'nt

wasn't NOT was'nt
weren't NOT were'nt

doesn't NOT does'nt
don't NOT do'nt

hasn't NOT has'nt
haven't NOT have'nt

**15d(2)**   **Do not confuse *its* and *it's*.**

*Its* is a special word which means that something belongs to *it*.

Turn down that radio; *its* music is too loud.   [The music from the radio is too loud.]

*It's* is a contraction meaning *it is*.

Turn down that radio; it's too loud.   [The radio (it) is too loud.]

**15d(3)**   **Do not use 's when you need only add s to form the plural of a word.**

Only the special uses given in **15e** call for 's for plurals.

WRONG   Both front tire's were flat.
RIGHT   Both front *tires* were flat.

## EXERCISE 4

Add apostrophes where needed to show contractions in the following sentences.

1. Trudy said that they wouldnt be late.
2. My brother graduated in the class of 68.
3. The crowd lost its temper.
4. I dont know whats happening, but its something important.
5. Mary really liked that dress; its too bad that its sleeve is torn.

**15e** **Use the apostrophe to form the plural of numbers, letters, and words referred to as words.**

> The printer put *s*'**s** after all of the names, and half of the 5'**s** are upside down.
> Put circles around the *and*'**s.**
> He spells his name with two *l*'**s.**
> Your paper would be better if you left out the *wow*'**s** and *oh*'**s.**
> The 1920'**s** were called the Jazz Years.

*Note:* Decades can also be written without the apostrophe.

## EXERCISE 5

Add apostrophes where they are needed in the following paragraph. Refer to the example that you have just studied if you need help in deciding where the apostrophes should be used.

> Corinne came dashing up the stairs with her new coat over her arm. She tossed Kevins book on the table and shuddered to see that it was seven oclock. Mrs. Watts car was to be ready and waiting at seven-thirty, and they were going to the reunion for the Class of 72. "Ill never make it," she muttered to herself as she dressed. "I need something to wear with this dress; its so plain. Theres Jills bracelet; its sparkle will really help, and shell never miss it."

# 16

## *Quotation Marks*

**Use quotation marks around the exact words of a writer or speaker and for some titles. Quotation marks may also be used to indicate words used as words.**

**16a** When the exact words of a writer or speaker are repeated, or quoted, by another person, the words are enclosed in quotation marks.

The speaker may be named before, after, or in the middle of the quotation. The name of the speaker is not included in the quotation marks.

> Eloise said, "Jane spent all of her money at the grocery store."
> "Jane spent all of her money at the grocery store," Eloise said.
> "Jane spent all of her money," Eloise said, "at the grocery store."

Notice that each quotation begins with a capital letter and is separated from the name of the speaker by a comma. (See also **13f.**) If the quotation is broken or separated within a sentence, the first word of the second part does not begin with a capital letter.

**16a(1)** If the quotation has more than one sentence, the end quotation mark is placed at the end of the last sentence.

> "The family reunion was a wonderful event," Callie said. "We met cousins we had never heard of before. Everyone brought food, and we all had a good time."

Notice that the quotation marks are placed after the comma or period that ends a quoted section.

**16a(2)** **If more than one speaker is quoted, begin a new paragraph each time the speaker changes.**

"Help!" screamed Laura.
"Can you hold on?" yelled George. "I'll be there in a minute."

Notice that a comma is not used between the quotation and the name of the speaker if an exclamation point or question mark is needed.

**16a(3)** **A quotation within a quotation is enclosed in single marks.**

"The correct quotation is: 'A penny saved is a penny earned,'" he said.

See Section **28** for a more complete discussion.

**16a(4)** **Do not enclose an indirect quotation in quotation marks.**

You will probably use indirect quotations in most of your writing, so learn the difference between direct and indirect quotations. The quotation is indirect if the exact words of the speaker are not used, but such words as *for*, *that*, or *if* are used to tell what the speaker said.

| | |
|---|---|
| DIRECT QUOTATION | Mr. Graves asked, "Did you count the tickets?" |
| INDIRECT QUOTATION | Mr. Graves asked *if* we had counted the tickets. |
| DIRECT QUOTATION | Edward said, "I will go tomorrow." |
| INDIRECT QUOTATION | Edward said *that* he would go tomorrow. |

**16a(5)**   **When other marks of punctuation are used with quoted material, all punctuation marks should be in the correct order.**

Place periods and commas inside quotation marks except for the period or comma that follows identification of the speaker.

> "If you wait," I said, "you'll miss the bus."

Place colons and semicolons outside the quotation marks unless they are part of the quotation.

> Most of us recited "The Raven"; only three chose "Kubla Khan": Eddie, Julia, and Sam,   [The colon and semicolon are not part of the quoted material.]

> Read and summarize "Diets: Good and Fad" by Thursday.   [The colon is part of the quoted material.]

Place question marks, exclamation points, and dashes inside the quotation marks if they apply to the quotation only and outside the quotation marks if they apply to the whole sentence.

> Jimmy asked, "Did you bring the bread and the pickles?"   [Only the quotation is a question.]

> Did that sign say "Detour Ahead"?   [The sentence is a question.]

**EXERCISE 1**

Add quotation marks where they are needed in the following sentences.

1. The professor said, Read the next chapter and answer the questions at the end of it.
2. I'm not sure I understand, said Henry. Will you repeat the directions?
3. Why doesn't he listen? grumbled Gerald.
4. What a beautiful day! sang Tillie as she danced down the street.
5. Is your ticket marked Use only on Tuesday?
6. Jack said that all of the material would be ready soon.

**16b** Use quotation marks to enclose the titles of short stories, songs, articles in magazines, parts of books, television programs, and short poems when they are referred to in other written material. (The titles of complete books or magazines and other long works are underlined or italicized [see **19a**].)

> "Checkpoint" is the first chapter of *The Spy Who Came In From the Cold.*
> The rock group played "Boo-Hoo, Baby."
> Did you read "Land Use and Capital" in the last issue of the *Freeman?*
> The children watched "Sesame Street" every afternoon.

Notice that the names of the things referred to are *not* separated from the rest of the sentence by a comma. The sentence is punctuated just as though the quotation marks were not there. The quotation marks tell the reader that the words they enclose are the name of a song, title of a chapter of a book, or name of an article. Quotation marks are frequently used in this way in school writing.

Do not use quotation marks around the title of your own paper. The title of your paper is original, and it should not be treated as quoted material unless you have taken a quotation to use as a title.

Here is an example of the title of a paper.

My First Job

I am sure that I will never forget my first job because the experience taught me . . .

**16c** Do not use quotation marks around common nicknames, technical terms, or well-known expressions.

| | |
|---|---|
| WRONG | I saw "Bill" yesterday. |
| RIGHT | I saw Bill yesterday. |

| | |
|---|---|
| WRONG | When "Lefty" ran in, all of his friends cheered. |
| RIGHT | When Lefty ran in, all of his friends cheered. |

|         |                                                                 |
|---------|-----------------------------------------------------------------|
| WRONG   | Use a "vernier caliper" to obtain an accurate measurement. |
| RIGHT   | Use a vernier caliper to obtain an accurate measurement. |
|         |                                                                 |
| WRONG   | Anyone can learn to "tune" a motor.                             |
| RIGHT   | Anyone can learn to tune a motor.                               |

**16d**   **Words used as words may sometimes be enclosed in quotation marks, or they may be underlined. (See also 19a[4].)**

The important thing to remember is that it is usually better *not* to underline words or enclose them in quotation marks unless there is no other way to express the idea.

|         |                                                                 |
|---------|-----------------------------------------------------------------|
| WEAK    | The word "love" makes some people interested and makes others yawn. |
| WEAK    | The word *love* makes some people interested and makes others yawn. |
| BETTER  | The thought of love is interesting to some people, but others may yawn at the idea. |
|         |                                                                 |
| WEAK    | That "mysterious atmosphere" is just propaganda. |
| BETTER  | That mysterious atmosphere is just propaganda. |

Notice that the same ideas can be expressed without the use of quotation marks or underlining. Good writers hold their readers' attention with well-chosen words and do not have to sprinkle a page with quotation marks.

**EXERCISE 2**

Add quotation marks where they are needed in the following paragraph.

The last pep rally was really a bomb even though the school newspaper had tried to create interest with an article called School Loyalty. The band was out of tune during the playing of Hail to Alma Mater, and Pudge Barker, the song leader, forgot some of the words. However, the team responded the next night with three touchdowns and two conversions and a landslide victory.

# 17

# *The Period and Other Marks*

**Use the period, the question mark, the exclamation point, the colon, the dash, parentheses, and brackets correctly in your writing.**

The period and the question mark are used more frequently than the other marks of punctuation, but all are important in your writing. The period, the question mark, and the exclamation point all show the end of a complete, or finished, sentence.

| | |
|---|---|
| STATEMENT | The classroom is very crowded. |
| QUESTION | Is the classroom crowded? |
| EXCLAMATION | That classroom is too crowded! |

The period also shows the end of most abbreviations. The colon, the dash, parentheses, and brackets are used within the sentence to call attention to a part of the sentence.

**17a** Use a period to end a statement, a request, or an indirect question, and after most abbreviations. Use ellipsis marks to show the omission of a word or words from quoted material.

**17a(1)** Use a period to end a statement, or telling sentence.

Most of the sentences you write will be statements; in them, you are telling about something.

The boy ran.
The tall, thin boy ran home after school.
The tall, thin boy in blue jeans and a green sweater ran rapidly
down the street after school.

All of the above sentences are statements. It does not matter
that one is very short and the other two are longer. Each is a
telling sentence, or statement, because it tells what the subject *(boy)* did *(ran)*.

### EXERCISE 1

In the following paragraph, begin each sentence with a
capital letter and end each sentence with a period.

my sister Mary and her husband are moving into a house
near us all of the rooms need paint and new furniture everyone
in the family has promised to help Mary and Ben get the house
ready even little Billy said that he would build a house for the
dog when we are through, the house on Dempsey Street will be
nice to live in

**17a(2)**    **Use a period to end a sentence that requests something
or gives a mild command.**

This type of sentence may tell someone what to do. It
requests or commands, but the command is not a strong one.
If the sentence were spoken instead of written, it would be
said in a normal, calm tone of voice.

Remember to close the windows and lock the front door when
you leave.   [The person spoken to *(you)* is requested to do
something.]
Follow the pattern exactly and cut each piece carefully.   [This
sentence commands or gives directions.]
Committee members, please be there by seven o'clock.   [Cer-
tain members are requested to arrive at a special time.]

The subject of the sentence may not be included, but it is
always the person spoken to, *you* (understood). (See **1b[4]**.)

**17a(3)**  **Use a period to end an indirect question.**

Do not confuse an indirect question with a direct one. An indirect question is a type of statement. If the sentence states that someone asked a question, it is a telling sentence and needs a period at the end.

WRONG   Our neighbors wanted to know where the boxes came from?

RIGHT   Our neighbors wanted to know where the boxes came from. [The sentence is *telling* what the neighbors wanted to know.]

WRONG   Mrs. Hildreth asked me to come to work the next day?

RIGHT   Mrs. Hildreth asked me to come to work the next day. [The sentence is *telling* what Mrs. Hildreth wanted me to do.]

**EXERCISE 2**

Begin each of the following sentences with a capital letter and end each with a period. After each sentence, tell whether it is a statement, a request, or an indirect question.

1. please send two students to the campus meeting tomorrow
2. the little town in the valley was sheltered by the surrounding hills
3. a small girl asked for three hamburgers and five large orange drinks
4. complete each of the forms and return them to the office by tomorrow
5. the man in the tan coat wanted to know where Mr. Sam Wilson lived.

**17a(4)**  **Use a period after most abbreviations.**

The period is used after abbreviations, or short forms of words. The use of a person's initial instead of the name is an abbreviation.

In most of your writing, you should be careful to use complete words, but there are some titles, degrees, ranks, and other words which are usually abbreviated. Many of the abbreviations end with a period.

> I saw Mr. Bronson last week.
> Mrs. Saunders has a B.A. in history.
> Lt. Wilbur Carson, Jr., lives on South Hampsted Avenue.
> [The full words are *Lieutenant* and *Junior*.]

Do not abbreviate words such as *hour, inch,* or *foot*. Measurements of time or space may be abbreviated in some cases, but for your papers and themes it is always best to use the complete words.

> WRONG   I worked an hr. after lunch.
>   RIGHT   I worked an *hour* after lunch.
>
> WRONG   Billy is over six ft. tall.
>   RIGHT   Billy is over six *feet* tall.
>
> WRONG   Mercer lives on a st. near the college.
>   RIGHT   Mercer lives on a *street* near the college.

Abbreviations in common use include the following:

> Mr., Mrs., Ms., Dr., C.O.D., A.M. OR a.m., P.M. OR p.m., B.C., A.D., R.S.V.P. OR r.s.v.p.

Abbreviations of the names of large organizations, government agencies, and some technical terms are frequently used without periods.

> NAACP, GOP, YMCA, NATO, HEW, FBI, TV, FM, AM, CB

**17a(5)**   Use ellipsis marks, which are three spaced periods (. . .), to show the omission of a word or words from quoted material.

If the ellipsis mark is at the end of a sentence, it is followed by another period, a question mark, or an exclamation point. Ellipsis marks are frequently needed in a library paper or other long formal paper.

> A large group heard his inspiring words: "The strength of the movement . . . is real and enduring."

*Note:* Do not use a period at the end of the title of a song, paper, book, magazine, or newspaper. (See **27**.)

TITLE USED IN A SENTENCE   The trio played "My Blue Heaven" while Sally danced.
TITLE BY ITSELF   An Unforgettable Day
TITLE USED IN A SENTENCE   *The Bridges at Toko-Ri* is an exciting book.
TITLE BY ITSELF   *American Opinion*

**EXERCISE 3**

Add periods where they are needed in the following sentences. Spell out any words which should not be abbreviated.

1. The rain finally stopped The ave was flooded with water and littered with branches several ft long
2. Mr Wilson finished mowing the grass in twenty min
3. The TV was not working yesterday when Dr Adamson wanted to watch a special program on the CIA
4. Mrs George M Craig will speak Saturday at the club meeting on the advantages of owning a CB radio
5. Jamie wanted to know why we were not going on the trip I asked his father to explain the many reasons

**17b**   Use a question mark to end an asking sentence.

Why is Ted leaving?
Are you taking History 186?
Did Marcie wear that old dress and coat to the party?
When will people learn that they must help each other?

The above examples are asking sentences, or questions. Each sentence is asking for information, and each sentence uses asking words such as *when* or *why* or begins with part of the verb.

Remember that an indirect question does not end with a question mark. The indirect question is really a statement about what is being asked, and the correct end mark is a period.

## EXERCISE 4

End each of the following sentences with a question mark or a period.

1. Why did Lynn leave her books in the car
2. Did Mrs. W. J. Jerret bring the programs for the meeting
3. Tom wanted to know how many students would go to the convocation
4. What did he mean by that last statement
5. I did not know where we were going

## EXERCISE 5

Copy the first sentence of each of the following pairs of sentences. Then write your own sentence, using the beginning given and following the italicized pattern.

1. When will *Susie take the books to the library?*
   When did _____ ?
2. The committee *asked Millicent to explain the plans.*
   The students _____ .
3. He forgot *where he had put the package.*
   She remembered _____ .
4. Are all *of the dishes broken?*
   Is each _____ ?
5. Did Jackie *take the pictures to her math class?*
   Did Herbie _____ ?

**17c**  Use an exclamation point at the end of a sentence that shows strong feeling or surprise or one that gives a strong command.

Some sentences show strong feeling or surprise, or they may let you know that something is happening suddenly. You might yell or shout if you were saying the sentence instead of writing it. Such sentences are exclaiming sentences, and they end with exclamation points.

Help! The house is on fire!
I'll hate you as long as I live!

Hold on, Ginny!
We want a touchdown!
It was a wonderful surprise!

Shouting or exclaiming sentences are usually short. They can add strength and feeling to your writing, but they should not be used often. When you use an exclaiming sentence, be sure that the idea you are expressing is truly one of strong or sudden feeling.

### EXERCISE 6

Copy the first sentence of each of the following pairs of sentences. Then write a similar exclaiming sentence of your own, using the beginning given and ending with an exclamation point.

1. Get *out of this house!*
   Run _____
2. What *a beautiful picture!*
   What a _____
3. Someone *help me quickly!*
   Come _____
4. There's *that noise again!*
   Here _____
5. Call *a doctor at once!*
   Tell _____

## 17d  Use the colon correctly.

### 7d(1)  Use a colon to call attention to something that follows.

Only one word may follow the main part of the sentence, but frequently there is a list, a quotation, or an explanation.

WRONG    Please bring the following supplies paper, pencils, eraser, and reference book.   [A mark is needed to separate the list of supplies from the rest of the sentence.]

WRONG    Please bring the following supplies, paper, pencils, eraser, and reference book.  [A comma between *supplies* and *paper* makes the word *supplies* part of the list of things to bring.]

WRONG    Please bring the following, paper, pencils, eraser, and reference book.  [The word *supplies* can be left out, but if a comma is used before *paper*, it is used before the first word of a list and this is wrong.]

RIGHT    Please bring the following: paper, pencils, eraser, and reference book.

RIGHT    Please bring the following supplies: paper, pencils, eraser, and reference book.

[Both of the above sentences are correct. The colon calls attention to the fact that the things that follow the colon are to be brought.]

WRONG    In conclusion, remember the famous quotation that says: "The only way to have a friend is to be one."  [The quotation is introduced with the verb *says* and therefore should be separated from the rest of the sentence by a comma. If the verb is not used, then a colon is correct.]

RIGHT    In conclusion, remember the famous quotation which says, "The only way to have a friend is to be one."

RIGHT    In conclusion, remember the famous quotation: "The only way to have a friend is to be one."  [The colon takes the place of the verb *says*, which introduces the quotation in the other correct example.]

The colon is used after the beginning, or salutation, of a business letter. This is considered a formal beginning; a friendly letter uses a comma.

Dear Sir:
Dear Senator Townley:
Dear Martin,

**17d(2)**    Use a colon to separate the figures that give hours and minutes, or chapter and verse in the Bible.

WRONG    I told Kevin I would be ready at 730, but at 645 the doorbell rang, and there he was.

RIGHT    I told Kevin I would be ready at 7:30, but at 6:45 the doorbell rang, and there he was.

Because

when

after

Since

If

Before

Although

As

While

whether

WRONG   Exodus 203 is the first of the Ten Commandments.
RIGHT   Exodus 20:3 is the first of the Ten Commandments.

*Caution:* A colon is used more frequently in formal writing than in informal writing. Do not confuse the colon and the semicolon; the names and the marks may seem to be similar, but the semicolon joins two sentences and the colon calls attention to something that follows it.

### EXERCISE 7

Copy the first sentence of each of the following pairs of sentences. Then write your own sentence, using the beginning given and making correct use of a colon.

1. There are five important ingredients: *apples, sugar, water, nutmeg, and cinnamon.*
   You need three basic items: _____ .
2. Mark has one driving ambition: *success.*
   Jarrell fears only one thing: _____ .
3. The words of an old song kept running through his mind: "*Oh, you beautiful doll.*"
   Her cries startled the neighbors: _____ .
4. The first bell rings at *8:15 in the morning.*
   The last train leaves at _____ .
5. The farmers were expected to remember the idea in Leviticus *20:22.*
   The chaplain read Genesis _____ .

**17e** Use a dash to show a sudden or abrupt break in a sentence.

A dash may also set off a word or a group of words that summarizes the sentence. Do not confuse the dash with the hyphen (see **12b**). In handwriting, the dash is a line as long as two or three hyphens.

The girls on our street are all the same — except Louanne.
Good grades, a diploma, a fine job — these are his immediate goals.

**17f**    Use parentheses to enclose certain words, figures, or letters.

Parentheses are always used in pairs. Use parentheses to enclose figures or letters that go with items in a series.

> It is important to (1) use the correct materials, (2) follow the directions carefully, (3) observe all safety precautions, and (4) have proper storage for the finished product.

Use parentheses to enclose explanation or comment within a sentence. Periods and commas that are not part of the information enclosed in parentheses should be placed outside the parentheses.

> Although Frank had not expected to do well in college (he had started because he had nothing else to do), he found himself near the top of the dean's list.

**17g**    Use brackets to enclose a word or words of comment or explanation within quotation marks or parentheses.

The words in brackets are *not* part of the quotation.

> "It should be understood [the message continued] that the situation cannot be tolerated any longer."

> Write clearly and logically; do not use complex structures if they can be avoided. (They are usually [as here] difficult to follow.)

**EXERCISE 8**

Add any needed colons, dashes, parentheses, or brackets in the following paragraph.

> Complete sentences, correct punctuation, related ideas   these things make up a good paragraph. You can write good paragraphs if you follow these steps (a) plan what you are going to write about, b get your ideas in order, c  write the paragraph,  d  proofread and correct (This is a very important and frequently overlooked step. , e make a good final copy.

# 18

# *Capitals*

## Learn when to use a capital letter and when not to use one.

**18a**  Capitalize the first word of a sentence.

Show your reader exactly where each sentence begins by starting the first word of the sentence with a capital letter. If two short sentences have been joined to form a long sentence, only the first one begins with a capital.

My favorite sport is basketball.
Why do children rebel against their parents?
Many new ideas have been developed; however, not all of
them are valid.

### EXERCISE 1

Copy the following sentences. Add any capitals that are needed.

1. some butterflies are very small.
2. did you see your friends yesterday?
3. the wind is cold, and the air is fresh and clean.
4. water pollution is a serious problem.
5. three men walked slowly toward the house.
6. not all states have the same laws; what is forbidden in one
   may be legal in another.

**18b**  **Capitalize proper names.**

A proper name is the name of a specific, or particular, person, place, or thing.

| | | | |
|---|---|---|---|
| people { | man<br>woman<br>child | specific people { | **T**om **H**. **L**arson<br>**J**ulia **C**ardin<br>**S**ally |
| places { | city<br>state<br>nation | specific places { | **B**altimore<br>**C**alifornia<br>**F**rance |
| things { | car<br>book<br>day<br>camera | specific things { | **C**hevrolet<br>**B**ible<br>**T**uesday<br>**K**odak |

**18b(1)**  **Names of persons are capitalized. The initials of names stand for those names and are capital letters.**

Did **J**ohn **W**. **T**rasmon tell **K**elly about the new school?

Specific names of animals or pets are also proper names and begin with capital letters.

One of Walt Disney's most popular creations was **D**umbo, the little elephant with the big ears.

**18b(2)**  **A title used before a name is capitalized.**

We all thought that **U**ncle Wilbur should go with us.
They saw **P**resident Carter leave the meeting.
Did **P**rofessor Ritter call the office?
My neighbors have met **C**aptain Farley.

A title not followed by a name is not usually capitalized.

A club **p**resident should be able to maintain order.
Ask your **p**rofessor about the old book.
The **c**aptain of the men came forward.

Degrees and titles after a name are part of the name and are capitalized.

> Mason R. Barkley, **J**r., **P**h.**D**.
> Carson D. Sommervale, **A**ttorney at **L**aw

The name of the profession is not capitalized.

> Carson D. Sommervale is a **l**awyer.

**18b(3)**   *I* is capitalized.

When you use the word *I*, you are talking about a very specific person: yourself. *I* is used in place of your own name, and it is always a capital letter when used in this way.

> When **I** looked up, **I** saw people jumping from the windows.
> **I** thought **I** saw two people in the car.

**EXERCISE 2**

Copy the following sentences. Add capitals where they are needed.

1. My sister josephine looks like something you would find in the comic page.
2. Her dentist is dr. t. l. osmondson.
3. the tall policeman talked to mr. johnson.
4. they saw sam and haley leave the yard together.
5. Did you hear professor Dixon's lecture on clean air?
6. when i walked to the store, i saw sally and Jill.
7. The program chairman introduced mrs. jason f. tomkies, sr.
8. when lieutenant halder opened the door, he saw five men waiting for him.
9. Did i miss all of the program?
10. the captain of the team is responsible for calling the plays.

**18b(4)**   The names of specific cities, states, countries, and continents are capitalized.

> We lived in **D**es **M**oines when I was a child.
> John has never driven in **C**alifornia.

Her report is about **A**rgentina, but mine is about another country.

Notice that words such as *city, state, country,* and *continent* are not capitalized unless they are part of the name of a particular city, state, country, or continent.

The **c**apital of a **s**tate may not be its largest **c**ity.

**18b(5)**   The names of specific avenues, streets, and routes are capitalized.

Bill took the car to 714 **G**ayle **A**venue, and I walked to the next street.
They live in the large yellow house on **B**ridge **S**treet.
Did you locate U.S. **R**oute 66 on the map?

Notice that words such as *avenue, street,* or *route* are not capitalized unless they are part of the name of a particular avenue, street, or route.

All the **r**outes in the town have **a**venues or **s**treets leading into them.

**18b(6)**   The names of specific mountains, parks, bodies of water, planets, and buildings are capitalized.

They visited **M**ount **R**ushmore and **Y**ellowstone **N**ational **P**ark while they were on a vacation trip.
Charles A. Lindbergh was the first person to fly alone across the **A**tlantic **O**cean.
Life on other planets, especially **M**ars, has long been a favorite theme of writers.
Many people visit the **E**mpire **S**tate **B**uilding each year while they are in New York City.

Notice that words such as *mountain, lake,* or *park* are not capitalized unless they are part of the name of a particular mountain, lake, or park.

The picnic can be held at the **l**ake in the new **p**ark.

**EXERCISE 3**

In the following paragraph, capitalize the names of any specific places.

The people of south america live between the atlantic ocean and the pacific ocean. The city of natal in brazil is an important port. The amazon river flows from the andes mountains into the atlantic ocean. There are many rivers and cities in brazil, which is a very large country.

**18b(7)** The names of months, days of the week, and holidays are capitalized.

> My favorite month is **N**ovember.
> In the United States, **M**ay and **J**une are warm months.
> The class will meet for three hours each **M**onday for the next five weeks.
> There will be a parade on **V**eterans **D**ay.

Notice that words such as *month*, *day*, *week*, or *holiday* are not capitalized unless they are part of the name of a particular month, day, week, or holiday.

> There are **m**onthly meetings scheduled every **d**ay for the next two **w**eeks.

**18b(8)** The names of departments and branches of government, political parties, companies, and organizations are capitalized.

> The **J**ustice **D**epartment occupies several large buildings and has many employees.
> A rally was planned by the **R**epublican party.
> The **M**etropolitan **I**nsurance **C**ompany has an office on Main Street.
> The large building on the corner belongs to **M**eglo **C**orporation.
> The **C**hesapeake **H**istorical **S**ociety meets every month.

**18b(9)**   The names of historical events and documents are capitalized.

> The **B**attle of **W**aterloo was an important event in French history.
> The **R**evolutionary **W**ar marks the beginning of our nation.
> The **T**reaty of **V**ersailles was signed in France.

**18b(10)**   Words that refer to God, religious denominations, and sacred books are capitalized.

| | |
|---|---|
| Words referring to God or the Deity | our Maker<br>Allah<br>the Trinity<br>the Messiah<br>Jesus<br>the Lord<br>the Almighty |
| Religious denominations | Catholic<br>Jewish<br>Buddhist<br>Moslem<br>Protestant |
| Sacred books or writings | the Bible<br>the Koran<br>the Old Testament<br>the Scriptures<br>Vedas |

**18b(11)**   Words that come from names that are capitalized are themselves capitalized.

| | |
|---|---|
| San Francisco | a **S**an **F**ranciscan |
| England | an **E**nglish course |
| Rotary Club | the **R**otarians |

See **19b(5)** for information on the abbreviation of capitalized words.

Use the following reference list as a guide.

| CAPITALIZED (SPECIFIC) | NOT CAPITALIZED (GENERAL) |
| --- | --- |
| Valley High School | high-school days |
| the Conservative party | a political party |
| the Exchange Club | a club for civic leaders |
| Chase Bank Building | the bank building |
| the Medal of Honor | a medal for bravery |
| an All-Star game | a basketball game |
| the Richmond Coliseum | a sports arena |
| the Churchland Raiders | a football team |
| History 312 | a course in history |
| Emporia College | a college |
| the Spanish people | people of another country |
| the Middle Ages | an era in history |
| Pepsi-Cola | a cola drink |
| New York State | the state on the map |
| the Orient | an oriental country |
| the Blue Ridge Mountains | some mountains in Virginia |
| Veterans Day | a day to honor veterans |
| the Southern Railway System | a railway network |
| Cousin Jimmy | a cousin |
| Golden Gate Bridge | a long bridge |
| Christmas in December | a day in winter |
| Springdale Acres | a housing development |

## EXERCISE 4

Add capital letters where they are needed in the following sentences.

1. Beginning spanish will be offered on monday and wednesday at nine.
2. We went to the football game on thanksgiving day.
3. Susan met her friends at the large department store on center avenue and vine street.
4. winter came early that year, and october was cold and rainy.
5. john belongs to the golden gate toastmasters club.
6. This country gained a large area of land by means of the louisiana purchase.
7. i went to kemper high school for two years.
8. The women of greensville methodist church cook and serve delicious meals every thursday evening.

9. We will study the talmud and the koran next year.
10. our basketball team lost the game to maytown high last
    saturday.

## 18c Capitalize the first, last, and important words in the titles of books, plays, songs, and poems. Capitalize the second part of important hyphenated words.

> The class will discuss **A**nimal **F**arm next week.
> Study the first two chapters in **H**istory of the **B**order **S**tates.
> The group sang "**T**he **S**tar-**S**pangled **B**anner."
> Her first published poem was called "**L**eaves of **A**utumn."

Notice that little words like *the, a, an,* and *of* are not capitalized unless one of these words begins or ends the title.

> The article was called "**A** Talent I Know **O**f."
> She sang "Do You Know **of a** Beautiful Home?" while the
> group assembled.

## 18d Capitalize *I* and *O* when they are used as words.

> All of the books which **I** wanted were very expensive.
> Tell me, **O** reader, how to solve this problem.

The word *O* is always spelled with a single capital letter. The word *oh* begins with a capital letter only when it is the first word of a sentence, title, or quoted material. Review **18b(3)** for additional information on the word *I*.

## 18e Capitalize the first word of quoted sentences.

> Tom said, "**T**he game is over, and we lost."
> "**W**hen the bell rings," said Miss Johnson, "everyone may
> leave quietly."
> The man exclaimed, "**I** do not know who you are. **W**hat right
> have you to question me? **T**ell me your name, and then I
> may talk to you."

**EXERCISE 5**

Add capital letters where they are needed in the following paragraphs.

mrs. lassiter walked up to the platform with a grim expression on her face. "can anyone here lead us in some songs?" she asked.

a tall man in the back of the room stood up. "perhaps i can. at least i'll be glad to try," he said. as he walked to the front of the room, the pianist started pounding out "my wild irish rose" and oh what a noise ensued!

**18f**  Do not use more capitals than you need.

**18f(1)**  Do not capitalize the name of a school subject unless it is the name of a specific course or a language.

My favorite **s**cience course is **B**iology 309.
Sue made low grades in **E**nglish and **h**istory, but she made an honor grade in **c**hemistry.

**18f(2)**  Do not capitalize the names of seasons or directions.

The flowers were beautiful in the **s**pring.
Every **w**inter I have trouble with my car.
Turn **w**est after you pass the school and the shopping center.

**18f(3)**  Do not capitalize the names of trees, fruits, vegetables, birds, or flowers.

Huge **o**ak trees were planted on each side of the street.
The **c**herry trees make spring in Washington a beautiful sight.
The girls brought **p**eaches, **p**ears, and **g**rapes.
Six **c**rows sat on the fence and selected the **c**orn that they would have for dinner.
The **r**obins and the **c**ardinals started to build nests.
All of the **r**oses were in bloom.

**18f(4)**   Do not capitalize the names of games or sports unless the name is a trademark.

> Tables were arranged for checkers, Scrabble, Monopoly, bridge, and dominoes.
> The tennis game was not very lively.
> Our football team went to see the Redskins in the playoff.
> The great American sport is said to be baseball, but the spectators far outnumber the players.

Notice that the names of specific teams are capitalized.

**18f(5)**   Do not capitalize the name of a disease unless it is named for a person, and then do not capitalize the word *disease*.

> The school was closed because many of the students had the measles.
> A young child may be very ill with pneumonia.
> I didn't realize how serious Hodgkin's disease could be.

**18f(6)**   Do not capitalize the names of musical instruments.

> I wear ear plugs when my sister practices on her violin.
> Eddie enjoys playing the drums in the school combo.
> The large Baldwin piano stood in the middle of the stage.

Notice that the names of the companies that manufacture the instruments are capitalized.

### EXERCISE 6

Add capital letters where they are needed in the following paragraph.

> The room was warm and comfortable. several large chairs were scattered about, and there were many books on shelves and tables. laura settled down to watch "the edge of night," and gary looked for his favorite song in a pile of tapes. A bowl of asters and roses made a spot of color, and the chinese paintings added a calm, quiet feeling.

# 19

# *Underlining, Abbreviations, and Numbers*

## Use underlining, abbreviations, and numbers correctly.

It is important to know how to use the standard forms for underlining, abbreviations, and numbers because even if you do not use them in your writing, you will be reading them in material which other people have written.

**19a**  Underline the titles of books and some other published materials; titles of works of art; names of ships, trains, and other special vehicles; and some words when you refer to them in your papers.

Some words or groups of words are underlined in handwritten or typewritten papers. If the material is printed, the underlined words are shown in italic type.

HANDWRITTEN  *She read an article in the Review of the News.*

TYPEWRITTEN  She read an article in the Review of the News.

PRINTED  She read an article in the *Review of the News*.

211

**19a(1)** Underline the titles of works that are published separately, such as books, periodicals, newspapers, bulletins, motion pictures, plays, and long musical compositions.

Underlining shows that you are writing about things that someone else has written.

> Fred Gipson's <u>Old Yeller</u> is a novel about frontier life of the 1860's in America.
>
> The <u>Flight of the Phoenix</u> is the story of a desperate struggle for life.
>
> Did you see the <u>Reader's Digest</u> this month?
>
> Shakespeare's <u>Romeo and Juliet</u> was given a modern musical setting in <u>West Side Story</u>.
>
> Handel's <u>Messiah</u> is usually performed at Christmastime.

Study the examples and notice the following points:

1. The words *a, an,* or *the* are underlined or italicized when they begin the title of a book; frequently they are not underlined when they begin the title of a periodical or newspaper.
2. The name of an author is not underlined or italicized.

A few references are not underlined.

1. Do not underline references to the Bible or its divisions.
2. Do not underline references to legal documents.
3. Do not underline the titles of your papers, because a title is not italicized when it stands at the head or beginning of a book or other separate publication.
4. Do not underline the titles of short stories, songs, short poems, articles from periodicals, and subdivisions of books; these titles are usually enclosed in quotation marks. (See **16b**.)

**19a(2)** Underline the names of works of art.

> Winslow Homer's painting <u>Breezing Up</u> shows both the power and the magnificence of the sea.

**19a(3)**   Underline the names of ships, trains, and other vehicles that have names.

Do not underline the names of companies that operate the vehicles.

> My father often recalled with pleasure his trip to Europe aboard the Cunard Line's <u>Queen Elizabeth</u>.
> The <u>George Washington</u> was a luxury train operated by the Chesapeake and Ohio Railway Company.
> Tom Moreland stepped out into space from <u>Skylab V</u>.

**19a(4)**   Underline words, letters, and figures used as illustrations or spoken of as such. (See also **16c**.)

> The words <u>right</u> and <u>write</u> sound alike.
> The word <u>fear</u> may mean many different things.
> Plurals of most names of things are formed by adding <u>s</u> to the singular word.
> The last <u>7</u> in the list should be a <u>1</u>.

**19a(5)**   Do not use underlining for emphasis or stress if it can be avoided.

Use stronger or more specific words in place of those words you may tend to underline.

> WEAK   The noise was <u>awful</u>.   [Underlining is used for emphasis.]
> BETTER   The noise hurt our ears and shook the walls.   [Underlining is not needed.]
>
> WEAK   The movie was <u>swell</u>.
> BETTER   The movie was excellent and enjoyable.

**EXERCISE 1**

In the following sentences, underline the words which should be underlined in your writing.

1. Martha read and reviewed Wuthering Heights.

2. Broiled snails were served for lunch on Air Force I.
3. The drama department presented Dark of the Moon last spring.
4. All class members are expected to read five articles from Modern Science or Chemistry Review.
5. The Mona Lisa hangs in the Louvre.
6. Wells's War of the Worlds is an exciting book.
7. Read the editorial in the Wednesday Sun Times.
8. Is the figure in the third line a 6 or an 8?
9. John Melton has a sailboat named Gypsy Moth.
10. Place a dot over every i and cross each t.

**19b**   **Abbreviations are shortened versions of names or titles and are often used where there is not much space.**

Some abbreviations are accepted in all kinds of writing, but most of the time it is better to spell out the words.

**19b(1)**   **Use the abbreviations *Mr.*, *Mrs.*, *Ms.*, *Dr.*, and *St.* (for *Saint*) before proper names.**

> *Mrs.* James Timmons and *Dr.* Stanley Wood were in charge of the meeting.
> It rained on *St.* Swithin's Day last year.

Spell out *doctor* and *saint* when they are not followed by proper names.

> Did you see the *doctor* before he left?
> She has some very beautiful pictures of *saints*.

**19b(2)**   **Some abbreviations, such as *Prof.*, *Rep.*, *Hon.*, *Gen.*, and *Capt.*, may be used before full names or before initials and last names. They should not be used before last names alone.**

> WRONG   Sen. Harmon spoke to the group.
> RIGHT   *Sen.* James Harmon spoke to the group.
>                     OR
>             *Senator* Harmon spoke to the group.

WRONG   She invited Rev. Wilson to have dinner with them.
RIGHT   She invited *Rev.* K. R. Wilson to have dinner with
  them.                    OR
  She invited *Reverend* Wilson to have dinner with
  them.

WRONG   I saw Capt. Allison in the library.
RIGHT   I saw *Capt.* C. W. Allison in the library.
                    OR
  I saw *Captain* Allison in the library.

**19b(3)**   It is customary to abbreviate titles and degrees if they appear after proper names.

Jr., Sr., Esq., D.D., Ph.D., M.A., M.D., C.P.A.
R. H. Bryant, *Jr.*, lives on the next street.

**19b(4)**   It is customary to abbreviate words used with dates and figures.

A.D., B.C., A.M. OR a.m., P.M. OR p.m., no. OR No., $

At 9:30 A.M. the television sets went on sale for $376.59.

**19b(5)**   It is customary to abbreviate the names of many organizations, expressions, and government agencies usually referred to by their initials.

Remember to use capital letters for each word that is capitalized in the full name or expression.

North Atlantic Treaty Organization   NATO

GOP   FBI   NASA   HEW   FHA   USA

The *AMA* published a report on the new medicine.

**19b(6)**   Use D.C. to designate the District of Columbia.

Washington, D.C.

Mr. Kermit Wells, Jr., lives in Washington, *D.C.*

**19b(7)**     Spell out the names of states and countries, months and days of the week, units of measurement, names of courses of study, and first names.

> Karen lives in *California*, but she spends several months each year in *Mexico*.
> The workshops are scheduled for the third and fourth *Wednesdays* in *April*.
> Please bring me five *pounds* of sugar and a *quart* of salad oil.
> *George* [NOT Geo.] Caton is taking *biology*, *history*, and *Spanish* this quarter.

**19b(8)**     Spell out words such as *Avenue, Street,* and *River* when they are part of proper names.

> Oakhill *Avenue* is the prettiest street in town.

**19b(9)**     Do not use **&** (for *and*), *Inc., Co.,* or *Bros.* unless such an abbreviation is part of an official name or title.

> Harcourt Brace Jovanovich, *Inc.*, is a large publishing company.
> The House **&** Grounds *Company* builds and repairs houses.

**19c**     Spell out numbers that can be expressed in one or two words.

> There are *seven thousand* students at my college, but only *fifty-five* are taking physics.

Use numerals for large numbers that need more than two words to express.

> The building cost *$14,700,000.*

**19c(1)**     Use numerals for figures in a series or in statistics.

> The lot is *250* feet long and *365* feet deep.

**19c(2)** Use numerals for addresses and zip codes.

Jim lives at *702* Farley Court, Perkins, Oklahoma *74059*.

**19c(3)** Use numerals for decimals and percentages and for money used with $.

Interest on the loan was figured at 7 percent.
Marian wrote a check for *$350*.

**19c(4)** Use numerals for pages and divisions of books.

Read pages *8* and *9* in Chapter *1*.

**19c(5)** Use numerals for identification numbers, such as television stations, serial numbers, and telephone numbers.

He watched Channel *10* every evening at six o'clock.

**19c(6)** Use numerals for dates and specific times of day.

The package arrived on April *21, 1975*.   [Not April 21st, 1975.]
OR
The package arrived *21* April *1975*.

Tomorrow the sun will rise at *5:53* A.M.

*Note:* Spell out a number at the beginning of a sentence, or rewrite the sentence.

WRONG   7:30 o'clock is the time for the dinner.
RIGHT   *Seven-thirty* is the time for the dinner.
OR
The dinner will begin at *7:30*.

WRONG   117 boys are in the class.
RIGHT   There are *117* boys in the class.

## EXERCISE 2

In the following sentences, underline the correct word in parentheses. Review the information on abbreviations and numbers if you are not certain which item is correct.

1. I saw (Wm., William) Swanson yesterday afternoon at the (doctor's, dr.'s) office.
2. Did you hear (Sen., Senator) Barnes last night on Channel (Three, 3)?
3. Maria works for (Prof., Professor) Harrison, who lives on Maple (Ave., Avenue).
4. Did you ever visit (Me., Maine)?
5. Classes will be held in Room (3190, three thousand one hundred and ninety) on the (3rd, third) (Tues., Tuesday) of each month.
6. He poured (2, two) cups of sugar over (5, five) pounds of fruit.
7. Lloyd Armstrong, (Jr., Junior), can tell you the difference in total cost between (8, eight) percent and (9, nine) per-cent interest.
8. Did you review Chapter (6, six) and write (10, ten) sen-tences about (biol., biology) and chemistry?
9. (HEW, Health, Education, and Welfare) and (OEO, Office of Economic Opportunity) have large offices on the (7th, seventh) floor.
10. (10, Ten) men from this campus are attending the confer-ence in Washington, (D.C., District of Columbia).

# PART FOUR

# *Words*

# 20

# *Learning to Use the Dictionary*

**Learn to use a dictionary to help you
find the best words to express your ideas
and to help you spell the words you use.**

**20a**  **Learn to find the words you want to use.**

To find a word in a dictionary, all you have to know is the
alphabet, because the dictionary is simply a long alphabetical list of words. A word with the information about it is
called an *entry*.

The guide words printed at the top of each page of a
dictionary help you find the word you are looking for.

Here are the guide
words found at the
top of a dictionary
page.

*Beaker* is the first | | *Beat* is the last
entry at the top of | **beaker  beat** | entry at the bottom
the left-hand col- | | of the right-hand
umn of the page. | | column of the page.

All the entries that
come alphabetically
between *beaker* and
*beat* can be found on
this page.

Do not be surprised if your dictionary entries are not exactly the same as the examples given in this section. Not all dictionaries are exactly the same, but these examples should give you a general idea of the way most dictionaries are organized and the kinds of information they give you.

### EXERCISE 1

In each numbered item below, the words on the left represent the guide words that would appear on a dictionary page. The words on the right represent entries that might appear on that page. Choose the entries from the right that you would find on a dictionary page having the guide words given on the left.

| GUIDE WORDS | ENTRIES |
|---|---|
| 1. prude . . . psychology | prune, psychopathic, probe, pseudo |
| 2. empty . . . enchantment | empire, enamel, en-, endeavor |
| 3. calmly . . . cameo | calm, calf, camel, calorie |
| 4. resistor . . . response | resole, resort, respiration, respond |

**20b** **Learn the kinds of information given in a dictionary.**

Now that you see how words are arranged in a dictionary, you need to know some of the things you can learn about a word from a dictionary.

You can learn more from a dictionary than just how to spell and define a word.

### EXERCISE 2

Using the following dictionary entries, answer the questions below them.

**As to ri a** (as tô′rē ə *or* as tō′rē ə), *n.* city in NW Oregon that was established as a fur-trading post by John Jacob Astor in 1811. Population 11,000.

**brain y** (brān′ ē), *adj.* **brain i er, brain i est.** *Informal.* intelligent; clever. **brain i ness,** *n.*

**C.O.,** 1. Commanding Officer. 2. *Informal.* conscientious objector.

**Dic ta phone** (dik′ tə fōn), *n.* Trademark. instrument which records and reproduces words that are spoken into it.

**Ed wards** (ed′ wərdz), *n.* 1. Jonathan, 1703-1758. American clergyman, theologian, and metaphysician. 2. his son, Jonathan, 1745-1801. American clergyman.

1. Does the abbreviation C.O. always have the same meaning?
2. Is the Dictaphone a new type of telephone?
3. Was Jonathan Edwards's son a preacher?
4. Would you say someone was brainy if you were writing a formal letter of recommendation for him?
5. Had the city of Astoria been established when the first Jonathan Edwards was born?

**20b(1)** Use a dictionary to learn how to divide and pronounce a word.

Two things you can learn about a word from the dictionary are how to divide the word when you write it and how to pronounce it when you say it.

**ko·a·la** (kō·ä′·lə)

The dictionary uses dots (•) to show you where you can divide the word. The heavy stress mark (′) shows you which part of the word should be said with greatest emphasis.

Do not include the dots or the stress marks when you write a word in a sentence. If you need to divide a word at the end of a line as you are writing, use a hyphen, as shown in the next sentence.

When we went to Australia last summer, we saw a ko-ala in a eucalyptus tree.

In a dictionary entry, do not confuse the dot (•) with the hyphen (-).

ko•a•la       self-assured

## EXERCISE 3

Use your dictionary to look up the following words. Write the words, using a hyphen to show where you would divide them at the end of a line.

**Example**   insinuate

insin -uate

1. illustrate
2. primarily
3. sensational
4. determination
5. warranty
6. authority

In most dictionaries, the key to the sound symbols used to show you how to pronounce each word is found at the bottom of the page on which the word appears.

**ko·a·la** (kō·ä′·lə)

hat, āge, cãre, fär; let, bē, tèrm; it, īce; hot, gō, ôrder; oil, out; cup, pùt, rüle, ūse; *ch*, child; *ng*, long; *th*, thin; ŦH, then; *zh*, measure; ə represents *a* in *about, e* in *taken, i* in *April, o* in *lemon, u* in *circus*.

This key to the sound symbols used in the entry above tells you that the *o* in *koala* sounds like the *o* in *go*, the *a* sounds like the *a* in *far*, and the last *a* (ə) sounds like the *a* in *about*.

## EXERCISE 4

Use the dictionary key below to figure out the following sentences. Write the sentences correctly.

hat, āge, cãre, fär; let, bē, tèrm; it, īce; hot, gō, ôrder; oil, out; cup, pùt, rüle, ūse; *ch*, child; *ng*, long; *th*, thin; ŦH, then; *zh*, measure; ə represents *a* in *about, e* in *taken, i* in *April, o* in *lemon, u* in *circus*.

**Example**   Ū kan′ot trust ə smīl′ing kat.
You cannot trust a smiling cat.

1. Sèrf′ing duz′nt māk Travis tīrd.
2. Stud′ē ing duz māk Travis tīrd.
3. Rēd′ing gùd bùks iz härd wèrk fôr Travis.
4. Hiz fā′vər it rēd′ing iz ŦHə sen′tər fōld in *Fun Tīm Mag′əzēn*.

**20b(2)**   Use a dictionary to learn how and when to use a word.

You already know that you can find out what a word means by looking it up in a dictionary. You can also find out how and when to use, or not to use, certain words by looking them up in a dictionary.

Here are the five most common labels used in dictionaries to indicate how and when to use, or not use, certain words. If there is no label given, the word is considered Standard or Formal.

*Informal*   The word or meaning is used in everyday speech or writing but not in formal speech or writing.

   **brain•storm** (brān′·stôrm), *n. Informal.* a sudden, inspired idea.

*Slang*   The word or meaning is used in very informal speaking situations only.

   **jerk** (jèrk), *n. Slang.* an unsophisticated or stupid person.

*Dialect*   The word or meaning is used only in the informal speech of a particular region or group.

   **pone** (pōn), *n. Dialect. Southern U.S.* 1. bread made of corn meal. 2. loaf or cake of the bread.

*Substandard*   The word or meaning is not acceptable in general standard English speech or writing.

   **bust** (bust), *v.* 1. *Substandard.* burst.

*Archaic* or *Obsolete*   The word or meaning is very rare except in old books, or in books written
in the style of an earlier period.

**per•chance** (pər′chans *or* pər chans′), *adv. Archaic.* perhaps.

## EXERCISE 5

Use your dictionary to find any labels explaining when
and how to use, or not to use, the following words. Write
the word, the label(s) your dictionary gives it, and its
meaning.

1. blow      4. gobbledygook
2. ain't     5. alarum
3. br'er

## EXERCISE 6

Use your dictionary to find the following information
about each of the words listed below. Copy each word
and write the information beside it.

a. What the word means
b. How to divide the word (dots)
c. How to pronounce the word (sound symbols)
d. How and when to use, or not to use, the word (*Informal, Slang,* and other labels)

1. solder (as a verb)
2. pandemonium
3. than
4. crib
5. bootlicker
6. library
7. pass

**20c**   **Use a dictionary to spell words correctly.**

Dictionaries often have sections that explain the general
rules for spelling, adding prefixes and suffixes, and forming

plurals of words. Locate the spelling aids in your dictionary and learn to use them.

**20c(1)** Use a dictionary to confirm the spelling of a word.

If you are not certain about verb forms, endings of words, or irregularities of spelling, confirm or correct the spelling by using a dictionary. Especially in a paperback dictionary, you may need to look for a word at the end of a dictionary entry. For example, if you looked for *informality* as a separate entry, you would not find it because it is part of the entry for *informal*.

> **in•for•mal** (in fôr′ ml), *adj.* 1. not formal; not in the regular or prescribed manner. 2. done without ceremony. 3. used in everyday common talk, but not used in formal talking or writing. —**in•for•mal•i•ty,** *n.* —**in•for•mal•ly,** *adv.*

A dictionary will help you to spell verb forms correctly because the main forms of the verb are given if there is any irregularity in spelling. The forms are usually near the beginning of an entry.

> **run** (run), *v.,* **ran, run, running,** 1. move the legs quickly; go faster than walking.

Some dictionaries may give this type of information at the end of the entry.

> 2. go hurriedly; hasten. 3. flee. —**ran, run, running.**

See Section **7** for additional help in spelling verb forms.

**20c(2)** Use a dictionary to correct misspelled words.

When a paper is returned to you, there may be the symbol *sp* or the number *12* written by or over a word; this indicates that the word is not spelled correctly. When the problem in spelling is at the beginning of the word, you may have trouble locating the word in a dictionary if you do not know the beginning letters. Here are some useful hints to help you locate words that you have misspelled.

1. The letter *c* may sound like *s* or *k*. If you cannot locate a word in the *s* or *k* section of the dictionary, you may have to look in the *c* section.

   capsize   *c* sounds like *k*
   certain   *c* sounds like *s*

2. The sound of *ch*, as in *church*, may be spelled *tch*, *te*, *ti*, or *tu*. Although the alternate spellings of the sound may not be the first letters, they may still keep you from locating the word easily.

   hatch       the *ch* sound is spelled *tch*
   righteous   the *ch* sound is spelled *te*
   question    the *ch* sound is spelled *ti*
   future      the *ch* sound is spelled *tu*

3. The letters *ch* may have the sound of *k*, as in *chemistry*.
4. The sound of *f* may be spelled *ph*, as in *photograph*.
5. The sounds of *g* and *j* are easily confused if the *g* has a soft sound. The words *generally*, *gentle*, *ginger*, and *gymnast* all sound as though they begin with *j*.
6. The letters *in* and *en* may sound alike at the beginning of a word. The beginnings of words like *enchant*, *encircle*, or *endure* all sound very similar to the beginnings of *indent*, *incubate*, or *indirect*. Learn to look for such words in both the *in* and *en* sections of the dictionary.
7. Words that sound as though they begin with *n* may have a silent letter before the *n*.

   *pneumonia* sounds like "newmonia"
   *knife* sounds like "nife"
   *gnaw* sounds like "naw"
   *knot* sounds the same as *not*, but the meaning is different
   *know* sounds the same as *no*, but the meaning is different

8. The sound of *r* may be spelled *rh* as in *rhyme* or *rhythm*.

9. The sound of *sh*, as in *she*, may be spelled many different ways.

| sure | the *sh* sound is spelled *su* |
| ocean | the *sh* sound is spelled *cea* |
| machine | the *sh* sound is spelled *ch* |
| mention | the *sh* sound is spelled *ti* |
| issue | the *sh* sound is spelled *ss* |
| special | the *sh* sound is spelled *ci* |

10. Some words that begin with a *w* may sound as though they begin with a different letter, because the *w* is silent. There may be another word that sounds the same, so be sure that you are using the word you mean to use.

*wring* sounds the same as *ring*
*write* sounds the same as *right*
*wrap* sounds the same as *rap*

The *wr* beginning for a word is quite common, so remember to look in the *wr* section of the dictionary if you cannot find the word in the *r* section. Additional examples of such words are *wreck*, *wrestle*, *wrong*, and *wrought*.

**20c(3)**    **A word may be marked "misspelled" because you used the wrong word.**

By leaving off the ending letters, you may spell a different word. For example, *fine* is a describing word that means "not coarse," or a verb that means "to impose a punishment by requiring payment of a sum." The word *fine* is a word in the dictionary, but if you meant "locate," then you should have spelled the word *find*. Do not stop with the spelling of the word; look at the definition and be sure that you are using the word you mean to use.

Do not forget the *h* in words such as *where* and *while*. If you use *were* for *where* and *wile* for *while*, you are using words that are different in both meaning and pronunciation.

See Section **21** for additional help in deciding on the correct word.

## EXERCISE 7

Use your dictionary to spell the following words correctly.

1. Use *f* or *ph* to spell these words that begin with an *f* sound.
_____anatic   _____antom   _____orum   _____ysical
2. Use *c*, *k*, or *ch* to spell these words that begin with a *k* sound.
_____aracteristic   _____ibitzer   _____onsecrate
3. Use *j* or *g* to spell these words that begin with a *j* sound.
_____ypsy   _____ealousy   _____ocular   _____esture
4. Use *n*, *kn*, *pn*, or *gn* to spell these words that begin with an *n* sound.
_____eumatic   _____atural   _____uckle   _____arled
5. Use *r*, *wr*, or *rh* to spell these words that begin with an *r* sound.
_____eumatism   _____umble   _____eckage   _____inkle

# 21

# *Using the Right Word*

## Use words correctly.

The words you choose help give your reader a good or a bad reaction to what you write. It is important to use the words you mean to use and to use the best words you can think of or find in a dictionary.

**21a** Use the words you mean to use.

You can ruin a perfectly good sentence by using the wrong word. If you are in doubt about a word, consult a good dictionary. If you can possibly help it, don't use a word that doesn't exist or that doesn't say what you think it says. It is better to use a word that sounds too simple to you than to use a word that is incorrect.

WRONG   Some foreign cars are considerated better investments than American cars. [*Considerated* does
        not exist.]

RIGHT   Some foreign cars are *considered* better investments
        than American cars.

INACCURATE   Customers will sit down at the counter and indulge in the tempting food.

ACCURATE   Customers will sit down at the counter and *eat*
           the tempting food.

INACCURATE   Gas rationing should be reinforced.
ACCURATE   Gas rationing should be *reinstated.*

| INACCURATE | They chalked their sticks frequently as the game prolonged. |
|---|---|
| ACCURATE | They chalked their sticks frequently as the game *continued*. |

## 21b  Use clear or specific words.

Sometimes a word will be used correctly, but it will not be the very best word you could have used. The best word is the one that gives the reader the clearest picture of what you mean to say. Which of the words below give you the clearest picture of what the writer is saying — those in the left-hand column or those in the right-hand column?

| a fat man | a man weighing over three hundred pounds, with a short neck, three chins, and a body shaped like a barrel |
|---|---|
| an old car | a 1958 Buick sedan |
| a happy woman | a woman who feels as if she has just found a million dollars. |
| a broken record | a record that was smashed to bits |

Of course, the words on the right are much more vivid and give the reader a clearer picture of what the writer is describing than those on the left. It really will improve your papers if you choose words that give your readers a clear, not a vague, picture of what you want to tell them.

| VAGUE | I like Amanda because she has a nice personality. |
|---|---|
| CLEAR | I like Amanda because she laughs at my jokes and doesn't get angry — even when I tell her I'm going to be late picking her up. |

| VAGUE | My room is very cheerful. |
|---|---|
| CLEAR | My room has plenty of sunlight; a warm red rug; big, soft yellow chairs; and a Welcome sign hanging on the door. |

| VAGUE | People buy all kinds of ridiculous things for their pets. What's more, there is now a variety of clothing and accessories to choose from. |
|---|---|
| CLEAR | A few of the many products for pets include gold jewelry, evening gowns, top hats and tails, and pajamas. If your pet is a little flabby, you can get him a jog-a-dog machine for $575. Also available are |

clip-on diapers, wigs, false eyelashes, mascara, and
nail polish in a dozen colors.

## EXERCISE 1

Rewrite the following paragraph, putting in clear or
specific words and details to illustrate the italicized
vague words.

Daydreaming used to be called "woolgathering." Usually
people daydream about *agreeable things.* In a daydream you
can revisit *the past* or place yourself in *the future.* Daydreaming makes possible *the impossible.* It allows you to rid yourself
of *unhappy feelings.* It is creative and essential for natural
growth. In our daydreams, all that we want to happen does
happen. Daydreaming offers us a release from *the cares of
society.*

## 21c Learn how to use these problem words.

Here is a list of some confusing words that have caused
students problems in writing. Be sure that you know how
these words are used.

| | |
|---|---|
| **a** | is used before a consonant sound. |
| **an** | is used before a vowel sound. |
| | *a* beer, *a* cork, *a* habit. |
| | *an* alligator, *an* elevator, *an* hour. |
| **accept** | means to "receive." |
| **except** | means "not included." |
| | I *accept* your apology. |
| | Everyone *except* my St. Bernard was invited to the cookout. |
| **affect** | means "to influence." |
| **effect** | usually means "result." |
| | President Nixon's resignation speech *affected* me deeply. |
| | Who knows what the *effect* of a nuclear war would be? |
| **a lot** | is not spelled *alot.* |

| | |
|---|---|
| **already** | means "before now" or "by this time." |
| **all ready** | means "completely prepared." |
| | The crowd is *already* assembled. |
| | We are *all ready* to go. |
| | |
| **always** | means "all the time." |
| **all ways** | means "every manner." |
| | Judy is not *always* prepared for class. |
| | I try to be helpful in *all ways*. |
| | |
| **between** | refers to two persons or things. |
| **among** | refers to more than two persons or things. |
| | A woman shouldn't have to choose *between* marriage and a career. |
| | The will divides his money *among* several heirs. |
| | |
| **borrow** | means "to get, with the intention of returning." |
| **lend** | means "to let someone have something you expect to get back." |
| | I *borrowed* some money from my brother. |
| | Lisa didn't want to *lend* me any of her clothes. |
| | |
| **bought** | means "purchased." |
| **brought** | means "caused to come here." |
| | Liz *bought* a ticket for the Sweepstakes. |
| | I *brought* along my knitting. |
| | |
| **bring** | means "to cause to come here." |
| **take** | means "to cause to go there." |
| | *Bring* that photograph album to me. |
| | *Take* that nasty cuspidor into the other room. |
| | |
| **effect** | See **affect, effect.** |
| | |
| **except** | See **accept, except.** |
| | |
| **fewer** | means "not as many." It is a plural word. |
| **less** | means "not as much." It is a singular word. |
| | I have *fewer* problems than I had ten years ago. |
| | I have *less* money than I had ten years ago. |
| | |
| **foot** | is singular. |
| **feet** | is plural. |
| | The stool is less than a *foot* tall. |
| | I am five *feet* tall. |
| | When the measurement comes before the person or thing it describes, however, use the word *foot*. |
| | This is a ten-*foot* ladder. |

| **from** | Do not use *off* or *off of* when you mean *from*. |
| **off** | The meanings are often similar, but *off* usually means "from the top of." |
| | WRONG  Jim copied off my paper. |
| | RIGHT  Jim copied *from* my paper. |
| **hole** | See **whole, hole, hold.** |
| **in** | means "located within." |
| **into** | means "toward the inside" of a place. |
| | We were all gathered *in* my aunt's room. |
| | Joe just walked *into* my aunt's room. |
| **its** | means "belonging to it." |
| **it's** | means "it is" or "it has." |
| | Virtue is *its* own reward. |
| | *It's* a small price to pay for being beautiful. |
| **learn** | means "to gain knowledge." |
| **teach** | means "to pass on knowledge." |
| | I *learned* how to surface-dive from my brother. |
| | Let me *teach* you how to stay awake in class. |
| **leave** | means "to go away from." |
| **let** | means "to allow to." |
| | I am *leaving* my past life behind. |
| | I will *let* him have my answer soon. |
| **lend** | See **borrow, lend.** |
| **less** | See **fewer, less.** |
| **loose** | means "not tight" or "unfastened." |
| **lose** | means "to allow to get away" or "to misplace." |
| | Susie seems to have a *loose* tooth. |
| | It's sad to *lose* an old friend. |
| **off** | See **from, off.** |
| **passed** | means "went by." |
| **past** | means "former times" or "belonging to former times." |
| | The parade *passed* through the town. |
| | It is often sad to remember the *past*. |
| **teach** | See **learn, teach.** |
| **than** | is used in a comparison. |
| **then** | can mean "at that time." |
| | George is faster *than* lightning. |
| | Wait awhile; Lou will *then* be free to help you. |

| | |
|---|---|
| **that** | See **who, which, that.** |
| **their** | means "belonging to them." |
| **there** | means "in that place" and sometimes introduces the subject of a sentence. |
| **they're** | means "they are." |

Let them have *their* own way.

*There* are many reasons for avoiding those rock concerts.

*They're* here! *They're* here!

| | |
|---|---|
| **to** | means "toward" or "in the direction of." It also appears before the verb in expressions like *to want* and *to have.* |
| **too** | means "also" or "more than enough." |
| **two** | means "one plus one." |

We all hate *to* go *to* the dentist.

I am *too* angry to speak.

I tried *two* or three times to reach Lisa.

| | |
|---|---|
| **to** | means "toward" or "in the direction of." |
| **at** | means "near" or "in the location of." |

WRONG  They arrived to our house.

RIGHT  They arrived *at* our house.

OR

They came *to* our house.

| | |
|---|---|
| **who** | refers to persons. |
| **which** | refers to things. |
| **that** | can refer to persons or things. |

Betsy Ross is the woman *who* made the first American flag.

*Which* of these stories did you prefer?

This is the wrench *that* I need for the job.

| | |
|---|---|
| **who's** | means "who is" or "who has." |
| **whose** | means "belonging to what person." |

*Who's* at the door?

*Whose* jellybeans are these?

| | |
|---|---|
| **whole** | means "entire." |
| **hole** | means "opening." |
| **hold** | means "to keep." |

I can't believe I ate the *whole* pie!

Every doughnut has its *hole*.

I won't believe I have the money until I *hold* it in my hand.

**your**          means "belonging to you."
**you're**        means "you are."
                  Take *your* seat.
                  I think that *you're* mistaken.

## EXERCISE 2

Write *to*, *too*, or *two* in each of the blanks in the following sentences.

1. Americans drive cars that burn _____ much gasoline.
2. I was _____ tired _____ understand what I was doing.
3. The nail was _____ inches _____ long.
4. Celia has dedicated her life _____ her family.
5. I was _____ proud _____ admit that I wasn't ready to be on my own.
6. _____ much freedom makes people lazy.
7. Tom was _____ afraid _____ stay home alone.

## EXERCISE 3

Write *a* or *an* in each of the blanks in the following sentences.

1. That elephant had _____ unbelievably long trunk.
2. Compare Providence to _____ uncrowded city, and you'll see in _____ instant what I mean.
3. My boyfriend is twenty-seven; I never thought I could fall in love with _____ older man.
4. It only took them _____ hour to find _____ place to eat.
5. Eve wanted to get _____ job in _____ office.
6. You can hang _____ clothesline in the yard.
7. Leo is _____ good quarterback.

## EXERCISE 4

Write *their, there,* or *they're* in each of the blanks in the following sentences.

1. _____ own land was rich farmland.
2. _____ going to be late if they don't hurry.
3. I'll never learn all _____ is to learn about a subject.
4. George had never been _____ before.
5. _____ are many stresses that can bring on a heart attack.

## EXERCISE 5

Underline the correct word in parentheses in the following sentences.

1. I walked (in, into) the kitchen and saw my mother frying bacon.
2. When the firefighters arrived (at, to) our house, they wanted to know where the fire was.
3. My uncle is (in, into) his workshop.
4. If you can get (to, at) the store by 10:30, you probably won't find it crowded.
5. It looks as though the crowd is already (at, to) the ball park.

## EXERCISE 6

If any of the italicized words in the following sentences is incorrectly used, change it to *who* or *which.*

1. He is the only man *that* I have ever loved.
2. Pick up the pliers *which* are on the workbench.
3. The attendant *which* parked your car doesn't seem to be around right now.
4. Kris Kristofferson, *who* has written some great country tunes, was once a Rhodes scholar.

## EXERCISE 7

Underline the correct word in parentheses in the following sentences.

1. (Who's, Whose) clothing did Elaine borrow this week?
2. It's easy to tell (whose, who's) put too much squash on his plate.
3. Guess (who's, whose) coming to dinner!
4. I wonder (who's, whose) been nibbling at this cake.
5. Just as we started to relax, the sergeant called out, ("Whose, "Who's) gear is this piled on the floor?"

## EXERCISE 8

Underline the correct word in parentheses in the following sentences.

1. My father is afraid to (learn, teach) any of us to drive.
2. Radio and TV have a great (affect, effect) on public taste.
3. People who have the blues (alot, a lot) have other emotional problems.
4. Mimi will (accept, except) whatever is right.
5. Since you have (brought, bought) gas for less money than that, you must know that it is possible to do it.
6. Before zip codes were put into (affect, effect), clerks had to look up all the names of small towns.
7. Lucy is willing to (accept, except) the job even though it has (fewer, less) benefits than her old one.
8. If you misplace (your, you're) wallet, (your, you're) in trouble.
9. We began to (loose, lose) sight of the ground as we (past, passed) through the clouds.
10. (Let, Leave) us make up our minds once and for all.
11. I wanted to (lend, borrow) a chain saw (from, off of) my uncle, but he was afraid to (lend, borrow) it to me.
12. (Bring, Take) those books back to the library before you have to pay a fine.
13. Mr. Emerson asked the salesgirl to (whole, hole, hold) that camera for him until payday.
14. On Friday nights my friend Jim is always trying to (lend, borrow) me ten dollars or so until I can get a job.
15. (Its, It's) a good day for staying at home by the fire.

16. The answers to the difficult questions are (always, all ways) hidden (in, into) the back of the manual.
17. (There's, Theirs) no point in rushing; (your, you're) (already, all ready) late.
18. Naomi is a beautiful, five- (foot, feet)-tall blonde.
19. The election comes down to a choice (among, between) two very good candidates.
20. It takes (fewer, less) people than you might think to make up a good basketball team.

# 22

# *Too Few Words*

## Do not leave out necessary words.

Many times readers can understand what a writer means to say even if the writer leaves out an occasional word in a sentence, but it is not a good idea to omit words. Most people omit words in their writing because they are careless, because they have developed the habit of leaving out certain words in writing, or because they often omit these words in speech and this habit has been transferred to their writing.

**22a** Do not develop the careless habit of leaving out short words like *the, and, he, she, it, his, her, of,* or *that.*

WRONG    As I got to swamp, I knew I had to go in.
RIGHT    As I got to *the* swamp, I knew I had to go in.

WRONG    It was my letter convinced my sister to come and see what was going on.
RIGHT    It was my letter *that* convinced my sister to come and see what was going on.

WRONG    He dribbles well also assists in points made by other players.
RIGHT    He dribbles well *and* also assists in points made by other players.

In particular, if you are giving directions, do not carelessly omit the words *it* and *the.* You may see such omissions in cookbooks and technical manuals, which try to save space, but you should include these words in your own papers.

WRONG    Take from bowl second half of dough and roll the same way you rolled the first piece.

RIGHT    Take from *the* bowl *the* second half of *the* dough and roll *it* the same way you rolled the first piece.

WRONG    Pull out locking rod and remove cylinder. Push rod with wire tip through barrel.

RIGHT    Pull out *the* locking rod and remove *the* cylinder. Push *the* rod with *the* wire tip through *the* barrel.

Remember to include *of* in expressions like *kind of, type of,* and *sort of.*

WRONG    He is the type person you don't want to mess around with.

RIGHT    He is the type *of* person you don't want to mess around with.

**22b**    Sometimes when you say a sentence quickly, you leave out the verbs *is, are, was,* or *were.* Do not make this mistake in writing.

WRONG    This a description of my brother.
RIGHT    This *is* a description of my brother.

**22c**    When you compare two people or two things, do not leave out any words that would make your comparison clear.

WRONG    Use our product. You'll feel cleaner than your soap. [You can't compare a person and a soap.]

RIGHT    Use our product. You'll feel cleaner than *you would using* your soap.

### EXERCISE 1

Insert any words that are needed to complete the meaning of the following sentences.

**Example**  Be sure that your air conditioner properly
grounded.
Be sure that your air conditioner *is* properly
grounded.

1. I give all the work that I do in school.
2. The first thing came into my mind was that Bob's body was in good physical shape.
3. Disney World offers many games and rides for family.
4. Even with his great size wouldn't hurt the smallest animal.
5. It was end of summer.
6. The Squires still had many promising young players as Ticky Burden and Mack Calvin.
7. My sister and her husband been late for our family reunion every year.
8. It was the weather made us decide to stay home instead of going to the beach.
9. John is the type man you wouldn't trust with much of your money.
10. I like Elvis Presley's singing better than Bob Dylan.

# 23

# *Too Many Words*

Leave out any words that repeat
something you have already said or that
serve no purpose in your sentence.

**23a**  Do not use the same word too often in a single
sentence or short paragraph.

Sometimes it is difficult to think of a word that has the same
meaning as the one you have just used. Finding a new word is
usually worth the effort, though, if you can thus avoid repeating yourself needlessly. Usually a little thought will suggest a
better way to say something.

REPETITIOUS  Jerry West was chosen coach of the Lakers
because he was well qualified for coaching
the team.  [There is no need to repeat the
idea that Jerry West is a coach.]

BETTER  Jerry West was chosen coach of the Lakers
because he was well qualified for the job.

REPETITIOUS  The section to be plated has to be roughed in
order to be plated.  [There is no need to
repeat that the section is to be plated.]

BETTER  The section to be plated has to be roughed
first.

**23b**  Do not use a synonym (a word that has the same meaning as a word you have already used) unless it serves a definite purpose.

Don't bore your reader by repeating an idea that doesn't have to be repeated.

| | |
|---|---|
| REPETITIOUS | Moving your fingers on the frets or neck of the guitar will give you the desired sounds you want. [*Desired sounds* and *sounds you want* mean the same thing. Only one of the expressions is needed.] |
| BETTER | Moving your fingers on the frets or neck of the guitar will give you the desired sounds. |
| REPETITIOUS | Replace the jack back in the trunk. [*Replace* means "to put back." Omit the word *back*.] |
| BETTER | Replace the jack in the trunk. |
| REPETITIOUS | My brother is neither fat nor thin, which helps him play football because of the way he is built. [*The way he is built* is unnecessary because the sentence says that he is *neither fat nor thin*.] |
| BETTER | My brother is neither fat nor thin, a fact which helps him play football. |

Avoid using expressions that are themselves repetitious.

REPETITIOUS
ink pen
school teacher
the modern world of today
In my opinion, I think

BETTER
pen
teacher
the modern world
I think

Do not repeat the subject by using *he, she, it,* or *they* right after the subject you have just named.

| | |
|---|---|
| REPETITIOUS | The coach, he is just there to help the quarterback decide what plays to run. |
| BETTER | The coach is just there to help the quarterback decide what plays to run. |

## EXERCISE 1

Rewrite the following sentences, eliminating any unnecessary words.

1. Edward Kennedy's refusal to run for President is based on his emotional feelings.
2. When I practiced my speech, some of the contents of my speech were twisted, which caused distortion in the development of my speech.
3. Through the years, bikes have been improved and made better.
4. Many violent films are rated *R* because of their violence.
5. Rembrandt, he was the greatest art painter of all time.
6. Do not hold or depress the tongue down.
7. You will have to return that dress back to the store.
8. In my opinion, I feel television will play an important role in our modern society.
9. Champ can catch a ball in his mouth and return it back to you.
10. I have decided what to do about the problem I am having getting a job in an office and what is needed to solve this problem.

**23c**   **Train yourself to say things plainly.**

Many beginning writers (and unfortunately some experienced ones) think that in order to have an effective style they have to use words that "sound good." Others think it is better to lead up to a point instead of making it directly. Actually, in most types of writing, the best style is the simplest one. Decide that after you have written something, you will take time to cross out unnecessary words and to reword sentences to make your work shorter and clearer. Ask yourself whether every word or group of words is really necessary to the meaning of a sentence.

Here are some sentences that are wordy (that contain unnecessary words). How could they be simplified?

WORDY   My sister dressed up to assume the appearance of Goldilocks. [*To assume the appearance of* is a pretentious way of saying *as.*]
BETTER   My sister dressed up as Goldilocks.

WORDY    College prepares you for the field you may be entering, or if you aren't planning to work, it still helps you talk about things in a conversation that is interesting to you and other people. [This could have been said in far fewer words.]

BETTER    College prepares you for an occupation and makes you a good conversationalist.

Avoid groups of words that add length but not clarity to your sentences.

| WORDY | BETTER |
|---|---|
| our modern world in which we live | our world |
| It tends to seem to this observer that | I believe that |
| To me, I think | I think |

## EXERCISE 2

Eliminate wordiness in the following sentences. Rewrite any sentences where it is necessary.

1. Put the jack in a position where it will lift the car in a way so that you can change the tire.
2. To me, I believe that the jet plane has changed the entire course of existence in this modern world in which we now live.
3. I was wondering what it was possible for me to do about the problem I was having deciding whether to go back to school or to look for some kind of job.
4. The snow began to reach a higher level on the ground on which it lay.
5. When I was in high school, I never studied enough to accumulate the knowledge of the many and varied important things I needed to know.
6. Quite a few people have a limited amount of time to engage in shopping. Most of those individuals find that a large part of this time is spent searching for desired yet hard-to-locate bargains in the many stores that line the streets of our major cities.
7. Mismanagement of the coupons causes them to be used up before the rationing period ends, resulting in a loss of ability to buy more rationed items until the next period.

**23d** Avoid long introductions and the repetition of words and ideas you have used elsewhere.

Be certain that everything you write has a definite purpose. This passage shows that the writer was groping for ways to fill up space.

> One of the most difficult adjustments any individual has to make is learning how to get along with others. People have individual differences in appearance, personality, and personal habits. Knowing that people are all different in the above-mentioned ways and aspects makes a person feel confused about how to adjust to others. There are several essential behavior patterns that all people have in common. It is each person's job to look for these patterns in order to understand and adjust to others.

As you can see, the writer never gets anywhere in this passage. Once the point is made that certain patterns of behavior exist in all individuals, the writer says nothing further.

**EXERCISE 3**

Eliminate all unnecessary repetition in the following paragraphs by writing the essential ideas in one or two sentences.

1. The team is an eleven-man unit. This means that every man works as a part of the team and that they all work together toward the same objective. If every man does his job in the right situation, the play will be successful.

2. Many people find commercials on TV very vexing because they interrupt the programs. Some programs have commercial breaks eight to ten times every half hour. A viewer watching pay TV is not distracted by continual advertising urging him to buy a special cleaner or hear about the heartbreak of hemorrhoids. Quite a few people have a limited time to watch TV. A large part of this time is spent watching commercials. If they had pay TV, they could watch more programs without the wasted time of commercials.

PART FIVE

# *Moving Toward the Complete Paper*

# 24

# *Improving Sentences*

## Improve your sentences by giving them variety, point, and clarity.

**24a**  Vary the length of your sentences. Avoid a series of short, choppy sentences.

If your papers are now fairly free of really serious mistakes like unfinished sentences and verb errors, you probably feel very much relieved. But there are still some things you must concern yourself with if you want to keep your reader's attention and interest. Sooner or later, all writers have to give some thought to the length and variety of their sentences if they want their readers to enjoy what they have written.

Read the following paragraph.

> On Saturday I went to a new club. The name of the club is the Dockside. It really is a nice club. It has the kind of atmosphere that makes you have a good time. It has red lights. It's a large club and has a dance floor. The tables are big, and the chairs match them. There's a bar as you walk in. There's another bar in the back. It has a gold carpet on the floor.

As you read that description of the Dockside, you probably noticed that you got a pretty good idea of what the club looked like. There were many specific details about the color and size of the furnishings. Yet the paragraph seemed monotonous. Did you notice that all the sentences were about the same length? Using the same information, the writer could

251

have written a better paragraph by varying the length of the sentences and combining some of them.

> On Saturday, I went to a new club called the Dockside. It really is nice. It has the kind of atmosphere that makes you have a good time. It is large and has a dance floor, big tables and matching chairs, and two bars. The red lights and gold carpet add color to the room.

### EXERCISE 1

Vary the length of the sentences in the following paragraph. Combine sentences when possible to avoid choppiness.

> The owner gave me a tour of his farm. It is 1½ miles off Route 32. He showed me how to feed the hogs. He showed me how fast they gobbled up food from the feeder. He said, "The hogs are always starved."

## 24b   Give your sentence a point.

### 24b (1)   Avoid strung-together *and* and *but* sentences.

If you write:

> My second year in high school I was in chorus, and I sang first soprano, and I was in mixed chorus, and I was in regional chorus also.

your sentence doesn't really have a point. You are not saying anything in particular about your singing career, but are just listing singing activities during a particular year. If you mean to make a list, it would be better to write:

> During my second year in high school, I sang first soprano in mixed and regional chorus.

Don't be an *and* sentence writer. Although some sentences joined by *and* or *but* may be useful, too many are as dull as a series of short, choppy sentences. In addition, they suggest to the reader that you haven't really sorted out your ideas.

In the following example, the writer overused *but* to join sentences. It is difficult for the reader to see what the point of the sentence is.

> My little brother wanted to see *The Exorcist*, but my mother wouldn't let him because of its X rating, but I don't think she knew what was in it.

Is the point that the writer's brother wanted to see *The Exorcist*, that his mother wouldn't let him, or that his mother didn't know much about the movie?

> Because of *The Exorcist*'s X rating, my mother kept my brother from seeing the movie, without really knowing what was in it.

You can now tell that the writer is emphasizing the fact that his mother wouldn't let his brother see the movie.

**24b(2)**   Make it clear when the thing talked about in one sentence *causes* the thing talked about in the next sentence. Use the word *because* or *since*, and join the sentences.

When one thing happens because another thing happened, make that idea clearer by using the word *because* or *since* and joining the two sentences. Notice that if the sentence begins with *because* or *since*, you have to put a comma where the sentences are joined. (See **13o** for more information.)

You can say:

> His bus was not on time. He was late for work.

You can join these ideas with *and:*

> His bus was not on time, *and* he was late for work.

These sentences do not make it very clear that one event caused the other. You can show the connection between the sentences by writing:

> *Because* his bus was not on time, he was late for work.
> OR
> He was late for work *because* his bus was not on time.

**24b(3)** Sometimes when you write two short sentences, you want to suggest that one thing happens after, before, or at the same time as another thing. You will make this point more clearly if you use the word *when, before, after*, or *while* and join the sentences.

> UNCONNECTED  My dog Clarence missed his footing on the boat dock. He plunged head first into the muddy water.
>
> BETTER  *After* my dog Clarence missed his footing on the boat dock, he plunged head first into the muddy water.
>
> UNCONNECTED  We ate peanut butter sandwiches and chocolate chip cookies. We talked about our plans for the rest of the summer.
>
> BETTER  We talked about our plans for the rest of the summer *while* we ate peanut butter sandwiches and chocolate chip cookies.

Notice that when the word *when, before, after*, or *while* introduces the sentence, you have to put a comma where the sentences are joined.

**24b(4)** Use words like *if, unless*, and *although* and join two short sentences to help give your sentence a point.

If you want to say that you wish you were a millionaire, it is not as clear to say

> I am pretty happy. I wish I had a million dollars.

as it is to say

> *Although* I am pretty happy, I wish I had a million dollars.
>
> OR
>
> I wish I had a million dollars *although* I am pretty happy.

Notice that you have to use a comma where the sentences are joined only when words like *if* and *although* introduce the sentence.

## EXERCISE 2

Give each sentence a point by using words such as *because, when,* and *although.*

**Example**   I overslept this morning, and I missed breakfast, and my whole day went wrong.
*Because* I overslept this morning and missed breakfast, my whole day went wrong.

1. I left the house this morning, and my car wouldn't start, and there was no gas in the tank.
2. I decided to go to driving school, and I knew I couldn't afford it, but I went anyway.
3. All the TV shows went off, and we all listened to the radio, and finally everybody got sleepy, and we all went to bed.

## EXERCISE 3

Improve each of the following pairs of sentences. Begin each pair with an introductory word — such as *because, since, when, after, before, while, if, although,* or *unless* — and join the two sentences.

**Example**   I got to know Michael. I started to like him.
*After* I got to know Michael, I started to like him.

1. Robert introduced me to his sister. He told me we both had the same name.
2. You are so angry with me. I am afraid to ask a favor of you.
3. The game started. We had already taken our seats.
4. I got my car started. I was on my way to work.
5. Fred likes it here. He would rather be at the beach.
6. Beth will let me know when you get here. I can meet you at the station.
7. Gus read your letter. He didn't know you were planning to visit us.
8. Rabbits sure do dig up a garden. They make nice pets for children.
9. I heard your uncle George lost his job last week. I started worrying about my own job.
10. Hank's wife left him for the milkman. He just hasn't been the same.

**24c** When you are describing a person or thing, one well-developed sentence is usually better than two short sentences.

WEAK    My father's old felt hat looks like it has been through the wars. It is sitting on the mantel.

BETTER    My father's old felt hat, which looks like it has been through the wars, is sitting on the mantel.

WEAK    Joe Louis was undoubtedly the greatest heavyweight fighter of all time. He is now practically penniless.

BETTER    Joe Louis, who was undoubtedly the greatest heavyweight fighter of all time, is now practically penniless.

WEAK    *Jaws* was the biggest moneymaker in years. It kept thousands of frightened teenagers away from the Atlantic coast beaches.

BETTER    *Jaws*, the biggest moneymaker in years, kept thousands of frightened teenagers away from the Atlantic coast beaches.

WEAK    Janet Guthrie was the first woman to race in the Indianapolis 500. She is also a successful New York physicist.

BETTER    Janet Guthrie, the first woman to race in the Indianapolis 500, is also a successful New York physicist.

**EXERCISE 4**

Combine each of the following pairs of sentences, following the pattern given in the example.

**Example**    Carl Simpson left a cigarette on the car seat.
He found a burning hulk when he returned.
Carl Simpson, *who left a cigarette on the car seat*, found a burning hulk when he returned.

1. Aunt Agatha watches all the horror movies on TV. She sometimes can't sleep at night thinking about them.
2. My dog Fred never bit a soul. He has a sign on his outdoor kennel which reads "Beware of Dog."
3. Marilyn's mother-in-law was never sick a day in her life. She is always worried about her health.

4. My father thinks he is an expert on politics. He was positive that Ronald Reagan would be the next President.

## EXERCISE 5

Combine each of the following pairs of sentences, using the italicized pattern given.

**Example**    My sister is the biggest baby in the world. She cried when she stubbed her toe on the screen door.
My sister, *the biggest baby in the world*, cried when she stubbed her toe on the screen door.

1. Robert Redford is my favorite actor. He sends goose-bumps up and down my spine.
2. Their only son is a real loser. He wrecked both their cars last year.
3. Johnny Bench is the best catcher in baseball. He has been in the All Star Game many times.
4. The new boy in school was named Jim McDonald. He seemed to have more money than the rest of us.

## EXERCISE 6

Combine each of the following pairs of sentences, using one of the patterns given.

**Example**    My house is a real white elephant. It will not bring much money on the market.
My house, *a real white elephant*, will not bring much money on the market.
OR
My house, *which is a real white elephant*, will not bring much money on the market.

1. My sister's hope chest is a standing joke in our family. It will probably never leave our house.
2. The garbage can is full to overflowing. It should have been emptied two days ago.
3. Our car is an antique according to my father. It sure runs like an antique.
4. Brighton Beach is a recreation area. It is not very far from downtown Manhattan.

**24d**  Make your writing more interesting by varying the beginnings of your sentences.

The following paragraph shows the need for such variety.

> My friend is not very athletic, but she is interested in sports. Her favorite sports are basketball, tennis, and baseball. She doesn't dislike any kind of game. She wishes she had more natural ability.

One of the reasons this paragraph is dull is that all the sentences start with the subject, which is followed immediately by the verb.

| Subject | Verb |
|---|---|
| My friend | is |
| Her favorite sports | are |
| She | doesn't dislike |
| She | wishes |

Here are some ways that sentences can be varied:

1. Put another sentence beginning with words like *when, if, although,* or *because,* before one of the short sentences, and join the sentences.

   Although her favorite sports are basketball, tennis, and baseball, she doesn't dislike any kind of game.

2. Begin the sentence with a word or short group of words that adds something to the sentence. Introductory words like *as a matter of fact, in addition, without a doubt, at that time, suddenly, unbelievably, in the morning,* and *after dinner* give variety to sentences.

   She doesn't dislike any kind of game. As a matter of fact, she wishes she had more natural ability.

3. Occasionally, use a question, a command, or a statement of surprise for variety.

   Let me tell you about my friend Anne. She is not very athletic, but she is interested in sports, especially basketball, tennis, and baseball. Would you believe that in spite of her lack of talent, she doesn't dislike any kind of game? It's amazing! She only wishes she had more natural ability.

## EXERCISE 7

Write a sentence using each of the following beginnings.

1. Unexpectedly,
2. Unless you get a letter tomorrow,
3. At the same time,
4. After a long bath,
5. In the past,
6. In the first place,
7. As soon as possible,
8. In spite of your objections,
9. Next to the door,
10. For this reason,

## EXERCISE 8

Write a paragraph of three sentences. Make one of them a question, a statement of surprise, or a command.

## EXERCISE 9

List the types of sentences you see in this paragraph.

I don't believe it! I overslept and missed my final exam in Math 121. What can I say to explain this stupidity? Unless I think of a good excuse, I don't dare face Professor Grinder. Come on, Horace, think of something.

Remember, to improve your sentences,

1. avoid too many short, choppy sentences.
2. avoid too many sentences joined by *and* or *but*.
3. use *because* or *since* and join short sentences when you want to say that one thing caused another.

4. use *when, after, before,* or *while* and join short sentences when you want to tell when something happened in relation to another thing.
5. use words like *if* and *although* and join two short sentences to express the relationship between one idea and another.
6. when describing persons or things, try to combine two short sentences into one clear sentence.
7. vary the beginnings of your sentences. Use introductory words, questions, commands, and statements of surprise.

## EXERCISE 10

The following paragraphs contain short, choppy sentences. Rewrite them, varying the length and beginnings of the sentences.

1.     I live in a quiet neighborhood. It is well established. It is the oldest area in Norfolk. The area is called Ghent. The downtown plaza is nearby.
2.     Most rare electric guitars were produced in the 1950s. Most guitarists prefer Gibson or Fender brands built during that time period. These instruments are very scarce and expensive. The Fender "telecaster" model is still very popular today. Today's production model looks exactly like the 1955 version. There is no comparison in the craftsmanship. The mid-fifties Gibson brand Les Paul model is probably the most popular of all old guitars. The Les Pauls produced today are considered the finest on the market.

# 25

# *The Paragraph*

## Learn to write clearly developed paragraphs.

A paragraph is a group of sentences about one idea, or topic. Physically, a paragraph is easy to see on a page, because its first word is indented from the left margin.

A paragraph looks like this:

| | |
|---|---|
| Sentence 1 | |
| | Sentence 2 |
| Sentence 3 | Sentence 4 |
| | Sentence 5 |
| Sentence 6 | Sentence 7 |
| | Sentence 8 |

The length of your paragraph will change with the type of topic you are writing about. That is, some topics are more difficult than others and take more words to develop. The average length of your paragraphs should be five to eight sentences, or about 50 to 150 words.

Your paragraphs should be about as long as the one on the following page.

### My Brother

My brother keeps himself physically fit. He runs four laps around a mile-long track twice in the morning and evening. In his spare time, he works out in the neighborhood gym, doing calisthenics and yoga, lifting weights, and sprinting. He always keeps two closets full of health foods and drinks. In the morning, he gets up at six o'clock and does one hundred sit-ups before he goes to work. If he keeps this up, he will either make the U.S. Olympic team or kill himself at an early age.

**25a** **Before beginning to write your paragraph, pick a topic or think about the topic you have been assigned.**

Be careful not to confuse a topic with a topic sentence.

| TOPICS | TOPIC SENTENCES |
|---|---|
| My brother's physical condition | My brother keeps himself physically fit. |
| Patience | Patience can be thought of as the ability to tolerate difficulties while hoping for better things. |
| Touring a movie theater | I read a newspaper article about the intricate brass and woodwork in some of the old movie theaters in the area and decided to take a look for myself. |
| Underwater explorations | Underwater explorations are far more important than most people believe. |

After you have your topic, jot down as many ideas as you can think of about it. You will use these ideas in writing your topic sentence now, and later in writing your paragraph.

**25b** **You may want to begin your paragraph with a topic sentence.**

The topic sentence tells what you're going to write about in the rest of your paragraph.

Be sure that what you write is a topic sentence, not just a topic. These are topics, not topic sentences:

| | |
|---|---|
| My friend Rodney | Rodney |
| Rodney's size | Rodney, my fat friend |

It is better to state directly the topic of the paragraph than to tell what you mean to say.

WEAK   In this paper I will tell about my friend Rodney.

WEAK   This paper will describe my friend Rodney.

WEAK   In this paragraph I will show that Rodney is the fattest young man I know.

BETTER   My friend Rodney is the fattest young man I've ever seen in my entire life.

### My Friend Rodney

TOPIC ⟶ SENTENCE

My friend Rodney is the fattest young man I've ever seen in my entire life. Although he is only eighteen years old, he weighs about three hundred pounds. Rodney's face appears to be inflated with air or helium because of the size of his jaws.

The topic sentence underlined above tells the reader that the rest of this paragraph will be about Rodney and the reasons that make him the fattest young man the writer has ever seen.

### EXERCISE 1

Pick out any good topic sentences you find in the following list. Do *not* write a paragraph.

1. My best friend
2. This paragraph will attempt to define fear.
3. An attack on the "blue laws"
4. Mercy killing is a very humane practice as long as it is not abused.
5. I believe capital punishment is a just punishment for murderers.
6. How to travel five miles without owning a car
7. The reaction to disaster in almost any part of the world is basically the same.
8. In this paragraph I will show that many of the conditions of

life at sea have changed tremendously during the last two
hundred years.
9. The role of the two-year college in higher education
10. My favorite sport is golf.

**25c**  **After you have written your topic sentence, decide
how you will develop your paragraph.**

In writing the paragraph, be careful to develop the topic sentence, not just the title. All the sentences in the paragraph
should give details about the topic sentence and should give
your reader a better understanding of the subject you are
writing about than the topic sentence alone does.

The following paragraph is not developed. Some of the
sentences do not give details about the topic sentence.

### My Cousin Kay

TOPIC ——————▶ My cousin Kay is very jealous when she is around me.
SENTENCE       When Kay comes to town to visit our relatives, she doesn't
even speak to me. Kay has short black hair and small brown
eyes. When I am around her, Kay is always talking to me. She
doesn't want to have anything to do with me. Kay has a big
mouth and a small nose. She talks about me behind my back.
Kay has small hands and is about five feet tall. I hope she finds
peace with herself.

To develop this paragraph, all the sentences should tell about
Kay's jealousy. Instead, some of the sentences tell how Kay
looks, and others tell how she acts. This paragraph is about
the title. "My Cousin Kay," but it is not about the topic sentence.

The following paragraph is better. All the sentences give
details about the topic sentence.

### My Cousin Kay

TOPIC ——————▶ My cousin Kay is very rude when she is around me.
SENTENCE       When Kay comes to town to visit our relatives, she doesn't
speak a word to me. When I am around her, Kay ignores me
completely, although when I'm not around her, her big loud
mouth is always talking about me behind my back. She probably acts like this because she dislikes me, and she doesn't
want to have anything to do with me. Kay is not an easy person
to get along with because she is rude and immature.

The sentence in this paragraph all tell about Kay's rudeness to the writer.

## EXERCISE 2

Read the following paragraph and write down any sentences that do not develop the topic sentence.

### The Worst Day in My Life

TOPIC ⟶ Working in an emergency room at a hospital gives a person
SENTENCE many opportunities to experience bad days, but my worst day came recently after a heavy rain and sleet storm. On the other hand, just last week I had three pleasant days in a row. On that day, our emergency room was overrun by drivers who were unused to the slick streets, little old ladies who had slipped on the ice, policemen who were hauling in the previously mentioned drivers, and a physician (only one) who was bleary-eyed and sneezing. The hospital staff physicians are poorly paid and don't seem to care about the patients. With a few more days like that one, I will be a good candidate for geriatric nursing. I hope I can get off early on Friday.

Here are some examples of the types of details you could use to develop some different types of paragraphs.

In a paragraph describing a person, use details that describe the person's

physical characteristics—hair, eyes, nose, size, age.
personality or character—happy or sad, generous or selfish, kind or cruel.
actions—things the person does that prove him to be the particular kind of person you say he is.

In a paragraph describing a place, use details that describe the place's

size.
residents.
points of interest.
condition.
history.
type (suburban, rural, urban).
good qualities.
defects.

In a paragraph describing an experience or event, use details that tell

> the time and place of the experience or event.
> the type of experience or event.
> the people involved, if any.
> what actually happened.
> the outcome.

In a paragraph explaining how to do something, use details that tell

> the materials, ingredients, talents, skills needed.
> the steps that must be followed.
> the reason(s) for any special step(s).
> any cautions that must be observed.
> the value of the finished product.

In a paragraph defining something, use details that give

> the origin of the word or thing.
> information concerning its discovery and development.
> synonyms for the word.
> a physical description.
> a description of how it works.
> an explanation of its uses.
> comparisons and contrasts of the word or thing with others.
> different types.
> examples and illustrations.

### EXERCISE 3

Choose one of the following topic sentences and list at least five details which could be used to develop it.

1. My mother is the most generous person I know.
2. On May 11, 1976, I was involved in a serious automobile accident.
3. In order to ride a skateboard successfully, you must master certain skills and follow several basic steps.
4. My hometown has changed so much since I moved away that I hardly knew the place when I went back for a visit last month.
5. The best definition of anger is an illustration of what the word means in action.

**25d** When you develop your paragraph, arrange the details so that the reader moves smoothly from one detail to the next.

One way to arrange details so that your reader can follow them easily is from what happens first to what happens last.

The details in the following paragraph are arranged from first to last.

How to Groom Your Cat

TOPIC ——————→ To groom your cat properly, you must follow a definite
SENTENCE        procedure very carefully. *First,* plan the procedure *before* your
cat knows you intend to groom him. *This procedure* should include gathering the necessary tools—such as comb, brush, and baby powder—and getting your cat's attention, maybe by playing with his favorite toy. *After* you've gathered the tools and lured your cat to a likely spot, the kitchen table, *for example,* you're ready to begin. *Now,* holding your cat firmly at the shoulders with one hand, begin brushing his coat with your other hand. *When* you come to a tangle that won't come out with the brush, use the comb to get rid of it. *Once* you have removed all the tangles, sprinkle a little baby powder into your cat's hair and brush through it again to make his coat look fluffy and clean. *Now* your cat should be ready to win a blue ribbon at any cat show.

The italicized words in the paragraph above,
$$\left\{\begin{array}{l} \textit{first} \\ \textit{before} \\ \textit{this procedure} \\ \textit{after} \\ \textit{for example} \\ \textit{now} \\ \textit{when} \\ \textit{once} \\ \textit{now} \end{array}\right.$$

join details and help the reader move smoothly from one detail to another.

The way you choose to arrange the details should be the way that develops your topic sentence best. Whatever way you choose, it should be clear to the reader and easy to follow.

**25e**   **Make the last sentence complete your paragraph.**

The following paragraph tells how to write a paragraph.

TITLE ————————————————————▶ Writing a Paragraph

TOPIC ————————————▶ To write a paragraph, you must follow certain basic steps.
SENTENCE          Writing a paragraph is a process you can learn if you are
BRIDGE TO ————▶ willing to think and plan before beginning to write, and to
DEVELOPMENT     follow your plan when you start to write. *First*, you must pick a
FIRST STEP ————▶ topic, or think about the topic you have been given. *Next*, you
SECOND STEP ———▶ must jot down as many ideas as you can think of about your
THIRD STEP ————▶ topic. *Then*, you should look back over your list and pick out
                the main points you will use in writing your topic sentence.
FOURTH STEP ——▶ *Now*, write your topic sentence. *After* you've written your topic
FIFTH STEP ————▶ sentence, you're ready to develop your paragraph using the
                main points included in your topic sentence. To develop your
SIXTH STEP ————▶ paragraph, *then*, write a series of sentences which explain your
                topic sentence. Be sure that all *these sentences* give details
SEVENTH STEP ——▶ about your topic sentence. *Finally*, you should bring your
                paragraph to an end by writing a sentence that makes the
                reader feel that your paragraph is complete. If you are careful
                in following the steps explained here, you will be able to write a
ENDING ————————▶ paragraph.

Now you know that a paragraph has certain basic characteristics.

1.  The topic sentence is a statement of the topic, or subject, of the paragraph.
2.  Details in a series of sentences develop the topic sentence.
3.  The ending is the last sentence of the paragraph. It should make the reader feel that the paragraph is complete.

## EXERCISE 4

Read the following paragraph. The topic sentence, developing details, and last sentence are scrambled so that the paragraph does not make sense. Rewrite the paragraph, rearranging the sentences so that the paragraph makes sense. Underline the topic sentence.

### The Community Recreation Center

From the lobby I wandered into the gym, where the paint was peeling off the walls in places and cigarette butts were scattered over the floor. The exterior of the building needed a new coat of paint, and the front door creaked on rusty hinges as I opened it. The neglect and abuse that the center had suffered made me want to leave as soon as possible, and as I walked back outside, I felt cold and sad. When I recently returned to the community recreation center I had enjoyed as a child, I was sadly surprised to see the playground full of weeds and trash. Inside, the lobby was dark and dirty; there was writing on the walls and a trash can was overflowing with paper cups and candy wrappers.

# PART SIX

# The Complete Paper

# 26

## *The Full-Length Paper*

### Learn to write a full-length paper of more than one paragraph.

You have just learned how to write a paragraph, a group of sentences about one subject. Now you can write a longer paper by writing a group of paragraphs about one subject. Such a paper may be called a full-length paper.

A full-length paper looks like this:

Paragraph 1
_____
_____
_____

Paragraph 2
_____
_____
_____

Paragraph 3
_____
_____
_____
_____

Paragraph 4
_____
_____
_____

As you can see, there are several paragraphs in a full-length paper, and you must indent each paragraph.

The length of your paper will change with the type of topic you are writing about. That is, some topics are more difficult than others and take more words to develop. The average length of your papers should be three to five paragraphs, or about 250 to 400 words.

Your papers should be about this long:

### Who Will Make the Squad?

I figured that since I was a sophomore I had a better than 50 percent chance of making the junior varsity basketball squad. Later, I learned that I had actually less than a 50 percent chance because the coach preferred to carry more freshmen than sophomores. He liked to let the first-year men gain as much on-the-court experience as possible to strengthen future teams.

These thoughts had to be placed second in my mind behind the desire to represent my school on the court. Practice was hard. It was all I could do to keep up with everybody else while running sprints. Fundamental drills were basically easy because I was able to hustle while running the drills. Through hustling I had hoped to catch the coach's eye. Hustling also had its price. Each night after practice I was bushed.

The first cut, which was to eliminate thirty of the sixty participants, rolled around after a week of practice. I was definitely pleased but not surprised to find my name on the list to report to practice that night. This was my first big break. It meant that I was halfway home.

That night at practice, I pushed myself harder than ever before with a desire that grew by the minute. With only one cut to go, tension mounted. The last night of practice was really hectic. Everyone played harder than he had ever played before. At the conclusion of the practice, everyone wondered if he would return the next night.

The next morning, the cut list went up. Everyone gathered around to see who made the team. Finally, I was able to wedge my way through the crowd to see the all-important list. Dejection ran through my blood when I saw nothing of my name. Bitterness was my reaction toward the coach. But soon I learned to live with my disappointment. I realized that the world just wasn't quite ready for another Jerry West.

## 26a   Choose a usable topic.

Before beginning to write your paper, pick a topic or think about the one you have been assigned. If you have to pick a topic of your own, keep these things in mind:

1. The topic should be something you are interested in or know something about. Don't pick a topic that you think your instructor would like but that you know nothing about.
2. The topic should be something you can develop in the time and space you have to write your paper.

> TOO BROAD   The family
> BETTER   The disappearing American family

Many of your papers will be written in class, without advance preparation. When this happens, you must pick a topic that requires no research and that is limited enough to be developed clearly and completely in about 250 words, during a fifty- to sixty-minute class period.

### EXERCISE 1

List any of the following topics that you think could be developed in about 250 words during a fifty- to sixty-minute class period. *Do not write a paper.*

1. Sports
2. Basketball
3. How the Carlton Raiders won the state championship in 1976
4. Hurricanes
5. Hurricane patterns along the Gulf Coast of the United States
6. The destruction of Biloxi, Mississippi, by hurricane Camille
7. How to train your cat
8. The American Revolution Bicentennial celebration
9. Governmental scandal during the last two Republican administrations
10. My biggest problem in college

**26b**   **Write a good topic sentence.**

After you have picked your topic, you should use it to write your topic sentence. Remember that this sentence tells the reader what the rest of your paper is going to be about.

> WEAK   How to get rid of a man   [This is a topic, not a topic sentence.]
>
> WEAK   This paper will explain how to get rid of a man.   [This tells about the purpose of the paper. It doesn't state directly what the paper is about.]
>
> WEAK   In this paper I will explain to the reader the steps to follow in order to get rid of a man.   [This tells about the intention of the writer. It doesn't state directly what the paper is about.]
>
> BETTER   Getting rid of a man is easy enough to do if you are constantly complaining, criticizing his friends, and making him aware of his shortcomings. [This sentence states directly how to get rid of a man, which is the subject of the rest of the paper.]

**EXERCISE 2**

Pick a broad subject from the list below. Then limit it to a topic that you could use to write a paper of about 250 words during a fifty- to sixty-minute class period. Use the limited topic to write a topic sentence which states directly what your paper will be about. *Do not write a paper.*

1. A true experience
2. CB radios
3. Family traditions
4. Sports

**26c**   **Make a simple plan for your paper.**

After you have written the topic sentence, jot down as many ideas as you can think of to develop it. You should organize these ideas so that the paper will make sense to your reader. Try using a simple plan to organize your ideas.

Making a plan for your ideas is easy if you follow some basic directions:

1. Think about the topic sentence of your paper.
2. Write down, in any order, all the ideas you have about the topic sentence.
3. Pick out the three or four ideas you want to develop in your paper.
4. Arrange these ideas so that they make sense.
   a. Put a Roman numeral (I, II, III) before each idea.
   b. Write down the ideas in complete sentences.

Here are a sample topic and a topic sentence that could be written for it, a list of ideas about the topic sentence, and a plan to organize the ideas in a paper. Note that ideas that will not be used to develop the topic sentence have been eliminated from the list, and that ideas that will be used to develop the topic sentence have been written in sentence form and arranged in this plan for the whole paper.

| | |
|---|---|
| TOPIC | werewolves |
| TOPIC SENTENCE | The werewolf is a creature from folklore who has inspired horror throughout history. |

| LIST OF IDEAS | Mr. Adams reminds me of a werewolf. | bats |
|---|---|---|
| | | I have a friend who likes science fiction. |
| | What is a werewolf? | |
| | old legends | |
| | full moon | vampires |
| | witches | recent versions of werewolf legends |
| | Dracula | |

PLAN   Topic Sentence: The werewolf is a creature from folklore who has inspired horror throughout history.

    I. The legendary werewolf is a person who can turn into a wolf.
    II. Werewolf stories tell of people killed brutally, apparently by wolves.
        A. These killings usually occur when there is a full moon.
        B. Human tracks, not of the victims, are usually found nearby.
    III. The only way to kill a werewolf is to shoot him with a silver bullet.
    IV. Probably the most famous modern version of the werewolf legends are the Lon Chaney films.

## EXERCISE 3

Below is a list of ideas that you might use to write a paper on the advantages of attending a two-year college. Write a topic sentence that you could use for such a paper. Then eliminate any ideas from the list that you could not use to develop your topic sentence. Finally, write a plan for your ideas. Make sure that all parts of your plan are in complete sentences. *Do not write the whole paper.*

1. Low tuition
2. Specialized research facilities
3. Quality instruction
4. Small classes
5. Good football teams
6. Convenient location
7. Good preparatory programs
8. Wide variety of doctoral programs
9. Community services
10. Hot lunches

**26d**  Write the paper, making use of the plan you have made.

Now that you have your topic sentence and your plan for the ideas you will use to develop it, you are ready to begin writing your paper.

You may use the actual sentences from your plan as the topic sentences of the paragraphs in the paper.

Read the following plan and compare it with the paper that was written from it.

Life at Sea — Today and Yesterday

Topic Sentence: Even today life at sea is a challenge, but a comparison of daily living conditions two hundred years ago and today shows that many conditions of life at sea have changed tremendously.

I. Food is just one of the aspects of life at sea which has changed over the years.

II. Another aspect of life at sea which has changed a great deal is living conditions.

III. Besides these changes in living conditions, there have been major changes in working conditions at sea.

IV. Finally, there have been changes in the forms of discipline used at sea.

Conclusion: In spite of the differences in conditions throughout the years, the sea has called men since time beyond recall and still does so.


Life at Sea — Today and Yesterday

INTRODUCTION ——————▶ From the viewpoint of a sailor of two hundred years ago,
TOPIC                going to sea was like being jailed, with the added risk of drown-
SENTENCE OF          ing. Even today life at sea is a challenge, but a comparison of
WHOLE PAPER ——▶ daily living conditions two hundred years ago and today shows
                     that many conditions of life at sea have changed tremendously.
FIRST TOPIC               Food is just one of the aspects of life at sea which have
SENTENCE OF ——▶ changed over the years. Two hundred years ago when a ship
PARAGRAPH            went to sea, a typical sailor would not expect to see land again
                     for some time. Ships were small, men were crowded together,
                     and there was limited storage space, so the only foods that
                     could be taken were those that stored easily and would not

spoil readily. The normal fare was salted meat in barrels, hard sea biscuits that usually became worm-infested long before the cruise was over, and water that became so green and slimy in a short time that a sailor drank it only when necessary. A rare captain might provide some cheese or raisins, but since the cost of outfitting the ship came out of his pocket, extra rations were rare. Today when ships go to sea, sailors can look forward to a virtually unlimited variety of foods and beverages. Meals are planned for quality, quantity, and proper nutrition. Usually little is spared to satisfy the crew, and although they may occasionally gripe, they may never in their lives receive better meals.

SECOND TOPIC SENTENCE OF⟶ PARAGRAPH      Another aspect of life at sea which has changed a great deal is living conditions. It has only been in recent years that berthing of men aboard ship has even been considered. In early days a man slept wherever he could find a soft plank. In many cases, on warships, men were required to sleep near their battle stations. Men were not allowed to live ashore because of the high desertion rate, but they were allowed to have their wives aboard ship while in port. Many a lad was sired alongside a ship's cannon, giving rise to the old saying, "son of a gun." Today, living conditions are a major morale factor, and men enjoy spacious bunks, adequate locker space, and additional recreation areas. In some cases, seamen are lucky enough to have wardrooms to live in.

THIRD TOPIC SENTENCE OF⟶ PARAGRAPH      Besides these changes in living conditions, there have been major changes in working conditions at sea. In the days of sail it was considered too risky to allow idle hands. In consequence, a work day would last from sunrise to sunset. Men were divided into port and starboard watches. This routine allowed a man four hours' sleep out of his first thirty-two hours and eight hours' sleep out of his second thirty-two hours. Imagine living this routine for months at sea! This doesn't even consider the fact that all hands were required for such evolutions as changing sail. Nowadays, a sailor may work a normal eight-hour day with adequate time for recreation and relaxation. On merchant vessels he may get paid overtime for extra hours. Unhappily, the Navy hasn't reached this point yet.

FOURTH TOPIC SENTENCE OF⟶ PARAGRAPH      Finally, there have been changes in the forms of discipline used at sea. Life at sea creates its own unique community, which requires rules that a landlubber may not comprehend. In the Navy of two hundred years ago, the slightest infraction usually called for harsh punishment. The usual form of punishment was flogging with a "cat." A routine minor offense would require twelve lashes, and the number would go up with the severity of the offense. The worst punishment was usually a deceptive disguise for sure death—a dozen through the fleet.

In this punishment a man was given a dozen lashes, but he was tied in a boat and rowed to each ship in port where crews were called out to witness punishment. Multiply these twelve lashes by fifty ships in port! Discipline is still a problem, and men still must face the mast, but gone are the whippings and the cruel ways of bygone days. Men nowadays are fined, reduced in position, or jailed for serious offenses, but they have all the rights of every citizen and can appeal any cases. Justice at sea is very similar to justice in any of our courts. In spite of the differences

CONCLUSION ⟶ in conditions throughout the years, the sea has called men since time beyond recall and still does so.

Divide your full-length paper into paragraphs using your plan. Begin a new paragraph in your paper when you introduce a new point in your plan.

Here is a full-length paper that is not divided into paragraphs.

### A Temporary Home

It had been a long, exhausting trip, and we had arrived late. Without really thinking or caring what the place was like, I went to bed early. My wife cried herself to sleep, and I just lay in bed thinking what a mistake I had made. We had left our home, uprooted the children, and come halfway around the world to a tiny island called Guam. It was the sun that woke me in the morning. It hung in a sky that seemed to be a reflection of the clear blue ocean below. It shone so brightly that it hurt my eyes, and already the heat from it was heavy and oppressive. I dragged myself to the window to have a look at my new surroundings. The calm of the sea below was destroyed by huge waves that suddenly appeared from nowhere, crashed with a thunder upon the reef, and then were gone as mysteriously as they had come. I turned my attention to the land. There were palm trees that swayed in the gentle breeze of the trade winds. On my right were mountains that would have been considered hills on any continent. Covering the mountains were more palm trees and the impenetrable jungle. That was what my eyes saw my first morning on Guam. Everything was so different, so new, and we knew we had to live with it for two years. But as time went by we adjusted to our new home. In fact, when the two years were over, we found a crowd of friends coming to see us off, waving and crying and yelling for us to write. My wife cried the night we left, and I sat alone thinking what a mistake I was making.

This paper is easier to follow when it is divided into paragraphs every time a new point is introduced.

### A Temporary Home

It had been a long, exhausting trip, and we had arrived late. Without really thinking or caring what the place was like, I went to bed early. My wife cried herself to sleep, and I just lay in bed thinking what a mistake I had made. We had left our home, uprooted the children, and come halfway around the world to a tiny island called Guam.

It was the sun that woke me in the morning. It hung in a sky that seemed to be a reflection of the clear blue ocean below. It shone so brightly that it hurt my eyes, and already the heat from it was heavy and oppressive. I dragged myself to the window to have a look at my new surroundings. The calm of the sea below was destroyed by huge waves that suddenly appeared from nowhere, crashed with a thunder upon the reef, and then were gone as mysteriously as they had come. I turned my attention to the land. There were palm trees that swayed in the gentle breeze of the trade winds. On my right were mountains that would have been considered hills on any continent. Covering the mountains were more palm trees and the impenetrable jungle.

That was what my eyes saw my first morning on Guam. Everything was so different, so new, and we knew we had to live with it for two years. But as time went by we adjusted to our new home. In fact, when the two years were over, we found a crowd of friends coming to see us off, waving and crying and yelling for us to write. My wife cried the night we left, and I sat alone thinking what a mistake I was making.

## EXERCISE 4

Divide the following full-length paper, beginning a new paragraph every time you think the writer brings up a new point.

### Starting College Again

Going back to college at age thirty-five was not my idea of an enjoyable way to end the summer. It was entirely my husband's notion. Once the idea was fully discussed with the family, I decided to give it a try. Now I had to plan a course of study. Before, in my younger days, I had taken nursing as my major, but now that nursing is more paperwork than patient care, I decided to try a new field that I could possibly work at in my home if the need arose. Once the decision to major in accounting was made, things began to happen. The first problem was to find time to return to college. This meant I would have to give up several of my volunteer jobs. I did not mind not being the P.T.A. president or the ship's ombudsman, but I hated to give up my Girl Scout junior troop. The only position I kept was that of cheerleading coach, since that was only a job through the fall. Once those decisions were made, I had to select a schedule that would not conflict with my children's school schedules, as I feel it is important to be home when they arrive. This was arranged, and the baby (preschooler) was enrolled in a pre-kindergarten class which she loved. Now the only big problem remaining was what to wear. Faded blue jeans and T-shirts emblazoned with the profound messages of today's youth were definitely out but remained a standing family joke. Finally chosen were sport clothes and several pairs of comfortable shoes. Now that I have been back in school for a while, I have found that the whole family has gained from the experience. My school-age daughters have visited several classes, met the teachers, enjoyed the artmobile, and discovered that college is a place where people with all levels of education can meet in a learning atmosphere. I now have homework with the kids, and the homework sessions have developed into family get-togethers. We have met and become friends with interesting people from all backgrounds. My life is very full now; my enthusiasm for school has spilled over to my family, and we lead a more rewarding and interesting life because more things are happening to us as a family.

Use your plan to avoid writing incomplete paragraphs or paragraphs that are too short to do their part in developing the topic sentence of your whole paper. Do not put each sentence into a separate paragraph.

This full-length paper is divided into incomplete paragraphs.

### Radiological Control Surveys

There are three basic types of radiological control surveys. They are swipe, radiation, and air sample. They are taken on a routine basis to determine radiological control status.

Swiping an area is the method used to determine the surface contamination levels. In most areas, swipes are taken at least once during an eight-hour shift.

Swiping is performed by wiping one-inch-disc filter paper over a one-hundred-centimeter-square area. The filter paper is then measured with a Geiger counter to determine if it contains radioactive particles.

Radiation surveys are taken at least once every twenty-four hours.

This is done to determine the level of radiation that might be emitted from radioactive items in the area.

These surveys are performed by holding a radiation detector at about waist level and walking about the area to be surveyed.

Air samples are taken to determine if any radioactive particles exist in the air. They are taken twice during an eight-hour shift.

A cloth filter is placed in the intake side of a vacuumlike instrument. The instrument is operated for two minutes. The filter is then removed and measured with a Geiger counter to determine if radioactive particles are deposited on it.

These surveys—swipe, radiation, and air sample—are taken to maintain high standards of radiological control.

This full-length paper is divided into complete paragraphs. The writer begins a new paragraph every time a new point is introduced.

### Radiological Control Surveys

TOPIC
SENTENCE
INTRODUCTION

There are three basic types of radiological control surveys. They are swipe, radiation, and air sample. They are taken on a routine basis to determine radiological control status.

FIRST TYPE
OF SURVEY

Swiping an area is the method used to determine the surface contamination levels. In most areas, swipes are taken at least once during an eight-hour shift. Swiping is performed by wiping one-inch-disc filter paper over a one-hundred-centimeter-square area. The filter paper is then measured with a Geiger counter to determine if it contains radioactive particles.

SECOND TYPE
OF SURVEY

Radiation surveys are taken at least once every twenty-four hours. This is done to determine the level of radiation that might be emitted from radioactive items in the area. These surveys are performed by holding a radiation detector at about waist level and walking about the area to be surveyed.

THIRD TYPE
OF SURVEY

Air samples are taken to determine if any radioactive particles exist in the air. They are taken twice during an eight-

{ hour shift. A cloth filter is placed in the intake system of a vacuumlike instrument. The instrument is operated for two minutes. The filter is then removed and measured with a Geiger counter to determine if radioactive particles are deposited on it.

CONCLUSION ⟶ { Although these surveys are basically similar, each performs an important function in determining radiological control status. Swiping determines surface contamination levels. Radiation surveys measure radiation emitted from radioactive items. Air samples measure radioactive particles in the air. Thus, all three — swipe, radiation, and air sample — are needed to maintain high standards of radiological control.

## EXERCISE 5

Organize the following paper into complete paragraphs by putting all sentences about one point together. Avoid one-sentence paragraphs.

### An Electric Coffeepot

Before you make that next pot of coffee in your electric pot, take a minute to familiarize yourself with the assembly parts that work together to brew that delicious cup of coffee.

An electric coffeepot has four assemblies made up of two or more parts. These assemblies are the cover, the body, the basket, and the base.

The cover assembly consists of a cover knob (usually made of plastic), a round metal cover, and a spreader held together by an assembly screw.

The spreader has many small holes in it. This assembly fits into a lip of the body assembly to retain the liquid and heat in the body.

The body assembly has a metal body with a groove (or lip) at the top for the cover assembly.

At the bottom of the body on the inside is a pump well.

A plastic handle and spout are attached to the outside of the body with screws. The spout is hollow and fits over a hole in the body.

The body holds approximately ten cups of liquid.

The basket assembly consists of two parts: the basket and the pump.

The basket is perforated with many holes to allow water to drip through.

It fits onto a long, slender round tube called the pump.

The basket assembly rests in the pump well of the body.

The base assembly is the heart of the pot. The base, made of plastic, houses the parts that heat the liquid in the body.

Inside the base are a pilot light, a thermostat, and a control wheel mounted on a metal bracket. These parts are connected to a heating element and a terminal pin set by wires. The terminal pin set protrudes through the base so that an electrical cord can be attached.

The bottom of the base has a little window to allow the pilot light to become visible when it lights. The base assembly is connected to the body assembly by a screw.

You can see, then, that an electric coffeepot is a complex mechanism composed of four different assemblies that work together to give you a simple cup of coffee.

Now that you are more familiar with the construction of your coffeepot, go ahead and make that pot of coffee.

## 26e  Add a conclusion to your paper.

You should bring your paper to an end by writing a sentence or two that make your reader feel the paper is complete. Often an ending returns to the idea stated in the topic sentence of the whole paper.

Don't change your topic in the conclusion. Use the conclusion to finish what you were saying in the whole paper.

To end this paper, the writer needed a sentence or two about euthanasia as a humane practice.

Is Euthanasia Justifiable?

Topic Sentence: Euthanasia is a very human practice as long as the practice is not abused.

   I. Euthanasia is the act of killing someone painlessly for reasons of mercy.
  II. There are certain cases in which euthanasia is justifiable.
 III. Most arguments against euthanasia can be answered.

Conclusion: Many doctors have been involved in malpractice suits in recent years.

Instead, the writer changed the subject by writing a sentence about malpractice suits.

This plan shows an ending that finishes what the writer was saying in the whole paper.

### Is Euthanasia Justifiable?

Topic Sentence: Euthanasia is a very humane practice as long as the practice is not abused.

   I. Euthanasia is the act of killing someone painlessly for reasons of mercy.
  II. There are certain cases in which euthanasia is justifiable.
 III. Most arguments against euthanasia can be answered.

Conclusion: It is more humane to let a person die than to prolong his life when he is not really living.

## EXERCISE 6

Read the following full-length paper. Pick out the topic sentence and write it. Then write your own conclusion for the paper.

### How Does Radar Operate?

Have you ever noticed a police car parked on the side of the highway, monitoring automobiles electronically to determine if they are speeding? The device the police officer is using is known as radar. Regardless of type or size, all radar units use a transmitter, a receiver, and a presentation system to accomplish their assigned tasks.

The transmitter takes a small initial voltage and increases it to an extremely high voltage. The high voltage is then modulated to a certain frequency and is turned into energy to be transmitted into space in the form of pulses to strike an object.

When energy is transmitted, it strikes an unknown object and returns to its source in the form of an electronic echo. The echo is then processed by the receiver to determine the distance between the energy pulses. The narrower the distance between the pulses, the faster the unknown object is moving. The information processed by the receiver is then relayed to the presentation system.

A presentation system may take many forms. In a police car, it is the form of a speed indicator dial much like a speedometer. If an automobile is moving at a set rate of speed, the speed indicator dial will show the police officer the exact rate.

You should include the following things when you write a full-length paper.

1. The *topic sentence*, which states directly what the whole paper is about.
2. The *plan*, which organizes your ideas about the topic sentence so that your paper will make sense.
3. *Paragraphs*, which give details developing the topic sentence of the whole paper.
4. The *ending*, which makes your reader feel that your paper is complete.

## EXERCISE 7

Read the following full-length paper. The paragraphs are scrambled so that the paper doesn't make sense. Rewrite the paper, rearranging the paragraphs so that the whole paper makes sense. Underline the topic sentence and the ending sentence.

### How to Feed a Baby

The first thing you need, of course, is a baby. The next thing you need is a good highchair that has a strap to tie the baby down with. If you don't have a strap, you may substitute a dish towel, belt, or anything similar that is handy. An absolute must is a bib because without it you will find yourself bathing the baby and changing his clothes after you feed him. Have his food ready before you put the baby into the highchair. Babies don't like to wait in highchairs.

The last step is to remove the baby from the highchair and change his diaper. A baby's diaper always needs changing after he eats, and that job must be done right away. Experience is always the best teacher, but if you follow these simple steps, you will be much better off when you are given the task of feeding the baby.

The feeding should be progressing very well now, but the baby may stop eating at any time. If this happens, it is probably due to one of three reasons: (1) he may have decided he doesn't like the food; (2) he may just want to be coaxed; (3) he may be sleepy. You can deal with reasons 1 and 2. Just pretend the spoonful of food is a choo-choo about to go into a tunnel, and, complete with sound effects, shove the food into the baby's mouth. Or, you may feign gratitude and tell the baby how good he is to eat all his food. If reason 3 is the cause of the baby's refusal to eat more, just forget the remainder of the food and go to the next step.

Now you are ready to begin. Place the baby in the highchair, and strap him down with the strap to prevent him from getting out or falling out. Take a small amount of food on a spoon and allow him to swallow it. Don't push the baby. Let him take his time. Babies don't like to be forced and once angered are slow to forgive and forget.

Feeding babies is a skill every father should master. I have only become the expert that I am today by diligently studying under three children who have taught me, or should I say forced me to learn, almost every trick.

When the baby has eaten all he intends to, remove the bib and spoon. They will quickly become toys and cause more mess if you don't. Then clean the excess food off the baby. Food will probably be in his hair and all over his face and hands. This is still better than it would have been without the bib.

# 27

# *The Library Paper*

## Learn how to prepare a library paper.

You may first need to know what a library paper is and why it goes by such a name. The library paper is usually prepared from materials found in a library. The paper may also be called a research paper because it has taken research to locate the information. A library paper is not an original story or article; it is made up of numerous pieces of information that are put together to próve a point or develop an idea. But the paper should be original in the way in which the materials are selected and used. You must carefully record the location, or source, of the information, because you are using facts from someone else. This record, or documentation, is in the form of footnotes and bibliography, both of which are fully explained later in this section. A library paper may be longer than other papers you have written, but you may have more time to write it. If you plan your work carefully, follow the steps presented in this section, and use accepted writing skills, you will write a well-prepared paper. You may find that getting started is difficult, so choosing a subject will be the first step to be discussed in detail.

## 27a   Choose a suitable subject for a library paper.

Your paper will be more interesting to you and will be easier to write if you choose a subject that you like or know something about. For example, if you are writing a paper for an art course, you will have to work with a topic that is more specific than the general subject of art. But you may not have a clear idea about that specific subject until you do some looking (or research) and reading. Where should you begin? Your first ideas may come from the textbook you are using in the course. If the instructor has not assigned subjects for the papers, you will be free to find out something more about a subject that interests you. If you feel that the topic of modern art seems worth thinking and writing about, you are moving toward a subject limited enough for a library paper.

## 27a(1)  Use the card catalog.

The library card catalog is the next place to look. The catalog lists all of the books in the library. Information about the books is usually on cards filed in drawers, although the catalog may also be in large books or on microfiche or other film. Each book is listed separately by subject, title, and author, and the subject cards are usually in a different section of the card catalog from the author and title cards. Since you are trying to decide on a subject for your paper, you will be interested in the subject section of the card catalog.

### *A subject card looks like this*

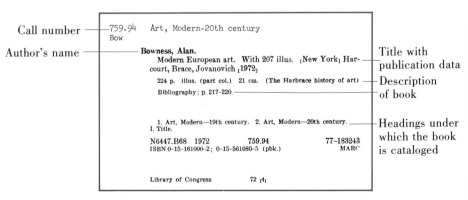

Call number

Author's name

759.94
Bow
    Art, Modern-20th century

**Bowness, Alan.**
    Modern European art. With 207 illus. ₍New York₎ Harcourt, Brace, Jovanovich ₍1972₎

    224 p.  illus. (part col.)  21 cm.  (The Harbrace history of art)
    Bibliography : p. 217-220.

    1. Art, Modern—19th century.  2. Art, Modern—20th century.
I. Title.
    N6447.B68  1972      759.94      77–183243
    ISBN 0-15-161000-2; 0-15-561080-5 (pbk.)      MARC

    Library of Congress      72 ₍4₎

Title with publication data

Description of book

Headings under which the book is cataloged

If there does not seem to be any material on the subject you are interested in, you may have to consult a subject-heading listing or guide (such as the Library of Congress Guide) or a *see also* card in the card catalog. The listing or cards will give other ways in which a subject may be listed; they will frequently list specific headings under the broad topics or headings.

### Subject-heading guide

**Art** — Technique
*also subdivision* Technique *under*
    Painting, Sculpture; *and*
    *similar headings*
**Art, Abstract**
    *sa* Modernism (Art)
**Art, Modern — 20th century**
    *sa* Art — History — 20th century
        Art, Abstract
        Dadaism
        Modernism (Art)
**Art, Modernist**
    *See* Modernism (Art)
**Art, Primitive**
*also subdivision* Antiquities *under*
    *names of countries, cities, etc.*

### A "see also" card

ART MOVEMENTS

See also

Abstract art
Classicism
Dadaism
Gothic art
Pop art
Surrealism

You are now ready to look through some of the available books in order to narrow the broad topic down to an interesting subject that could be covered in a paper of the assigned length. You may already be interested in one of the art movements.

**27a(2)**    Use indexes to magazines.

Books are only one of the sources of information available in a library. The *Readers' Guide to Periodical Literature* is a listing of articles in popular magazines, and it can serve as a valuable source of ideas for possible subjects for a paper. This group of books, usually one for each year, is located in the reference section of the library. Each article is listed in the *Readers' Guide* under subject, title, and author. Articles may be listed under several subject headings. The library you are using may not have all of the periodicals listed. If you are considering one of the art movements as the subject for a research paper, the *Readers' Guide* will let you know what articles appeared on the movement in any one year and will also give the name and date of the magazine and the page numbers of the article. An entry in the *Readers' Guide*\* looks like this:

> DADAISM
> Remember Dada: Man Ray at eighty. S. De
> Gramont. il pors N Y Times Mag p6-7+ S
> 6 '70

This entry tells that an article concerning Dadaism appeared in the *New York Times Magazine* on September 6, 1970. It was written by S. DeGramont and was a little more than two pages long. Any abbreviations and symbols used in the entries are explained in the front of the *Readers' Guide*. Many libraries also have specialized guides or indexes (such as the *Art Index*) that are concerned only with a narrow field of interest.

\* *Readers' Guide to Periodical Literature.* Copyright © 1970, 1971, by The H. W. Wilson Company. Material reproduced by permission of the publisher.

The topic of art movements is still a broad one. Suppose that you, like the student whose paper appears on pages 313–25, decide to write a library paper on the Dada movement. Now that you have chosen a specific subject, you can begin gathering the information that will go into the paper.

### EXERCISE 1

Find one book listing in the library card catalog and one article listing in the *Readers' Guide to Periodical Literature* for each of the following subjects. For each book, give the title, author, and date of publication. For each article, give the name of the magazine, date of issue, title of the article, and number of pages in the article.

1. Folk music
2. Automobile racing
3. Careers in business
4. Caring for house plants
5. Soybeans

## 27b   Take notes that will help you write your paper.

Now that you have decided on a subject, it is time to read what has been said about that subject. It is important to keep an open mind when you start to take notes. You may think you know where your research will lead you, but after you have read some books and articles on your subject, you may change your mind. For example, the student who wrote "Dada in America" (pages 313–25) originally intended to write a paper describing the Dada movement in general. When she started taking notes, she found much more material on the subject than she had expected, so she restricted her paper to Dada in this country. Once you have chosen a topic, you have made a good beginning; but it is only a beginning. Let your paper take final shape in your mind only after you have looked through the available material.

**27b(1)**   Gather your sources and prepare to take notes on them.

You have already consulted the *Readers' Guide* and the card catalog to help you decide on a topic. Now start gathering sources that may help you write your paper. It is a good idea to make a list of the possible books and articles on your subject. You will not be able to find all of the books and magazines you need in your library, but locate as many as you can in the card catalog. Your library may have a special card catalog for periodicals. On your list, put the call number of each possible source next to the name of that source. Then look at the sources available.

Be sure to consult the table of contents and the index of each book you use to be sure you have not missed any information on your subject. Also remember that the text, the footnotes, and the bibliography of a book or an article are often good places to look for the names of other sources. (See **27d** if you are not sure what footnotes and bibliography are.)

**27b(2)**   Prepare bibliography cards.

You should make a bibliography card for every book or article you plan to use in any way in your paper. Since you won't be certain, when you begin your research, whether a book or article will really be of importance, it is a good idea to make a card for each work that seems to have some information on your subject. On the bibliography card, list the call number, author, title, place of publication, publishing company, and date of publication of the book. For an article in a magazine or newspaper, list the title and the author of the article, the magazine or newspaper, the volume number, date, inclusive pages, and call number (if your library uses call numbers for periodicals). There are different forms for edited works, translated works, special collections, and so on (see pages 305–06 for other information that may be necessary for a correct biliography). Remember that even though you do not have to concern yourself about bibliographical form when you are just beginning your research, you can save yourself a lot of time when you are writing your paper if you note down all the necessary bibliographical information at the beginning.

BIBLIOGRAPHY CARD FOR A BOOK

BIBLIOGRAPHY CARD FOR AN ARTICLE

# 27b(3)   Prepare note cards.

Make at least one note card, in addition to a bibliography card, for every book or article that you consult and wish to mention in your paper. The number of note cards you use for each book depends on how valuable the book is as a source for your topic. On each card write the name of the author or the title of the book or article and the pages from which you are taking the information.

There are three basic types of notes you can take:

1. You can jot down a few words or a sentence on a note card to help you remember what was in the book or article. This type of note-taking is best if the book or article does not have much information directly on your particular topic. You may read a book for background information or may wish to list a book in your bibliography as a useful general source on your subject. You will probably not have many cards of this sort, since it is a good idea to limit your bibliography mainly to works that you have quoted or have referred to directly in your paper. Here is an example of this type of card:

*Abbate, pp. 69–153.*

*Chapter 2 gives a good picture of twentieth-century art.*

2. You may want to use a direct quotation from the author of a book or article, perhaps because you feel that the way he or she has said something is important. When you quote directly, be very accurate. Reproduce all marks of punctuation that appear in the material that you are quoting. If you leave out part of a passage, use ellipsis marks ( **. . .** ) to show that you have done so. If a complete sentence comes before the omitted part, put a period in front of the ellipsis marks.

| ORIGINAL MATERIAL | STUDENT'S QUOTE |
|---|---|
| It has only been in recent years that berthing of men aboard ship has even been considered. In early days a man slept wherever he could find a soft plank. In many cases, on warships, men were required to sleep near their battle stations. Men were not allowed to live ashore because of the high desertion rate, but they were allowed to have wives aboard ship while in port. | *It has only been in recent years that berthing of men aboard ship has even been considered.... In many cases, on warships, men were required to sleep near their battle stations. Men were not allowed to live ashore..., but they were allowed to have wives aboard ship while in port.* |

Be sure to record on your note card the correct page number for each quotation. Make up a new note card for each quotation. Your note card may look like this:

*Penrose, p 46*

*Man Ray said of his process: "It was thrilling to paint a picture, hardly touching the surface — a purely cerebral act, as it were."*

3. You may want to restate what the author has said, putting his or her ideas in your own words. You will probably use this type of note most often, since the material you read will be too long to be included whole. If you are taking notes on a really useful article, you may even choose to summarize the entire source on note cards. Your summaries may vary in length. If you are recording the general idea of the source, your summary may be one or two sentences. If you are summarizing an important book or article, your summary may take up several note cards. If you are summarizing several

passages, write only one passage on each note card, and include a page reference for each passage. Both of the cards below summarize the essay "Life at Sea" (page 279). The card on the top gives a one-sentence summary; the card on the bottom gives a longer summary.

*Life at Sea*

By comparing food, living conditions, working conditions, and discipline, one can see that the life of a sailor is much easier today than it was 200 years ago.

*Life at Sea*

The life of a sailor is much different today than it was 200 years ago. Because of the smaller ships and crowded conditions, few kinds of food could be stored. Now meals are well planned and varied. Sleeping conditions were crowded and uncomfortable, but now living accommodations are comfortable. Work days are shorter, and recreation time is provided. The formerly severe discipline is fairer. No matter what the conditions, however, men will always be attracted by the sea.

No matter how long your summary is, you should:

1. Keep the same proportions as the passage you are summarizing. If the author wrote one paragraph on the causes of a disease and two paragraphs on the symptoms of that disease, you might write one sentence on the causes and two sentences on the symptoms of the disease.
2. Use your own words, unless you are quoting.

Sometimes you will not want to summarize the entire source but only pick out some important passages. It is very important to put those passages in your own words whenever you are not quoting. Then you will be able to tell which passages are direct quotations when you look back over your notes. Remember that any time you use three or more words of an author in the same order that the author used them without enclosing the words in quotation marks, you are plagiarizing, or pretending that you have written the material yourself. Most people who plagiarize do not realize that they are doing so. Plagiarism can be easily avoided by careful note-taking.


## EXERCISE 2

Make two bibliography cards on your topic, being sure to include all the information mentioned on page 295.


## EXERCISE 3

Read the student paper "How Does Radar Operate?" (page 287). Make the following four note cards on that paper:

1. A few words to help you remember what was in the paper
2. A quotation from the paper
3. A one-sentence summary of the paper
4. A summary one-third as long as the paper


## EXERCISE 4

Read the student paper "Who Will Make the Squad?" (page 274). Which of the following summaries is likely to lead a student to plagiarize, or to pretend that he or she has written the paper?

### SUMMARY A

In "Who Will Make the Squad?" the student tells us that in spite of all his expectations and practice, he never made the basketball squad. "The world must not have been quite ready for another Jerry West."

SUMMARY B

In "Who Will Make the Squad?" the student counted on making the junior varsity basketball squad. He was able to hustle while running the drills. The last night he played harder than he had ever played before. But he had to realize that the world wasn't quite ready for another Jerry West.

**27c**  Organize your material and make your outline.

Now that you have taken all your notes, it is time to decide how to put your paper together. Spread out all your note cards on a large table and see what you have. The student who wrote "Dada in America" (pages 313–25) found that her cards could be put into several piles: the origin of the Dada movement; introduction of Dada to Americans; the American leaders of the Dada movement; and the results of the movement. When she started taking notes, the student knew that she wanted to write about the Dada movement in America, but she didn't know what precise statement she could make about the movement until after she completed her research. Now that you have finished your research, it is time for you to decide what precise statement you want to make. That precise statement is the central idea of your paper.

After you decide on your central idea, think about how to organize your material. Make several piles of note cards; each pile should contain only those cards that show a point that supports your central idea. You will find that some of the cards will have to be discarded because they have little or nothing to do with the main point. On a sheet of paper, list the points that lead to or support your central idea, and arrange them in logical order in the form of an outline. (If you have forgotten how to put together an outline, see the directions for making a simple plan on page 277.) It is probably best to make a *sentence outline,* since this type of outline will help you think through all the points clearly before you begin to write the paper. Be sure, then, that every point in the outline is a complete sentence. After you have made the outline, you can number your cards according to the place they have in the outline.

An outline for a research paper will be longer than the outline for an essay. It should be made of the central idea and two or three main headings or main points. Some main headings will be divided into subheadings, and some of these subheadings will have supporting points or details. Use Roman numerals (I, II, III) for main headings, capital letters (A, B, C) for subheadings, and numbers for supporting points. Indent as indicated below. This is a skeleton of an outline:

Central Idea

   I. Main heading
     A. Subheading
     B. Subheading
       1. Supporting point
       2. Supporting point
  II. Main heading
 III. Main heading
     A. Subheading
     B. Subheading

The student who wrote "Dada in America" used this skeleton to make the following outline:

Dada in America

Central Idea: Dada, an anti-art movement that originated in Europe after World War I and had a brief stay in America, changed the way Americans look at art today.

   I. Dada began in Europe.
     A. It originated in Germany.
     B. Its original purpose was to ridicule all institutions.
     C. Contradiction existed among the originators of the movement.
  II. Dada caught on slowly in America.
     A. The reaction to the Armory Show was unfavorable.
     B. The American temperament was not receptive to Dada.
       1. Americans did not have the same antiwar reactions that Europeans did.
       2. Americans were more used to realistic art than Europeans were and reacted badly to Dada.

III. Dada finally gained acceptance in America.
   A. Two European Dadaists did some important work in America.
      1. Picabia's work with machines was influential.
      2. Marcel Duchamp's *Nude Descending a Staircase* and his readymades gained attention.
   B. Man Ray was the most important American Dadaist.
      1. He invented the aerograph.
      2. He developed the rayograph.
   C. There were other minor Dadaists who contributed to the movement.
IV. The Dada movement gradually ended, yet it left its mark.
   A. Some artists moved on to other artistic pursuits.
   B. The Museum of Modern Art exhibition failed to revive interest in the movement.
   C. Its major significance was in its effect on contemporary art.

When you finish your outline, look it over to check the following things:

1. Make certain that your subheadings are really parts of the headings under which they appear.

INACCURATE

B. Man Ray was the most important American Dadaist.
   1. He invented the aerograph.
   2. Dada caught on slowly in America.   [Subheading 2 has nothing to do with Man Ray.]

ACCURATE

B. Man Ray was the most important American Dadaist.
   1. He invented the aerograph.
   2. He developed the rayograph.

2. Make certain that each heading is different from the others. There should be no overlapping.

OVERLAPPING

IV. The Dada movement gradually ended, yet it left its mark.
   A. Some artists moved on to other artistic pursuits.
   B. André Breton turned to surrealism.

NO OVERLAPPING

IV. The Dada movement gradually ended, yet it left its mark.
   A. Some artists moved on to other artistic pursuits.
   B. Its major significance was in its effect on contemporary art.

3. Make certain that each heading that you have divided has at least two subheadings. If you have a I, you need a II; if you have an A, you need a B; if you have a 1, you need a 2.

WRONG

I. Dada began in Europe.
   A. It originated in Germany.
II. Dada caught on slowly in America.

RIGHT

I. Dada began in Europe.
   A. It originated in Germany.
   B. Its original purpose was to ridicule all institutions.
   C. Contradictions existed among the originators of the movement.
II. Dada caught on slowly in America.

After you have a working outline, you are ready to start writing your paper.

## EXERCISE 5

This is an outline for the paper "Who Will Make the Squad?" (page 274). What mistakes has the author of the outline made? Rewrite the outline, correcting the errors.

Who Will Make the Squad?

Central Idea: While playing basketball in high school, I found out that high expectations and hours of difficult practice did not help me make the squad.

  I. Since I was a sophomore, I thought I had a good chance of making the squad.
 II. I practiced basketball every night.
   A. I wanted the coach to see how hard I was playing.
III. I survived the first cut.
   A. I was one of the thirty left after the first cut.
   B. We practiced hard to see who the five starters would be.
IV. The final list did not contain my name.
   A. I was not one of the five starters.
   B. I was bitterly disappointed.

**27d**    **Prepare a bibliography and notes.**

Because you are using information gathered from different sources to write your library paper, you must give credit to these sources for providing the information you need. The information is not your own, and if you do not credit the author, you are guilty of literary theft, or plagiarism.

To credit your sources, you must use a bibliography and notes or footnotes. A bibliography is a list of all the books, magazines, and other sources you use in writing your library paper. Each note or footnote gives the exact page in a particular book, magazine, or other source from which you took some specific information. *Footnotes* are placed at the foot, or bottom, of each page of the paper. *Notes* are placed on a separate page after the final page of the paper.

FOOTNOTES                                    NOTES

Notes
1
Elizabeth Stevens, "Dada and Son," <u>Atlantic</u>, July 1968, p. 104.

2
Stevens, p. 105.

1
Elizabeth Stevens, "Dada and Son," <u>Atlantic</u>, July 1968, p. 104.

2
Stevens, p. 105.

**27d(1)**    **Prepare a bibliography.**

Each bibliography entry has three basic parts:

1. Author (Write last name first; begin at left margin.)
2. Title (Underline and capitalize correctly; give sub-title.)

3. Publication information (Give place of publication, name of publisher, and latest copyright date.) For journals, give first and last pages of article.

Bibliography entries are listed in alphabetical order according to the author's last name. If a book or article does not have an author given, use the title of the book or article to place it in the list alphabetically.

## *Sample bibliography entries*

A book by a single author:

> Canaday, John Edwin. <u>Mainstreams of Modern Art.</u> New York: Holt, Rinehart and Winston, 1959.

An article in a popular magazine:

> Goldin, Amy. "Alexander Calder, 1898–1977." <u>Art in America</u>, March–April 1977, pp. 70–73.

An article in a scholarly journal:

> Hamill, Pete. "Robert Grossman." <u>Graphis: International Journal of Graphic Art and Applied Art</u>, 32, No. 186 (1976/77), 342–47.

An edited book in its second edition:

> Hammel, William, ed. <u>The Popular Arts in America</u>. 2nd ed. New York: Harcourt Brace Jovanovich, 1977.

An article from an edited collection:

> Kauffmann, Stanley. "The Film Generation: Celebration and Concern." <u>The Popular Arts in America</u>. 2nd ed. Ed. William Hammel. New York: Harcourt Brace Jovanovich, 1977.

A book with a subtitle, written by more than one author:

> McQuade, Donald, and Robert Atwan. <u>Popular Writing in America: The Interaction of Style and Audience.</u> New York: Oxford Univ. Press, 1977.

## 27d(2)  Prepare notes.

When you use information in your paper from a particular source, place a number immediately after the information, a half-space above the line you are writing on. The first time you do this, the number you write will be *one*[1]. The next time, the number will be *two*[2]; the third time, *three*[3]; and so on. These numbers refer to the notes giving credit to the sources you used to get the information. Write the notes themselves on a separate page immediately following the final page of your paper.

The first time you write a note giving credit to a particular source, include this information:

1. Note number  (Write the same number here that you wrote in your paper after the information you took from this source.)
2. Author  (Write first name first.)
3. Title (Underline and capitalize correctly; give subtitle.)
4. Publication information (Give place of publication, name of publisher, and latest copyright date.)
5. Page number(s) (Write the page number[s] from which you took the information.)

*Sample first-reference notes*

A book with a subtitle written by more than one author:

[1]Donald McQuade and Robert Atwan, <u>Popular Writing in America: The Interaction of Style and Audience</u> (New York: Oxford Univ. Press, 1977), p. 56.

An article in a popular magazine:

[2]Amy Goldin, "Alexander Calder, 1898–1977," <u>Art in America</u>, March–April 1977, p. 71.

An article from an edited collection:

[3]Stanley Kauffmann, "The Film Generation: Celebration and Concern," in <u>The Popular Arts in America</u>, ed. William Hammel, 2nd ed. (New York: Harcourt Brace Jovanovich, 1977), p. 60.

A book by a single author:

[4]John Edwin Canaday, <u>Mainstreams of Modern Art</u> (New York: Holt, Rinehart and Winston, 1959), p. 95.

An article in a scholarly journal:

[5]Pete Hamill, "Robert Grossman," <u>Graphis: International Journal of Graphic Art and Applied Art,</u> 32, No. 186 (1976/77), 345.

An edited book in its second edition:

[6]William Hammel, ed., <u>The Popular Arts in America</u>, 2nd ed. (New York: Harcourt Brace Jovanovich, 1977), p. 10.

The second time you write a note giving credit to a particular source, use a shortened form:

1. Author's last name
2. Page number(s) (if different from that given in the first-reference note for this source)

If you use works by two or more authors with the same last name, give the authors' first initials when you write second-reference notes giving them credit.

If you use more than one work by the same author, give both the author's last name and the title of the work you are giving credit to when you write a second-reference note for it.

### Sample second-reference notes

```
5Goldin, p. 72.
6McQuade and Atwan, p. 60.
7Kauffmann, p. 62.
```

Credit for different information also taken from page 72 of Goldin's article:

```
8Goldin.
9Canaday, p. 105.
```

### EXERCISE 6

Arrange the following information in correct bibliography form so that the entries are listed as they actually would be in a bibliography for a paper. Be sure to punctuate and abbreviate correctly. Omit any unnecessary information.

Charlotte Willard; 1971; *Famous Modern Artists: From Cezanne to Pop Art*; Platt and Munk; New York; pages 16–21.

*New York Times Magazine*; "Remember Dada: Man Ray at Eighty"; DeGramont, S.; pages 6–7; September 6, 1970.

Pages 55–57; *Saturday Review*; Katharine Kuh; Volume 4; "Preservation of the Avant-Garde"; October 30, 1976.

June 20, 1966; "Love and Hiccups"; *Newsweek*; page 67; vol. 66.

Baldwin, James; *The Popular Arts in America*; New York; edited by William Hammel; 2nd ed.; 1977; "Mass Culture and the Creative Artist"; p. 30; Harcourt Brace Jovanovich.

J. Canaday; pp. 28–31; March 24, 1968; *New York Times Magazine*; "Dada and Its Offspring; Exhibition at Museum of Modern Art".

Holt, Rinehart and Winston; *Purposes of Art*; Pages 38–42; Elsen, Albert; 1967; New York.

## EXERCISE 7

Arrange the information given in Exercise 6 in correct first-reference note form so that the notes are listed as they would actually appear on a note page in a library paper. Number the notes consecutively, beginning with any source you wish. Use any page numbers you wish.

Write second-reference notes for three of the sources given. Number these consecutively with the first-reference notes.

## 27e   Write the paper.

Using your outline and note cards, first write a rough draft of your library paper. To write your paper, you must organize in a unified way all the information you have gathered from various sources. That means you cannot simply copy your note cards in the order your outline calls for. Instead, you must make sure that the information you have gathered is put together smoothly and logically with sentences and paragraphs that join ideas for your reader.

This quoted information is used without anything to join ideas:

> Contradiction existed even among the Dadaists themselves. Kurt Schwitters was "absolutely, unreservedly, twenty-four hours-a-day, PRO art." "The whole swindle that men call war was finished. . . . I felt myself freed and had to shout my jubilation out to the world."

This quoted information is used with words and sentences to join ideas:

> Contradiction existed even among the Dadaists themselves. For example, one of the members of the movement, Kurt Schwitters, was not anti-art. He was, according to Hans Richter, "absolutely, unreservedly, twenty-four hours-a-day, PRO art." He believed that everything was art. Though most of the Dadaists joined the movement because of their feelings of despair about the war, Schwitters became a Dadaist for just the opposite reasons: "The whole swindle that men call war was finished. . . . I felt myself freed and had to shout my jubilation out to the world."

Just as you do for any paper you write, you must proofread the rough draft of your library paper carefully to eliminate errors and to make sure that what you have written is clear. Then, using the principles in Section **28** of this text, or any specific directions your instructor has given you, type the paper in final form.

Your final library paper should include:

1. Title page
2. Outline page
3. Paper itself
4. Notes page
5. Bibliography page

You may also be asked to submit, with your final paper, your note cards, original outline, and rough draft.

DADA IN AMERICA

by

Ellen Robey

Outline

Central Idea:   Dada, an anti-art movement that originated
                in Europe after World War I and had a brief
                stay in America, changed the way Americans
                look at art today.

I. Dada began in Europe.

    A. It originated in Germany.

    B. Its original purpose was to ridicule all institutions.

    C. Contradiction existed among the originators of the
       movement.

II. Dada caught on slowly in America.

    A. The reaction to the Armory Show was unfavorable.

    B. The American temperament was not receptive to Dada.

       1. Americans did not have the same antiwar
          reactions that Europeans did.

       2. Americans were more used to realistic art than
          Europeans were and reacted badly to Dada.

III. Dada finally gained acceptance in America.

    A. Two European Dadaists did some important work in
       America.

       1. Picabia's work with machines was influential.

       2. Marcel Duchamp's <u>Nude Descending a Staircase</u> and
          his readymades gained attention.

B. Man Ray was the most important American Dadaist.

   1. He invented the aerograph.

   2. He developed the rayograph.

C. There were other minor Dadaists who contributed to the movement.

IV. The Dada movement gradually ended, yet it left its mark.

A. Some artists moved on to other artistic pursuits.

B. The Museum of Modern Art exhibition failed to revive interest in the movement.

C. Its major significance was in its effect on contemporary art.

Dada in America

A fur-lined tea cup, sixty-three coat hangers suspended from each other, a reproduction of the Mona Lisa with a mustache--these are examples of the Dadaist attack on rationality and logic in art and in all things. This paper will deal with how the movement began in Europe, how it came to America, how we reacted to it, and how it still affects American art today.

Although some Dadaist works were produced as early as 1913, Dada officially began in Germany in 1916 as a reaction to World War I. It was started by a group of men who were disillusioned and tired of the whole idea of war. Its aim was to ridicule and destroy all existing institutions, especially art movements. Dada was the first, and so far the last, anti-art movement.

The originators of the movement chose its name at random from a dictionary. (Dada is French baby-talk for "hobby horse.") They felt that for too long the emphasis in art had been placed on reason and logic. As Hans Richter put it:

> The myth that everything in the world can be rationally explained had been gaining ground since the time of Descartes. An inversion was necessary to restore the balance.
> The realization that reason and anti-reason, sense and nonsense, design and chance, consciousness and unconsciousness belong together as a necessary part of a whole--this was the central message of Dada.[1]

Contradiction existed even among the Dadaists themselves.
For example, one of the members of the movement, Kurt
Schwitters, was not anti-art. He was, according to Hans
Richter, "absolutely, unreservedly, twenty-four hours-a-
day, PRO art."[2] He believed that everything was art. Though
most of the Dadaists joined the movement because of their
feelings of despair about the war, Schwitters became a Dadaist
for just the opposite reason: "The whole swindle that men
call war was finished. . . . I felt myself freed and had to
shout my jubilation out to the world."[3]

The United States was first introduced to Marcel Duchamp
and Francis Picabia, two artists who were to become leaders
of the Dada movement, through the famous New York Armory Show
of 1913. The exhibition included many examples of cubist and
pre-Dadaist works. The public reaction was anything but
favorable. In fact, at one point, demonstrators had to be
held back by policemen, who outnumbered them.

It is not surprising that Dadaism was not as well accepted
in the United States as in Europe. This movement was brought
about by reaction to the war: a war that had a much greater
effect on Europe than America. America did not feel the fury
that Europe did. Also, realism had a stronger foothold in
America, and Dada, a totally new way of looking at art, came as

3

a shock.  At the start, very few of the paintings were sold, and it was not until years later that this new art movement was accepted in America.

Two men who were instrumental in bringing about this acceptance were Marcel Duchamp and Francis Picabia.  They had both been very active Dadaists in Europe.  Picabia's wife, Mme. Gabrielle Buffet-Picabia, said of the two that they "emulated one another in their extraordinary adherence to paradoxical destructive principles."[4]  Of the two, Francis Picabia was by far the wilder.  As a child he replaced his grandfather's original art works with copies he had made, and sold the originals to raise money for his stamp collection.[5]  Like many Dadaists, Picabia was fascinated by machines.  He would paint machinery and then give it a title that changed its meaning.  For example, one of his works, entitled Portrait of an American Girl in a State of Nudity, shows a large spark plug with the inscription "For Ever" under it.

Marcel Duchamp came from a family of artists.  His two brothers and his sister were all well-known artists; in fact, all four of the Duchamps were represented in the Armory Show. But none of them attracted as much attention as Marcel.  His Nude Descending a Staircase was the most controversial of all the works in the show.  It was a painting of a nude figure in the cubist style with repeating lines to give it a sense of motion. The painting created a scandal partly because it illustrated a radically new way of looking at art. Another objection was to the subject of the painting. In the words of Marcel Jean: "For a nude to be posed standing, lying down, or by the edge of a lake, remained entirely permissible; but that a nude, transformed into flashes of glacial lightning, should begin to descend a staircase"[6] seemed incredible to viewers. The painting became a symbol of madness for the American critics of the show. Perhaps it was the bad reception his Nude got that moved Duchamp to make his first anti-art objects, the readymades, in 1914.

The first readymade was simply a picture from a calendar to which he added two splashes of color. This work was then called Pharmacy. According to the Dadaist and art critic Andre Breton, the readymades are "manufactured objects promoted to the dignity of objects of art through the choice of the artist."[7] Sometimes the object is altered in some way; for example, Duchamp drew a mustache and goatee on a reproduction of the Mona Lisa. Several years later he produced an unaltered reproduction, and called it Shaved.

Although both Duchamp and Picabia were important figures in the Dadaist movement in the United States, neither one of

5

them was American.  The most important American Dadaist was
Man Ray, who contributed to the movement the techniques of the
aerograph and the rayograph.  Like many of the Dadaists, Man
Ray was interested in machines, but he went a step further
than others since he actually used them to paint with.  Using
a spray machine to apply paint to a canvas, he was able to
achieve a new effect.  Man Ray called the paintings he produced this way aerographs.  He said about his new process,
"It was thrilling to paint a picture, hardly touching the
surface--a purely cerebral act, as it were."[8]  Some examples
of his aerographs, made between 1918 and 1920, are The Rope
Dancer Accompanies Herself with Her Shadows, Hermaphrodite,
and The Suicide.  The Suicide was painted at a time when Man
Ray was receiving criticism for "destroying art by painting
by mechanical means"[9] and when he was having marital problems.
He had intended to use the painting as part of an elaborate
suicide scheme but gave up the idea because he felt people
might say that he destroyed himself as well as art by mechanical
means.

    Another technique Man Ray developed was called the rayograph.
He discovered it while he was developing some pictures he had
taken of his work.  While working in his darkroom, he was surprised to see the images of a few objects he had accidentally

placed on a light-sensitized sheet under a glass plate appear before his eyes. He described the images as "not quite a simple silhouette of the objects, as in a straight photograph, but distorted and refracted by the glass more or less in contact with the paper and standing out against a black back-ground, the part directly exposed to the light."[10] That night, he and a friend experimented, making rayographs from every nearby object that they could find. Man Ray continued to make the rayographs and to explore other photographic methods, but he still thought of himself more as a painter than as a photo-grapher.

Although Man Ray was the only really important American artist of the movement, there were other Americans who contributed to the movement in different ways. Walter Arensberg, for instance, a wealthy member of the New York avant-garde, patronized many of the Dadaist artists, including Picabia, Duchamp, and Man Ray. Alfred Stieglitz was a photo-grapher who owned a New York studio at 291 Fifth Avenue. He felt that photography should be considered an art. He also believed that it had replaced conventional art forms and that new ideas were needed. These new ideas could be seen in a Dadaist magazine that he published called <u>291</u>.[11] He also played an important role in the Armory Show.

7

Dada never gained a large following in the United States. Picabia and Duchamp returned to Europe, and Man Ray and others moved on to surrealism. In 1968, in an attempt to recapture the spirit of Dada, The Museum of Modern Art put together an exhibition called "Dada, Surrealism, and their Heritage," but without the anger of the times behind it, the art lost most of its meaning. In the words of art critic Katherine Kuh, "All that remains is wit, . . . visual puns, and play. What we miss is the total involvement, the acid intelligence, the bitter creativity . . . of authentic Dada and early Surrealism."[12]

In retrospect, it seems that the importance of Dada is not in the movement itself but in the feeling that inspired it and the effect it has had on contemporary art movements in America. Pop art, for example, owes a debt to Dada. So even though Dada did not succeed as a movement, it did accomplish its goal: to reverse the trend toward logic and realism in art.

8

Notes

1
Elizabeth Stevens, "Dada and Son," Atlantic, July 1968,
p. 104.

2
Calvin Tomkins, The World of Marcel Duchamp (New York:
Time-Life Books, 1966), p. 39.

3
Robert Hughes, "Out of the Midden Heap," Time, 1 March
1971, p. 64.

4
Marcel Jean, The History of Surrealist Painting, trans.
Simon Watson Taylor (New York: Grove Press, 1967), p. 29.

5
Jean, p. 30.

6
Jean, p. 34.

7
Tomkins, p. 36.

8
Roland Penrose, Man Ray (Boston: New York Graphic
Society, 1975), p. 46.

9
Penrose, p. 50.

10
Penrose, p. 76.

11
Jean, p. 57.

12
Katherine Kuh, "A Fury That Scorched," Saturday
Review, 27 April 1968, pp. 57-58.

9

Bibliography


Abbate, Francesco, ed. <u>American Art</u>. Trans. Simon Coldham.
    London: Octopus Books, 1972.

<u>American Paintings 1900-1970</u>. New York: Time-Life Books, 1970.

"Dada at M.O.M.A." <u>Newsweek</u>, 8 April 1968, pp. 132-33.

Goodrich, Lloyd. <u>Three Centuries of American Art</u>. New York:
    Praeger, 1966.

"The Hobby Horse Rides Again." <u>Time</u>, 5 April 1968, pp. 84-87.

Hughes, Robert. "Out of the Midden Heap." <u>Time</u>, 1 March
    1971, pp. 64-66.

Jean, Marcel. <u>The History of Surrealist Painting</u>. Trans.
    Simon Watson Taylor. New York: Grove Press, 1967.

Kuh, Katherine. "A Fury That Scorched." <u>Saturday Review</u>,
    27 April 1968, pp. 56-58.

Penrose, Roland. <u>Man Ray</u>. Boston: New York Graphic Society,
    1975.

Stevens, Elizabeth. "Dada and Son." <u>Atlantic</u>, July 1968,
    pp. 102-05.

Tomkins, Calvin. <u>The World of Marcel Duchamp</u>. New York:
    Time-Life Books, 1966.

Waldberg, Patrick. <u>Surrealism</u>. New York: McGraw-Hill, 1971.

# 28

# *Putting the Paper in Final Form*

**Be sure that your paper is in good form when you give it to your instructor to grade.**

## 28a  Use the correct materials.

Unless your instructor gives you special directions, use these materials when you *write* formal papers:

1. Standard-size, white, wide-lined paper, not torn from a spiral notebook
2. Blue or black ink

and use these materials when you *type* formal papers:

1. Standard-size, white, unlined paper
2. Black ribbon

## 28b  Write or type so that your paper is easy to read.

1. When typing, leave one-inch margins at the top, the bottom, and on each side of the page. When writing, leave one-inch margins at the right and bottom of each page and use the printed lines for top and left margins.
2. Write or type your name and the date at the top of the first page or on a title page.
3. Center the title at the top of the first page. Do not un-

derline or put quotation marks around the title. Capitalize the first, last, and all important words. Skip a line, or double space, after the title.

4. Indent the first word of each paragraph about one inch, or five spaces, from the left margin.

5. Double-space when typing. Write on every other line when writing.

6. Number the pages with Arabic numbers (1, 2, 3, . . .), beginning with page 2. Place the number at the top center or top right-hand corner of each page.

7. If you have to divide a word at the end of a line, look it up in your dictionary to find out where you can divide it. (See Section **20** if you need help in dividing words.)

8. Write each letter clearly. Be sure that your capital letters are different from your lower-case letters. Be sure that you cross your *t*'s and dot your *i*'s. Use solid dots, not circles, for periods.

9. When typing, avoid erasures and strike-overs. Use correction fluid to make corrections neatly.

**28c**   **Proofread your paper carefully.**

Correct any mistakes you find before you give your paper to your instructor to grade.

1. When writing papers in class, always reserve at least five minutes to proofread your paper carefully and make corrections.

2. When writing papers out of class, write your paper once, leave it for a while, and then proofread it carefully and make corrections.

3. After you have written two or three papers, you will begin to see the mistakes you make most often. Proofread your papers, looking especially for each of these mistakes. It is easy to find a mistake when you are looking for a particular one.

The following paragraph shows the changes the student writer made after proofreading.

The ~~Worse~~ *Worst* Day in My Life

It all started on October 26, 1972, the day I was inducted into the United States Army. On *the* twenty-sixth, I was ordered to report to the Greyhound *B*us *S*tation in Norfolk, *and* And from there proceed to Richmond for a complete ~~physican~~ *physical* and mental examination. I have never stood in line for such a great length of time *I* it was like nothing I had ever experienced before. After I completed my testing, I was released for lunch. After lunch, I had to report to the *t*Train *S*tation in Richmond, where I was told to board a train and stay on until the conductor said, "Fort Jackson, South Carolina,") my home for six weeks *of train-*basic tranning. October 26, 1972, was the worst day of my life, but it was also *the* first of many bad days I spent in the Army.

## EXERCISE 1

Copy the following paragraph, leaving enough room between lines to make corrections. Proofread the paragraph carefully and make any necessary changes.

### The Discotheque

The discotheque is where day ends and night life begins. On the outside of the discotheque there are neon lights flashing and blinking. People standing around laughing and talking listning to the loud music that echoes from the inside as they wait to get in. On the inside of the discotheque their are large number of people at the bar drinking beer some at tables and some anywhere they can find enough room. The discotheque is famous for it's loud music and draft beer. It has a small stage where go go dancers preform and men sit around drinking beer and watching the dancers. People talking loud to be heard over the music but saying nothing of very much importance. Despite the noise and the crowd, the discotheque is still favorite amoung many people it is a exciting way to spend a night after a dull work day.

**28d** **When your instructor returns your paper, be sure to make any corrections suggested.**

1. Find the correct section in this handbook.
2. Study the section that explains the change you need to make.
3. Make the necessary change on your paper.
4. If you need to make major changes in sentences and paragraphs, rewrite your paper.

If you follow this procedure, it will help you to understand why you need to make the changes your instructor suggests. It will also help you avoid repeating the same mistakes.

Here is a paragraph marked by an instructor using the section numbers found in this book.

The Old Telephone Building

Yesterday I made an appointment to see the old telephone

building, which is for sale. The building was in fair condition

on the outside, except the windows was boarded. As I enter the

building there was papers scatter in the halls and rooms. Going

upstairs was hazardous the steps was weak. The second floor

was an disgrace, with paint pilling off the walls piles of trash on

the floor. The building was a total lost.

Here is the same paragraph as it was corrected by the
student who wrote it.

### The Old Telephone Building

Yesterday I made an appointment to see the old telephone

building, which is for sale. The building was in fair condition

on the outside, except the windows ~~was~~ boarded. As I ~~enter~~ the
*22 that* *were 6a* *22 up* *7 entered*

building there ~~was~~ papers ~~scatter~~ in the halls and rooms. Going
*6a were* *7 scattered*

upstairs was hazardous. the steps ~~was~~ weak. The second floor
*3 T* *6a were*

was ~~an~~ disgrace, with paint ~~pilling~~ off the walls piles of trash on
*a 21* *12 peeling* *22 and*

the floor. The building was a total ~~lost~~.
*loss 21*

## EXERCISE 2

Copy the following paragraph, including the errors and
the instructor's marks. Make the necessary changes in
the paragraph, using the sections in this book to help
you.

### The Corner Grocery Store

I approached the store on the corner I could see it was a
*3*

poor store because of the rubbish outside. There was boxes,
*6a*

papers, and cans filled with trash on the street in front of the

store. I opened the door, and it slamed shut behind me as if
*12*

*12*

*6a*

some one else were closing it in anger. The store were filled

*22*                    *7*        *7*

with most of everyday needs, but it look overstock. The

*22*                         *22*

shelves filled and cases of canned goods sitting on the floor in

*12, 21*                            *22*        *7*

the isles. The clutter of the inside of store explain why the

*6a*                          *1, 12*

trash were piled outside in such large amount.

# Index